Atatürk on Screen

Atatürk on Screen

Documentary Film and the Making of a Leader

Enis Dinç

I.B.TAURIS
LONDON • NEW YORK • OXFORD • NEW DELHI • SYDNEY

I.B. TAURIS
Bloomsbury Publishing Plc
50 Bedford Square, London, WC1B 3DP, UK
1385 Broadway, New York, NY 10018, USA
29 Earlsfort Terrace, Dublin 2, Ireland

BLOOMSBURY, I.B. TAURIS and the I.B. Tauris logo are trademarks of
Bloomsbury Publishing Plc

First published in Great Britain 2020
This paperback edition published in 2021

Copyright © Enis Dinç 2020

Enis Dinç has asserted his right under the Copyright, Designs and Patents Act, 1988,
to be identified as Author of this work.

Series design by Adriana Brioso
Cover image: President of the Turkish Republic Mustafa Kemal Atatürk (1881–1938).
(© Hulton Archive/Getty Images)

All rights reserved. No part of this publication may be reproduced or transmitted
in any form or by any means, electronic or mechanical, including photocopying,
recording, or any information storage or retrieval system, without prior
permission in writing from the publishers.

Bloomsbury Publishing Plc does not have any control over, or responsibility for, any
third-party websites referred to or in this book. All internet addresses given in this
book were correct at the time of going to press. The author and publisher regret any
inconvenience caused if addresses have changed or sites have ceased to exist,
but can accept no responsibility for any such changes.

A catalogue record for this book is available from the British Library.

A catalog record for this book is available from the Library of Congress.

ISBN: 978-1-7883-1225-7
PB: 978-0-7556-4693-7
ebook: 978-0-7556-0204-9
ePDF: 978-0-7556-0203-2

Typeset by Deanta Global Publishing Services, Chennai, India

To find out more about our authors and books visit www.bloomsbury.com and
sign up for our newsletters.

*To the memory of
my mother Birten Dinç*

Contents

Acknowledgements		ix
Introduction		1
	Materials	7
	Chapter outline	11
1	Early cinema in the Ottoman Empire	15
	Public cinema in the Ottoman Empire	20
	Wartime cinema	28
	Conclusion	38
2	Filming the struggle for independence (1919–23)	49
	Domestic film producers	50
	Foreign film producers	64
	Orphan films	65
	Mustafa Kemal at the cinema	75
	Conclusion	77
3	Performing modernity: The film of Mustafa Kemal Atatürk on his Forest Farm	87
	The making of Mustafa Kemal's film	89
	Preliminary Speeches (Scene I)	90
	The Fountain (Scene II)	98
	The Garden (Scene III)	103
	The Cows (Scene IV)	104
	The Poultry (Scene V)	105
	The Sheep (Scene VI)	106
	The Tractors (Scene VII)	107
	The Machine Shop (Scene VIII)	108
	Woman, Lovely Woman (Scene IX)	109

	The fortunes of the film	111
	Conclusion	120
4	How to impress an American: The power of the motion picture	133
	Who was Julien Bryan?	135
	Arrival	136
	Bryan meets Atatürk	138
	The many afterlives of Bryan's footage	144
	Conclusion	151
5	Father of all Turks: How *The March of Time* newsreel series represented Atatürk	159
	Newsreel and *The March of Time*	160
	Father of all Turks	161
	Intertitle 1	163
	Intertitle 2	165
	Intertitle 3	166
	Intertitle 4	188
	Conclusion	192
Epilogue: Atatürk in retrospect		199
Bibliography		219
Index		233

Acknowledgements

As Atatürk did not single-handedly create Turkey, I have not crafted this book without help. There was an army of people who supported me throughout my journey, and I am indebted to them all. However, my greatest debts are to the supervisors of my PhD thesis, of which this book is a revised version. In the first place, I should like to thank Prof. Esther Peeren, who gave so much time, energy and attention to reading my work, commenting thoroughly on everything, and correcting my drafts endlessly. In the course of writing this book, she has always pushed me to achieve better writing and conceptual clarity, and encouraged me to combine my empirical research with theory. I am also grateful to Prof. Frank van Vree for his suggestions for improvement, expert advice on media and film history, and great reading recommendations in history and philosophy. But above all, I would like to thank him for giving me the positive energy I needed during the writing process. In addition, I would like to thank Prof. M. Şükrü Hanioğlu, who was immediately sympathetic to my research and extremely helpful, with factual corrections and valuable suggestions for improvement, particularly on late Ottoman and modern Republican history. I am especially grateful to Prof. Hanioğlu for inviting me as a visiting PhD student to Princeton University, which decisively changed the course of my research.

My greatest debts are also institutional, especially to the Amsterdam School for Cultural Analysis (ASCA) and the Amsterdam Centre for Globalization Studies (ACGS) at the University of Amsterdam, where I was a PhD fellow between 2012 and 2016. Their financial support made my extensive research possible. Many thanks go to a number of individuals who built, developed and continue to successfully manage these institutions, such as Prof. Jeroen de Kloet from ACGS, and Dr. Eloe Kingma and Jantine van Gogh from ASCA. I am also grateful to the Department of Near Eastern Studies (NES) at Princeton University, which gave me a wonderful opportunity to discuss parts of my research with a distinguished group of scholars and colleagues. I would like to especially thank Dr. Nilüfer Hatemi for inviting me to present my work at the Turkish Table Talks. The director of the Seeger Center for Hellenic Studies, Dimitri Gondicas, allowed me to present part of my research in their workshop series to a lively group of scholars from various disciplines. I want to thank him not only for offering me this opportunity, which I enjoyed very much, but also for his hospitality during my time in Princeton. Also at Princeton, Prof. Thomas Y. Levin's 'Early German Cinema' seminar was extremely helpful for increasing my knowledge of film history as well as providing me with new theoretical insights that were highly inspirational for this book.

I owe a particular debt to the Harvard-Koç Universities' Ottoman Summer School in Turkey, where I learned to read and translate Ottoman Turkish printed texts and manuscript documents. I should primarily thank Dr. Yorgos Dedes for accepting me into the school despite my unusual background, and for always being a great teacher. In particular, I should express my grandmother Hafize Ekinci's great appreciation of Dr. Dedes for finally teaching her grandson the 'eski yazı' properly. I would also like to thank Dr. Selim Sırrı Kuru, who developed my reading skills in Ottoman manuscripts further, and took the time to speak with me about my work in detail. He was also the one who made me aware of the power of language and literature. I am very grateful to Prof. Gönül Tekin for establishing such a great Summer School together with her husband Prof. Şinasi Tekin. I have to admit that without their school and its beautiful environment, I would have been much less attracted to learning Ottoman Turkish. I would like to express my gratitude to Prof. Evangelia Balta, not only for teaching me Karamanlidika but also for taking care of me as if I was her own son. Her love has inspired me to continually strive to become a better academic and a better human like herself. In the three summers spent at the Summer School, I learned a great deal about language, literature and history, and I accumulated invaluable experiences that helped me to grow as a young scholar; I hope I was able to reflect some of this in my work.

I also owe a great deal to the Turkish and foreign film archives I visited in the course of my research. I gratefully acknowledge the help of Dr. Levent Yılmazok and Prof. Asiye Korkmaz, who provided me with access to some of the films featuring Atatürk in the archives of the Turkish Film & TV Institute at the Mimar Sinan Fine Arts University (a.k.a. the Turkish Film Archives), and who shared their knowledge with me. I should also thank the archives of the Turkish Armed Forces Photo Film Center in Ankara for sending me a CD containing parts of several films featuring Atatürk. I am grateful to archivist

Carol Swain from the National Archives in Washington, DC, who helped me identify films and documents on Atatürk. Moreover, I thank her for showing me what it means to be an archivist and how much archivists can advance a researcher's work. I would especially like to thank a great man, Sam Bryan, who generously opened up his private archive in New York for me, and who searched tirelessly with me for the films, photographs and documents his father Julien Bryan produced on Atatürk. I am also grateful to Matthew Fisher, who helped me to find The *March of Time*'s promotional newsletter 'Photo Reporter' in the HBO Archives in New York and provided me with relevant information. I should also mention with gratitude the help of Greg Wilsbacher, Scott Allen and Benjamin Singleton at the Moving Image Research Collections (MIRC) at the University of South Carolina. With their help, I was able to discover the footage of Atatürk shot by the Fox Film Crew on Atatürk and Turkey, and be the first to write about it. Without the sympathy and generosity of all the people mentioned here, this book would not have been what it is now.

A number of scholars kindly shared their knowledge and published and unpublished works with me. In this respect, I should especially thank Prof. Erik-Jan Zürcher, Prof. Sibel Bozdoğan and Prof. Reşat Kasaba, as well as Dr. Ahmet Gürata, Dr. Güldem Baykal Büyüksaraç and Prof. Heath W. Lowry. Dr. Mustafa Özen, Dr. Günhan Börekçi and Saadet Özen kindly sent me their MA and PhD theses, and answered my questions, for which I am very grateful. I would also like to thank my colleagues Taylor Zajicek, Özde Çeliktemel-Thomen and Ali Özuyar for sharing their research with me. This book contains many parts that required translations from various languages into English; I must acknowledge the crucial contributions of my French teacher Emmanuelle Favreau, my American friend Daniel Fields, and the Turkish author Rıfat N. Bali for the translations.

I take special pleasure in thanking my friends and my best critics, Oscar Aguirre Mandujano, Paul Babinski, Uzma Abid Ansari and Jaimee Comstock-Skipp, who helped me with their constructive comments on this book from its introduction to its conclusion. The final shape of this book owes much to my publisher I.B. Tauris and editor Sophie Rudland, who kissed the frog and turned it into a prince. Finally, I should like to thank my wonderful family: my mother Birten Dinç and my father Sebahattin Dinç, my aunts Yüksel Ekinci and Zehra Dülger, and my grandparents Hafize and Kamil Ekinci, without whom I would not have been able to study. This book is dedicated to them.

Introduction

Although several general accounts of the history of cinema in Turkey exist,[1] there is no detailed study on the use of film as a means of communication by Mustafa Kemal Atatürk[2] and his followers during the struggle for independence and in building the Republic of Turkey as a modern nation-state (1919–38). Atatürk's attitude towards cinema is hard to reconstruct, yet it has generally been assumed to have been positive. This is not only because of the number of short films that exist documenting his life, but also because of some anecdotes and quotations that have been attributed to him, which have become part of a broader hagiographic tradition of quoting Atatürk as an authority on all matters.

Even today, when you visit the Turkish Film & TV Institute at Mimar Sinan Fine Arts University (a.k.a. the Turkish Film Archives), you see the following framed words of Atatürk extolling cinema on the wall:

> Cinema is such an invention that a day will come in which it will become clear that it has changed the face of world civilization, more than the invention of gun powder, electricity, and the discovery of new continents has done. Cinema will ensure that people living in the most distant corners of the world know and love each other. Cinema will erase differences of opinion and appearance. It will make the greatest contribution to the realization of the ideals of humanity. We need to give cinema the value it deserves.[3]

Although it is hard to verify the source of this frequently used quotation, it has taken its place among the other famous pronouncements of Atatürk invoked to attribute a prophet-like quality to him. Since these words are supposed to have been uttered by the founding father of the Turkish Republic, they gained an authoritative position regarding the cultural value of cinema, and are still referred to by his followers to legitimize, justify and increase the importance of cinema in contemporary Turkey.[4] Conversely, the more cinema as a medium gained in global popularity, the more Atatürk's astuteness and his supposed ability to see the future seemed to be proven. In this way, this and several other oft-quoted pronouncements by Atatürk served not only to justify the quality of the leader in the past but also to legitimize particular interests in the present.

In addition to the aforementioned dictum, several anecdotes attest to Atatürk's interest in film. According to one of these, Atatürk once asked Nurettin Baransel Pasha, who was in charge of making a documentary film on the Turkish War of Independence, when the project would be finished. Baransel answered that they were having difficulties completing it because the scenes showing Atatürk were mostly composed of motionless images. Thereupon Atatürk frowned and asked:

> I am alive. Since my documents, sword, and boots from the National Struggle are already there, did I not carry out the duty and mission that was given to me? Had you asked me, I would have accepted the role with pleasure, played it like an artist and brought the memories to life. This is a national duty. Because through this film it will be possible to vividly demonstrate to the Turkish youth how this struggle was won and to leave them with memories.[5]

According to the anecdote, despite wanting to, Atatürk was not able to act in the film because of health problems.[6] Regardless of whether it was true or not, this anecdote underscoring Atatürk's interest in film and his conceptualization of it as a 'national duty' is recounted not only to emphasize the importance of film for Atatürk but also to show his supposed capacity to envision an age in which film would become one of the most important forms of mass media. Moreover, the anecdote suggests that Atatürk realized not only the future potential of film but also its potential to aid in the project of nation-building that occupied him at the time. By serving as a mnemonic device, for him, film could create vivid memories of a shared history in its viewers, through which they – the Turkish youth in particular – would be brought together.

This study goes beyond these well-known quotations and anecdotes to explore in detail what Atatürk's relationship to cinema was like during his lifetime. Atatürk wanted to create an indisputably 'modern', 'democratic' and 'civilized' image for himself and his country. Cinema was a highly appropriate medium for the purpose of affirming Atatürk's and Turkey's modernity because it was considered the most modern and realistic medium available. Yet at the same time, not many films or film projects remain from the early republican period featuring Atatürk or Kemalist Turkey. This paradoxical situation made me curious about the precise role cinema played in the political agenda of Atatürk and his followers. In order to analyse its significance, my focus here is on film projects that were sponsored and supported by Atatürk or his government during the years he was in power (1919–38). On the basis of archival materials, including previously unknown films and documents, I reveal the cultural significance of film for Atatürk's political agenda and its vital contribution to constructing the public image of the leader and of the new Turkish state.

This study has three main objectives. The first objective is to analyse the image of Atatürk on film in order to better understand the evolution of his public image over the course of his time in power and its contribution to the developing concept of the Turkish nation. Although Atatürk's public image was central to the emergence and maintenance of the Turkish nation-state, it has not yet received the scholarly attention it deserves. It is particularly striking that there is no comprehensive study of contemporary media representations of Atatürk. This study seeks to remedy the lacuna.

Born into a middle-class, Turkish-speaking, Muslim family in Ottoman Salonica in 1881, Mustafa was an ordinary boy. Despite his successful military career, he was not a well-known army officer until he became the leader of the national resistance movement in Anatolia in 1919. Yet he managed to mobilize the Muslim population for the national cause to defeat the Allies' attempts at dividing the Turkish heartland of the Ottoman Empire, to overthrow the last sultan, and to declare the Turkish Republic, becoming its first president in 1923.

As president, he implemented numerous reforms in order to transform the outdated Ottoman imperial order into a new, modern, and Turkish nation-state, modelled after Western examples. Through his reforms, he also sought to turn the old traditional Ottoman-Muslim community into a new secular Turkish society with science as its guiding principle. In a prominent speech held on the occasion of the tenth anniversary of the republic on 29 October 1933, Atatürk proclaimed that the Turkish nation would rise to the level of the 'civilized nations of the world' and elevate Turkey's national culture above the level of 'contemporary civilization'. By contemporary civilization he meant modern Western civilization, as represented by Europe.[7]

Although the extent to which Atatürk succeeded in achieving his aims has been disputed in the twenty-first century and lies beyond the scope of this study, it is certain that he brought about a radical change within Turkish society. Even today, long after his death, he is regarded as one of the longest running personality cults in the modern world. How did he achieve this? Mainstream Turkish historiography has tended to explain his political success referring to the 'Great Man' theory.[8] According to this view, Atatürk almost single-handedly saved the Turkish nation from disappearing, and created the Turkish Republic out of the ashes of the Ottoman Empire.[9]

Others have linked his political success to charisma. In this view, Atatürk was a charismatic authority in the Weberian sense, a leader who – thanks to his exceptional personal qualities and accomplishments – inspired obedience from his followers.[10] Still others have criticized this view as being ahistorical, and have claimed that his supposed charisma was a by-product of the political position he achieved later in his career as well as the following of his state-sponsored personality cult.[11] Although the latter approach places Atatürk in his historical context, it does not explain sufficiently how the leader – whether he was charismatic or not – could have such a strong and lasting impact on Turkish politics and society, both during his lifetime and after his death.

This study suggests that the roots of Atatürk's success cannot be found only in political theory, but should be located in the culture of nationalism[12] and the place it assigns to Atatürk in the collective imagination. Although he was not well-known to the public, the effort and attention his government devoted to the creation of his public image gradually turned him into a superhuman in the eyes of many. By presenting him as a heroic figure, virtually omnipotent and omnipresent, the official, state-sponsored mass media played an important role in the creation and dissemination of his image, which allowed him to influence public opinion and to establish the new 'imagined community' of the Turkish nation.

The second objective of this study is that, unlike much Turkish historiography, which tends to view Atatürk as a man ahead of his time, it aims to place him in his historical context. The anecdotes and quotations so frequently used to describe Atatürk's interest in cinema are exposed as a questionable part of what might be called the 'myth' of Atatürk. By presenting his vision of cinema as far ahead of his time, Atatürk is isolated from his context and is separated from the social, cultural and intellectual milieu in which he was brought up: the Ottoman Empire of the late nineteenth and early twentieth centuries.

When Mustafa Kemal was a young cadet, there was already a cinema culture in the empire. Nevertheless, Ottoman cinema was limited to particular institutions, ethnic groups and social classes, segregated by gender and largely confined to those having a certain affinity with Western modernity. When Mustafa Kemal became a leader in the national resistance movement, however, he began to employ cinema not only as an effective tool for political communication at home and abroad but also as a cultural force, assisting him in the transformation of society and in building a modern Turkey. This study details how Atatürk used cinema in a distinctive way in order to answer the major social, cultural and political problems of his time.

The study's final objective is to understand the role of cinema in the modernization process during the late-Ottoman and early-Republican eras. Instead of understanding film as a mere record of what happened, this study shows how cinema was an active cultural force in history. By showing foreign ideas and lifestyles on the screen, cinema helped the Ottoman public imagine new communities in place of old ones. Conversely, cinema also helped to convey the new identity of the modern Turkish nation-state to foreign audiences. Furthermore, this study shows not only how cinema as a technological innovation changed social, cultural and political life but also how society's engagement with cinema shaped its specific development within the Turkish-Ottoman context. By analysing the dialectic between cinema and society in the transformation process from the Ottoman Empire to the Turkish Republic, this study hopes to bring a new cultural perspective to the politics of modernization and nationalism in Turkey.

The concepts of modernity or modernization, which are frequently used in this book, are highly disputable today. However, for Atatürk and his followers, modernity was a simple concept; when they talked about modernity, they were referring to the modernity of the West represented by the Europe of their day. The Western programme of modernity, as developed in Europe, defined itself by a number of features such as industrialization, urbanization, secularization, rationalization, professionalization, individualism, faith in progress through human action, mass politics, the emergence of the nation-state and its essential institutions (public education, modern bureaucracy and representative democracy), a market economy and others. Atatürk and his followers believed that Turkish society could only be improved by following the Western programme of modernity, including its ideological and institutional premises.

However, the Western programme of modernity, which provided the basic paradigm in the 1950s, has been challenged by the theorists of globalization, dependency school, world-system theory and other approaches in the last few decades.[13] Thanks to the recent criticism, we know today that the version of modernity defended by Atatürk and his followers in the 1920s and the 1930s was only one of several different types of modernities. As the author of this book, I do not believe that the Kemalist modernization project with its roots in the twentieth century can respond to the challenges of the twenty-first century, or serve as a model for further modernization projects in contemporary Turkey. Nevertheless, it can still help us to better understand today's Turkey by offering a historical perspective on Turkey's modernization process, and the positive and negative consequences of it affecting the country. Thus, the aim of this study is not to offer another critique of the concept of modernity or to offer alternative models, but rather to understand the concept of modernity from Atatürk and his followers' points of view and to explain how their engagement with a medium intimately associated with Western modernity unfolded within their specific cultural-historical framework.

This study concentrates on a single medium: film. Film was chosen for several reasons: (a) Although it was an important part of cultural history of the Kemalist period, film has not been analysed in detail before; (b) it was deemed particularly suitable for Atatürk's project of creating his own, and the new Turkey's image as 'modern' because film, as a medium, was strongly associated with Western modernity; and (c) by facilitating the presentation of Atatürk and Turkey's new image to both domestic and foreign audiences, the medium of film functioned as a catalyst for the nation-building process. Contemporary representations of Atatürk in film not only helped consolidate his power during his lifetime but also constituted – and continues to constitute – the archive or framework supporting the myth of Atatürk. Analysing Atatürk's evolving public image in film, this study aims to achieve a better understanding of the relations between media and power, and of the role these relations played in the making of a 'great man' and the modern nation-state in the early-twentieth century.[14]

In the remainder of this introduction, I will first provide details about the filmic materials I analyse and their sources; then, I will briefly outline the six chapters to come.

Materials

To meet the objectives identified earlier, this study makes use of various types of primary source materials. However, the main sources of this research are the films themselves. I analyse film footage featuring Atatürk during the years he was in power, asking how he used cinema: 'To say what, to whom and with what effect'?[15] Found in Turkish and foreign film archives, much of this film footage has not previously been identified or analysed. In Turkey, two archives were central to my project: the Mimar Sinan Film Archives (a.k.a. the Turkish Film Archives) in Istanbul, and the archives of the Turkish Armed Forces Photo Film Center in Ankara. Both own a number of films showing Atatürk, some of which they provided for my research. Although part of the film material from these two archives was only available in fragments or are incomplete in other ways, I tried to find different versions of the same film in other film archives outside of Turkey. Besides the films, I have made use of letters, memoirs and newspaper articles as well as reports, newsletters and production files to supplement my analysis.

Some of the issues I encountered when looking for films to analyse are common to film history, while the others are specific to the Turkish context and my focus on Atatürk. The films in question were produced in the 1920s and the 1930s, a period in which movies were filmed on nitrate film base, a highly flammable material that needs to be carefully stored to avoid decomposition over time. However, until the 1930s, not much attention was paid to the institutional preservation of films. Consequently, according to the British film historian James Chapman, 'it has been estimated that up to three quarters of the films made before 1930 no longer survive, while others exist only in fragments'.[16]

Although the archivists from Mimar Sinan University are currently carefully restoring some of the films analysed in this research, most of the restorations have not yet been finished or made available to the public. Besides, there is no guarantee that the films that survived from this period remain in their original form. Because of the film medium's specific features, such as the use of montage and editing, much of the footage may have been changed as it was used in different films over time. As this research will show, some films surviving in the archives differ from the original versions described in documentation and letters.

Beside these general technical problems, the legal conditions for accessing archival film materials as well as the copyright held by the archives in Turkey, which allow them to give access only to certain films, partly shaped the corpus of material I was able to analyse. Instead of choosing films from a catalogue according to their own search criteria, researchers are only shown – if they are lucky enough – a few films or parts of films a few times, according to the seemingly arbitrary criteria of the archivists. Since my research was about Atatürk, a delicate subject in Turkey, consulting the films was also considered somehow sensitive by the archivists. Finally, since almost no written records exist concerning the films, the archives themselves did not have much information on the footage they possessed.

Despite these limitations, the archivists kindly shared with me some of the films in their collections, on the basis of which I was able to conduct this research. In particular, I made use of two films provided by the Turkish Film Archives at Mimar Sinan University: *Lozan Sulh Heyetinin Karşılanması* (The Reception of the Lausanne Peace Committee, 1923), which is analysed in Chapter 2; and *Atatürk'ün Amerikan Büyükelçisi Joseph C. Grew'u Orman Çiftliğinde Kabulü* (The Reception of the American Ambassador Joseph C. Grew by Atatürk on the Forest Farm, 1930), which is the focus of Chapter 3. Parts of some films on Atatürk and documents provided by the Turkish Armed Forces Photo Film Center are used to compare my own and other researchers' findings in Chapters 1, 2 and 4.

To understand the full scope of Atatürk's use of film, I also had to consult films and documents related to Atatürk in archives outside Turkey. British Pathé, for instance, owns a number of films featuring Atatürk, two of which are analysed in Chapter 2: some silent footage titled *Mustapha Kemel* (1920–9) and a silent newsreel called *Mustapha Kemal* (1923). Besides visiting the major European archives, I conducted extensive research in the United States, where I found original films and documents about Atatürk that constitute a substantial part of this research. Three archives in the United States stand out as holding significant film material on Atatürk: the Moving Image Research Collections (MIRC) at the University of South Carolina, in Columbia, South Carolina; the National Archives in Washington, DC; and the private archives in New York of Sam Bryan, the son of the film-maker Julien Bryan who shot live footage of Atatürk in 1936.

In the MIRC, I found the film *Ataturk Entertains Grew on His Private Estate*, shot by Fox Films Inc. in 1930. This film is not just a slightly different version of the film *Atatürk'ün Amerikan Büyükelçisi Joseph C. Grew'u Orman Çiftliğinde Kabulü* (The Reception of the American Ambassador Joseph C. Grew by Atatürk on the Forest Farm, 1930) held by the Turkish Film Archives, but it is also a longer and less degraded version. It is highly probable that the MIRC version comprises the original footage shot by the Fox Films crew when they came to Turkey to film Atatürk in 1930. As I explain in detail in Chapter 3, I draw this conclusion on the basis of diplomatic correspondence concerning the filming of Atatürk on his farm by Fox Films Inc., written by the American Ambassador Joseph C. Grew to the Secretary of State. The way ambassador Grew describes it in his letter is much closer to the MIRC version than to the TFA version. The fact that the film was preserved by MIRC as part of the Fox Movietone News Collections also increases the likelihood that it is the original version.

Quite surprisingly, nobody in Turkey, including the archivists at the Turkish Film Archives working painstakingly on the restoration of Atatürk's films, seems to have been aware of the existence of this extended, less degraded footage held by USC. At the time of my writing this study, two videos displayed on the website for the Presidency of the Republic of Turkey are taken from slightly eroded versions of *Gazi Mustafa Kemal, Atatürk Orman Çiftliği'nde* (Ghazi Mustafa Kemal is on the Forest Farm) and *Gazi Mustafa Kemal'in Amerikalılara Hitabı* (Ghazi Mustafa Kemal's Address to the Americans).[17]

To reconstruct the story of the production of *Ataturk Entertains Grew on His Private Estate* more comprehensively, and to understand the intentions behind it, in Chapter 3, I compare the ambassador's version of the film as he describes it in his letter with the two different versions of the film in the TFA and USC archives. The disparities reveal a fascinating story regarding the making of the film and its fortunes. Although the primary source material of this study is film, here a diplomatic letter unexpectedly changed the course of my research, enabling the reconstruction of missing parts in the two archived versions of the film. At the same time, the letter offered further insight into the film by revealing what happened behind the scenes. In this way, it becomes clear that other sources, such as letters, can sometimes reveal as much as or even more about a film than the film itself.

Also important for my research in the United States were the National Archives in Washington, DC. There, I found an episode from *The March of Time* newsreels featuring Atatürk and entitled 'Father of All Turks', which was released in the United States on 19 February 1937. Published by Time-Life Incorporated, the newsreel episode, which is analysed in Chapter 5 in great detail, was not only screened nationwide in the United States but also in Europe when Atatürk was still alive. The study of the newsreels' production files led me to the film-maker Julien Bryan, who provided the majority of the footage for the episode, in particular the contemporary footage of Atatürk.

Although Julien Bryan is unfortunately no longer alive today, his son Sam Bryan, the executive director of the International Film Foundation, generously provided me with access to his private archives in New York where he preserves a significant part of his father's films, still photos and documents, including those of and relating to Atatürk. In these archives, I found evidence that Julien Bryan's footage of Atatürk was used not only for *The March of Time* newsreels but also for an illustrated lecture called *Turkey Reborn*, which he delivered throughout the United States from 1937 onwards.

According to my research and Sam Bryan's knowledge, the film *Turkey Reborn* has not survived in its original form. Some parts of the footage, however, were used in other films and documentaries, as will be discussed in Chapter 4. I was able to reconstruct the story of the footage's journey onto American screens by looking at materials from the period, such as letters, newspaper articles, publicity material and memoirs as well as photographs, films and reports, and by interviewing Sam Bryan who remembers significant details about the footage of Atatürk filmed by his father.

These findings allowed me to gain unique insight into the production and reception of Bryan's footage of Atatürk in the United States. Evidence of correspondence between President Franklin D. Roosevelt and Atatürk, for instance, provides interesting details about the reception of Bryan's film in the United States. Found in the Time Warner Inc.'s HBO archives in New York, *The March of Time*'s promotional newsletter, *Photo Reporter*, helped me to reconstruct the details of Julien Bryan's visit to Atatürk in the fall of 1936. Most importantly, Bryan's own report on Turkey, written retrospectively in 1961, provided wonderful insights into his personal experience of filming Atatürk.

Chapter 4 again shows that, alongside the films, other materials can play a crucial role in recreating the story of footage that was transformed and projected onto the screen in different versions and diverse ways. This underscores that films are artefacts that cannot be understood by narrative and visual analysis alone. They are complex products, whose form and content are the result of several processes that are social and cultural as well as political and economic in nature. Consequently, films have to be considered in relation to the particular contexts within which they were produced and consumed. By combining foreign and Turkish sources as well as textual and contextual analysis, this study intends to bring together the films made of Atatürk at his instigation or with his support. Such a larger picture is particularly relevant in the case of Atatürk, since he used film to create and project a modern and civilized image of himself and his country, not just inside Turkey but also in the international arena.

Chapter outline

This study is divided into six chapters. Chapter 1 transports us back in time to the Ottoman Empire of the late nineteenth and early twentieth centuries, and more specifically to the social and cultural environment in which Atatürk was born and raised. It compares the history of cinema in Europe and the United States with the history of cinema in the Ottoman Empire. By placing Atatürk in his historical context, the chapter reveals the general framework within which his ideas on cinema emerged. Unlike the mainstream view, which regards Atatürk as a man whose ideas anticipated cinema's future success, this chapter offers an alternative approach focusing on the social, cultural and political forces that shaped his vision of cinema. It shows that his supposed attitudes towards cinema, as well as his later use of the medium, owed a great deal to the period and the milieu in which he lived.

Chapter 2 concentrates on Mustafa Kemal's and the nationalists' use of cinema during the struggle for independence (1919–23) and its aftermath. It shows how they deliberately mobilized cinema to create a national consciousness and to gain public support for Turkey's independence. The chapter further demonstrates that their efforts to film the war not only served propaganda purposes during it but also shaped the depiction of the war in its wake by building an 'archive' of cinematic images for the future(in the sense of Jacques Derrida and Michel Foucault). Moreover, through close readings of three films from this period, *Mustapha Kemel* (1920-9), *Mustapha Kemal* (1923) and *Lozan Sulh Heyetinin Karşılanması* (The Reception of the Lausanne Peace Committee, 1923), the chapter reveals the cultural and political messages that Mustafa Kemal sought to convey to the Western world after his rise to power.

Chapter 3 compares an account of the making of a film about Atatürk on his farm by Fox Film Inc. in 1930, which was provided in a letter from the American ambassador to Turkey Joseph C. Grew, with the two surviving versions of the film. The chapter demonstrates how Mustafa Kemal used film to project an image of himself and of the new Turkey as modern, civilized and democratic to the Americans. This image was carefully designed to challenge established ideas about Turkey in Western Orientalist discourses. In addition, the chapter analyses Mustafa Kemal's own performance in the film, and explains why film as a medium of communication was both an alluring and a risky way to present the young Turkey's new identity to the American public.

Chapter 4 traces the journey of the American film-maker Julien Bryan, who shot exclusive pictures of Atatürk in Turkey in 1936, including those of his private life. Two films emerged from the footage: *Turkey Reborn* (1937) and 'Father of All Turks' (1937). The first was produced by Julien Bryan as an illustrated travel lecture and was screened nationwide in the United States, and the second, produced by The *March of Time* newsreel series of Time-Life Inc., was screened in the United States and Europe. This chapter reconstructs the story of *Turkey Reborn* and shows how, in the interwar period, Atatürk managed to impress many Americans, including President Roosevelt, through this film footage. By analysing the making of Bryan's film, the chapter emphasizes Atatürk's concerns about his public image and his conscious attempts to shape Western public opinion through film at a critical time in European and global politics. Finally, the chapter makes clear that Bryan's moving images of Atatürk impressed not only his contemporaries but also later generations, who would remember him through these images.

Chapter 5 focuses on the 'Father of All Turks' episode of the famous American newsreel series *March of Time* (MOT). It explores how a contemporary newsreel series represented Atatürk and the Kemalist modernization programme in Western media. The chapter focuses on Atatürk's personal role in shaping his public image on the world stage and in claiming a status for Turkey among the 'civilized nations' of the world. At the same time, a close look at the way Atatürk's self-representation is distorted in the newsreel suggests that he could not fully control the meanings ascribed to his cinematic image outside Turkey.

The Epilogue concludes the study by placing Atatürk's image in a historical perspective, comparing his practice of creating his public image through media, including film, to that of his predecessors and contemporaries, and identifying avenues for further research. First of all, it compares Atatürk with political rulers of his time and of earlier periods in order to better understand how their public image, communicated through different forms of media, but particularly cinema, influenced his attempts to construct and communicate his own image as a political leader. Since Atatürk's public image has been central to the creation and maintenance of the Turkish nation-state, the chapter also compares his image in the media of his day and in today's media. This shows how changes in Turkish political culture and society have been accompanied by transformations in Atatürk's image.

Notes

1 Giovanni Scognamillo, *Türk Sinema Tarihi* (İstanbul: Kabalcı Yayınevi, 2010); Nijat Özön, *Türk Sineması Tarihi, 1896–1960* (İstanbul: Doruk Yayımcılık, 2010); Savaş Arslan, *Cinema in Turkey: A New Critical History* (New York: Oxford University Press, 2011).

2 I will refer to the founder of the Turkish Republic as Mustafa Kemal in the period before he adopted the family name Atatürk on 24 November 1934. I will also refer to him as Atatürk when I speak about him in general.

3 In Turkish: 'Sinema öyle bir keşiftir ki, bir gün gelecek, barutun, elektriğin ve kıtaların keşfinden çok dünya medeniyetinin veçhesini değiştireceği görülecektir. Sinema, dünyanın en uzak uçlarında oturan insanların birbirlerini tanımalarını, sevmelerini temin edecektir. Sinema, insanlar arasındaki görüş, görünüş farklarını silecek; insanlık idealinin tahakkukuna en büyük yardımı yapacaktır. Sinemaya layık olduğu ehemmiyeti vermeliyiz'. M. Kemal Atatürk.

4 See Erman Şener, *Kurtuluş Savaşı ve Sinemamız* (Dizi Yayınları, 1970), 3; Atilla Dorsay, *Sinema ve Çağımız* (Istanbul: Remzi Kitapevi, 1998), 15; Yılmaz Özdil, *Mustafa Kemal* (Istanbul: Kırmızı Kedi Yayinevi, 2018), 416.

5 In Turkish: 'Ben hayattayım. Millî Mücadele'ye ait bütün evrakım, kılıcım, çizmem hali hazırda mevcut olduğuna göre, çağırdığınız anda bana düşen vazife ve görevi yapmadım mı? Böyle bir teklif karşısında kalsam memnuniyetle kabul eder, bir artist gibi filmde rol alır, hâtıraları canlandırırdım. Bu milli bir vazifedir. Çünkü Türk gençliğine bu mücadelenin kazanıldığını canlı olarak isbat etmek,

hâtıra bırakmak bu filmle mümkün olacaktır'. See Şener, *Kurtuluş Savaşı ve Sinemamız*, 31–2.
6 Ibid., 32.
7 Bernard Lewis, *The Emergence of Modern Turkey*, 3rd ed. (New York: Oxford University Press, 2002), 292.
8 Thomas Carlyle, *On Heroes, Hero-Worship, and the Heroic in History*, ed. David R. Sorensen and Brent E. Kinser (New Haven and London: Yale University Press, 2013).
9 Yakup Kadri Karaosmanoğlu, *Atatürk* (İstanbul: İletişim Yayınları, 2014).
10 Emre Kongar, *Devrim Tarihi ve Toplum Bilinci Açısından Atatürk* (İstanbul: Remzi Kitabevi, 2005), 125–213.
11 Erik-Jan Zürcher, 'In the name of the father, the teacher and the hero: Atatürk cult in Turkey', in *Political Leadership Leaders and Charisma*, ed. Vivian Ibrahim and Margit Wunsch (London: Routledge, 2012).
12 Benedict Anderson's book *Imagined Communities* was an inspiration for me in approaching the subject of nationalism from a cultural perspective, particularly his idea of the cultural roots of nationalism (in terms of conscious or unconscious attitudes towards fatality, religion, time, etc.) and his idea of the role of print capitalism in the emergence of national consciousness. See Benedict Anderson, *Imagined Communities: Reflections on the Origin and Spread of Nationalism* (London: Verso, 2006), 9–46.
13 Particularly, the Israeli sociologist Shmuel Noah Eisenstadt's critique of classical theories of modernization and his notion of 'multiple modernities' played a significant role in changing the understanding and meaning of modernity in sociological theory. See Shmuel N. Eisenstadt, 'Multiple Modernities', in the *Multiple Modernities*, ed. Shmuel N. Eisenstadt (New York: Routledge, 2017), 1–30.
14 The British historian Peter Burke's study of Louis XIV's public image from a constructivist perspective was a great inspiration for this book. See Peter Burke, *The Fabrication of Louis XIV* (London: Yale University Press, 2009).
15 In his famous formula, the American political scientist Harold D. Lasswell (1902–78) describes an act of communication in terms of who says what to whom through which channel with what effect. See Herold D. Lasswell, 'The Structure and Function of Communication in Society', in *The Communication of Ideas: A Series of Addresses*, ed. Lyman Bryson (New York: Institute for Religious and Social Studies, 1948), 37.
16 James Chapman, *Film and History* (Basingstoke: Palgrave Macmillan, 2013), 4.
17 They are probably taken from the Turkish Film Archives or Turkish General Staff Archives. See 'Video Galerisi', Türkiye Cumhuriyeti Cumhurbaşkanlığı, accessed 15 May 2016, https://www.tccb.gov.tr/ata_ozel/video/.

1

Early cinema in the Ottoman Empire

In the nineteenth century, several attempts were made to capture and display certain phenomena in motion pictures in Europe and the United States. The inventors of these cinematic technologies included scientists, photographers, showmen and others.[1] In the United States, the English-born Eadweard Muybridge, who was already a famous photographer, managed to project sequences of photos of a galloping horse in motion onto a screen by 1880. Following Muybridge and the work of several others, the French physiologist Étienne Marey was able to record multiple images of flying birds. According to Mary Ann Doane, the inventors of these technologies were dealing with one of the most important questions of modernity in the nineteenth century: how to make time visible, representable and storable so that the human struggle against its inexorable passage could be won.[2] Alongside other technological inventions such as the railway, the steamship and telegraphy, cinema was seen as a medium that could help people to achieve a triumph against time and space.

The intense nineteenth-century American and European interest in institutions such as archives, museums and zoos, and technologies such as photography and cinema may be seen as resulting from a desire for the preservation of time in a rapidly changing environment. By capturing motion instantaneously and then enabling this past experience to become a present experience in the future, visual archival technologies such as photography and cinema could emancipate human life from the boundaries of time.[3]

As the technical experiments of inventors produced successful results, inventor-entrepreneurs from the United States and Europe realized the commercial potential of motion pictures, and became interested in developing the experiments further. In 1894, the American inventor Thomas Edison managed to use his invention of the kinetoscope to project film to the public in the United States. Edison's kinetoscope, however, was technically limited and allowed only one person at a time to watch a moving film with an eyepiece. One year later, on 1 November 1895, Max and Emil Skladanowsky were able to screen nine films with their invention of the bioscope at the Wintergarten, a high-class variety theatre in Berlin. In December 1895, one month after the Skladanowskys' screenings, the Lumière brothers introduced their invention of the cinématographe by screening films for an audience of thirty-five people at the Grand Café in Paris. In 1896, they presented their films to a larger audience at the Empire Music Hall in London.

The pioneers of cinema provided motion pictures to be shown in arcades, cafés, theatres and travelling shows. In the initial years of cinema, it was not difficult to please an audience because they were easily intrigued by moving images on the screen. The Lumière brothers' catalogue, for instance, consisted of actuality films,[4] in which everyday activities, events and places were filmed without being structured into a narrative or a coherent whole. The subjects of the films made, such as *La Sortie de l'Usine Lumière à Lyon* (Workers Leaving the Lumière Factory in Lyon, 1895), *Repas de Bébé* (Baby's Meal, 1895), and *L'Arrivée d'un Train en Gare de La Ciotat* (The Arrival of a Train at La Ciotat Station, 1895), indicate that there was indeed a fascination with the recording and representation of movement in time.[5] During this period, therefore, cinema emerged from and contributed to the archival impulse of the nineteenth century.[6] However, unlike the other archival technologies, cinema could not only capture and store the experience of the present, but, through subsequent screenings, also offer this past experience as an experience of the 'present' for its spectators.[7]

As technological inventions were following each other at a dizzying speed in Europe and the United States at the end of the nineteenth century, the news of the 'moving pictures' also reached the Ottoman Empire. In particular, the publicity activities of the Lumière brothers for the cinematograph attracted the interest of non-Muslims working as photographers. Istanbul's famous photographers Théodore Vafiadis (of Greek origin) and Onnik Diradour (of Armenian origin) were already in correspondence with the Lumière brothers about their cinematograph in 1895–6.[8]

In 1896, the Lumière brothers sent their representatives to introduce the cinematograph in several countries, including the Ottoman Empire. Although there is some information about the Lumières' operators' filming activities in the Ottoman Empire,[9] it is not known whether they were allowed to screen their films for an audience. What is known is that the Lumières' operators faced some difficulties when they crossed the Ottoman border equipped with their new invention.[10] According to the Turkish cinema historian Nijat Özön, this was partly because the device was new to the Ottoman bureaucrats and partly due to Sultan Abdülhamid II's suspicion of any device that had a crank or functioned with electricity, a suspicion that extended to the Lumières' cinematograph, which required an electric lamp.[11] The Ottoman authorities were worried that the cinematograph's projection lamp could explode, cause a fire and harm the public.[12]

At the time, electricity was already being used as an energy source in major European capitals such as London, Paris, Berlin and Vienna, but the situation was different in the Ottoman Empire's capital, Istanbul. Frightened by the great fires that had plagued the city,[13] Sultan Abdülhamid II became extremely cautious about the use of electricity in his domains in general and Istanbul in particular, since its buildings were mainly made of wood. If there was a fault in an electrical connection, the resulting fire could potentially spread and turn the city to ashes. In addition, Istanbul's urban infrastructure was not geared for electricity as there were many European gas companies that had been granted concessions for the illumination of Istanbul. There was also a lack of technical knowledge among the sultan's subjects about electricity, and the number of fire brigades was small. Worse still, the sultan's political opponents could have easily used a fire caused by an electrical failure as an opportunity to criticize him. Thus, the sceptical attitude of Ottoman bureaucrats towards the new invention of the Lumières can partly be understood as an extension of the sultan's suspicion towards electricity.

However, the way Özön links the slow development of cinema in the Ottoman Empire to Sultan Abdülhamid II's suspicious attitude towards modern Western technologies and his oppressive rule ignores some important facts.[14] First, the sultan himself was strongly interested in new visual technologies such as photography and cinema.[15] He sent his collection of photographic albums as a gift to the Library of Congress in Washington, DC in 1893 and to the British Museum in London in 1894 for propaganda.[16] The albums were carefully designed to display the modernization efforts of the empire, emphasizing the progress achieved in science, education and culture as well as developments in health, military and industry since Sultan Abdülhamid II ascended the throne.[17] As photography was considered the most modern and 'realistic' medium of the time, the sultan saw it as a perfect means for presenting himself as an enlightened and modernizing ruler.[18]

The sultan also employed photography for practical and documentary purposes. Fearing terrorist attacks, he was mostly not willing to leave his palace; photography allowed him to follow important developments in his vast empire without his having to set foot outside.[19] His huge network of spies and informants employed photography to gather intelligence as well as to monitor significant events and governmental projects. Highly interested in physiognomy,[20] the sultan used photographs to assess convicts for amnesty and students for admission to the military colleges.[21] As a traditionalist, he valued the rich cultural heritage under his domain. To preserve it for posterity, he arranged for some monuments and buildings of Islamic and Classical civilizations to be photographed.[22] It is clear that Sultan Abdülhamid II had realized the documentary potential of photography and its ability to preserve the past for future generations.

Similarly, the sultan was interested in cinema. As in many royal courts in Europe, cinema quickly became a popular medium for entertainment in the Ottoman court. The sultan's daughter, Ayşe Osmanoğlu, mentions in her memoirs that a French magician, Bertrand, screened some films in the Yıldız Palace.[23] This means that one of the first film screenings in the Ottoman Empire took place in the imperial palace.[24] A Spanish showman called Don Ramirez also screened films for the sultan in the palace in order to get permission to use electricity in his travelling circus, which opened in Istanbul probably in 1899.[25]

Unlike his friend Kaiser Wilhelm II, Sultan Abdülhamid II did not like to travel much. Instead, he preferred to stay in his palace and enjoy special film screenings held by foreign film operators. In 1906, he even hired an English 'bioscope attaché' to show travel films for his private viewing.[26] Some of the film organizers and entrepreneurs were awarded medals and money by the sultan. For his contributions to cinema, for instance, the French inventor and manufacturer Pierre Victor Continsouza received the *Sanayi-i Nefise* (Fine Arts) medal together with two hundred shillings in 1898.[27] By awarding these prizes, the sultan presented himself as a munificent patron of modern science and technology.

Cinema was by no means only a technological curiosity for the sultan. Like photography, it helped him solve a communication problem by allowing him to follow recent political developments around the world without leaving his palace. In 1902, for instance, he ordered films from the Ottoman Embassy in Berlin for the palace, particularly on the situation in China after its war against Western powers and Japan.[28] After hearing of the screening of a movie in Barcelona called 'Ottoman Atrocities' concerning the Bulgarian insurrection in 1903, the sultan's government intervened via the Ottoman embassy in Madrid to prohibit the screening of the film, which, they argued, 'misinformed' the public.[29] The sultan also employed cinema to follow and propagate projects within his far-flung empire. To promote the recently built Anatolian Railway, for instance, he commissioned a cameraman whose job was to produce a number of films 'regardless of cost'.[30]

As with other technologies, Sultan Abdülhamid II was selective in his approach to cinema. To regulate the use of cinema and the magic lantern, a cinematography privilege was prepared during his reign in 1903.[31] Consisting of twenty-six articles, the privilege constituted the legal framework for the making and screening of moving images in the empire.[32] Ranging from stipulations about the rights of privilege owners, the screening sites and the content of the films to technical issues, the privilege offers fascinating glimpses into attitudes towards cinema during the Hamidian era. It suggests that there were conscious attempts to benefit from the new medium by propagating the regime's politics and by educating students, soldiers and peasants. At the same time, the privilege sought to restrict cinema's undesirable effects on public morality and state policies.

Although Sultan Abdülhamid II discovered that the new medium was a powerful force that could serve political ends, he generally avoided using it to portray himself. This was most likely partly due to the Islamic aversion to the visual representation of the human image and partly for security purposes.[33] Nevertheless, to make himself visible after the assassination attempt by the Armenian Revolutionary Federation in 1905, he appeared on camera during his *selamlık*[34] ceremony.[35] Likewise, to reclaim his power after the Young Turk Revolution of 1908, he allowed Sigmund Weinberg, the representative of Pathé Frères in Turkey, to film him during the *selamlık* ceremony at the Hamidiye Mosque.[36] The latter film was shown both in Istanbul and Germany. According to the Turkish-Dutch film historian Mustafa Özen, the sultan was also filmed while attending the inauguration of the new parliament in December 1908.³⁷

Initially, the sultan had been less opposed to electricity as well, going so far as to test its use at the end of the nineteenth century at the mansion of one of his most reliable officials, İzzet Pasha (a.k.a. Arab İzzet), in Istanbul. Turkish journalist Murat Bardakçı tells us what happened next. With the permission of the sultan, the electrification of İzzet Pasha's mansion in Beşiktaş was completed and the house was lit. The illumination of the mansion fascinated the dwellers of Istanbul. Despite this success, the cautious sultan wanted to wait and see what would happen in the long run. Bardakçı states that İzzet Pasha also obtained a cinema projector for watching silent films with his family and friends. On one of these movie nights, the electricity sparked and the flames set the house on fire, burning it down within a couple of hours. İzzet Pasha and his family survived, but a young female servant who had been sleeping on an upper floor died. The unfortunate incident reaffirmed the sultan's suspicions regarding the use of electricity and, as a consequence, Istanbul's residents had to wait for electricity until 1914.³⁸

However, the sultan allowed limited use of electricity in some other cities outside of Istanbul. In 1902, Tarsus became the first city in the empire to use electricity for illumination, followed by the major cities Izmir and Salonica in 1905. Electricity also began to be used in Istanbul before 1914 in exclusive places such as the Yıldız Palace, Tersane-i Amire (Imperial Dockyard) and a few shops in the district.³⁹

It is restrictive to link the slow development of electricity and cinema to the suspicious attitudes of the Ottoman ruling elite towards Western technologies. As mentioned earlier, Sultan Abdülhamid II was not per definition against products of Western modernity, but made selective and limited use of them during his reign. However, cinema's slow development in the Ottoman Empire in comparison to Europe and the United States did not depend on technology alone. Cinema also required favourable social, cultural, political and economic conditions to become a popular medium among the public.

Public cinema in the Ottoman Empire

Cinema quickly became an important part of the entertainment culture in the Ottoman palace, and it would not take long for it to reach audiences outside of the palace walls. It was a French painter named Henri Delavallée who introduced cinema to the Ottomans on 12 December 1896 by organizing a public screening at the famous brasserie Salle Sponeck in Pera (Beyoğlu), the most Europeanized neighbourhood of Istanbul.[40] The reaction of the audience members, who for the first time in their lives saw a motion picture, was not very different from reactions in other parts of the world; they were astonished. Some showed fear as they watched a bullfight, a train travel and much more.[41]

The astonishment of the audience points to a unique character of this new technology: its immediacy. Photography can fix a moment in the present and give a feeling of reality, but the captured moment immediately turns into an experience of the past, so that when we look at a photograph, what we see is a moment gone by. On the other hand, cinema's technical capacity to capture motion by juxtaposing several moments in time and displaying them in a sequence creates a feeling of real-time movement, a feeling of being in the 'here' and 'now', an enduring experience of presence for viewers.[42]

Just as the first film screening at the Salle Sponeck caused different reactions among the Ottoman audience, the new medium itself found diverse echoes within public discourse. According to Ercüment Ekrem Talu, one of the audience members at the screening, the Istanbul public intensively debated the event and the new medium for several weeks. Some people claimed that it was a sin to watch it and regretted that they had attended, while what Talu calls the 'progressive' people were delighted that another component of civilization had entered their country.[43]

As Leo Charney and Vanessa R. Schwartz note in their introduction to *Cinema and the Invention of Modern Life*, cinema was a medium in which several aspects of modernity merged. First, it was a new technology and a commercial product of modern capitalism. Second, it was an outcome and important part of urban culture, which addressed its audiences as a homogeneous mass. Third, by capturing and displaying actual movement in time, it went far beyond the capacities of the existing conventional visual media. Cinema surpassed the pre-existing forms of modern culture (the nineteenth-century realist novel, serial and melodrama) in many ways and became an original form of its own.[44]

In the Ottoman Empire, cinema largely remained a complementary medium until after the Young Turk Revolution of 1908. In the Islamic context, it was commonly employed to accompany traditional performing arts such as *Karagöz* (a shadow play), *Ortaoyunu* (Turkish comedia dell'arte)[45] and

Meddah (storytelling), especially during Ramadan (the Islamic month of fasting), and was also used in theatres, coffee houses and fairs in order to enrich the entertainment programme. Also in Europe and the United States, film screenings initially took place in venues of entertainment such as vaudevilles, magic theatres and fairs.

According to Doane, this feature of cinema points to another important aspect: its capacity to display contingency.[46] She suggests that, on the one hand, cinema was a technological invention that emerged out of the desire of capitalist modernity to structure and gain control over contingency and temporality by rationalizing them. On the other hand, the contingency that needed to be controlled still carried potential risks as well as a certain allure in resisting rationalization, system, structure and meaning.[47] Through the attraction of the spontaneous, the unpredictable and the unexpected, cinema rapidly became a popular form of entertainment. At the same time, it carried a potential risk in displaying such contingency, because too much contingency could easily threaten the control exercised over the representational totality[48] and therefore the control over meaning, as will be mentioned in the next chapter when looking closely at some of the films featuring Atatürk.

Cinema's entertainment potential raises an important question: Who were the people entertained by this new medium? In the Ottoman Empire, for a long time, cinema was considered a *gâvur* (non-Muslim or infidel) business and form of entertainment.[49] In its first years, cinema was primarily a popular form of entertainment in Istanbul's Pera, and the vast majority of the audience consisted of non-Muslims, Levantines and foreign nationals.[50]

Despite some criticism, the new invention was generally welcomed by Istanbul's Muslim public as well. Two months after his first film screening in the Salle Sponeck in Pera, in early February 1897, Henri Delavallée took his show to the famous coffeehouse Fevziye Kıraathanesi in Şehzadebaşı, the other centre of entertainment for Muslims in Istanbul. Later, different travelling operators and entrepreneurs from Europe and the United States held film shows in Istanbul and elsewhere for Muslim audiences.

After reaching the Ottoman Empire, cinema needed the right political climate to become a distinctive form of entertainment and to reach a broader audience.[51] On 30 January 1908, in the last year of Sultan Abdülhamid II's rule, a Jewish businessman named Sigmund Weinberg, who was the agent of Pathé Frères in Turkey, opened the first permanent movie theatre called

Cinémathéatre Pathé, in Tepebaşı, Istanbul.[52] After the Young Turk Revolution of 1908, the number of permanent movie theatres rose gradually. As the quantity of movie theatres and salons that displayed films grew, the number of representatives of foreign film producers from France, Britain, Germany and the United States also increased.

In addition to Istanbul, cinema showed a distinctive and rapid development in cosmopolitan port cities such as Salonica and Izmir, which had easy access to communications with Europe, access to electricity, and hosted a high proportion of foreigners and non-Muslims at the beginning of the twentieth century. Not a long time ago in 1881, Mustafa Kemal was born into a Muslim, Turkish-speaking, middle-class family in Salonica. The Ottoman Empire's own modernization efforts and its increasing incorporation into the Western capitalist economy in the late nineteenth century had brought with it visible changes to the cities' landscape such as street gas lighting, electricity, telegraph lines, trams, railways, docks, banks, new industrial buildings, printing houses and modern secular schools. The emerging Ottoman bourgeoisie, most of whom were non-Muslims, led also to the creation of new social settings such as Western-style cafes and restaurants, literary clubs and theatres, sport clubs and hippodromes, and parks and promenades.

Young Mustafa was highly influenced by the social, cultural and intellectual milieu in which he was born and raised. Significantly, he was educated in a Western-style civilian school called Şemsi Efendi in Salonica, and in military schools in Salonica, Monastir and Istanbul that were products of the reform era.[53] As a young man he witnessed many infrastructural transformations as well as leisure activities of foreign and non-Muslim bourgeoisie in Ottoman cities, who would provide him with a model of modernity.

Like many other modern technologies, it was the Western foreigners who first introduced photography and cinema to the Ottoman Empire in the nineteenth century. Nevertheless, initially it would be the non-Muslims of the empire who quickly adopted these technologies and made them part of their culture and lifestyle, such as the Manaki brothers photographers (of Vlach origin), who brought a bioscope film camera from London and created the first motion pictures in the Ottoman Balkans.[54] They made what many consider to be the first Ottoman film in 1905: a documentary film entitled *Grandmother Despina* showing their grandmother spinning in the village of Avdela in Monastir.

The pioneering role of non-Muslims in adopting the modern Western technologies of photography and cinema in the Ottoman Empire was partly due to the way certain religious and ethnic backgrounds were associated with certain crafts, and partly due to who had access to and interest in new technologies coming from abroad. The non-Muslim elites of the empire were familiar with Western culture thanks to their cultural and commercial relations with Europe. Some non-Muslim merchants, particularly the members of the local Christian bourgeoisie, benefited from the advantages of capitulations and other agreements in trading with Western countries in the nineteenth century. As a result, they were culturally more ready to adopt new visual technologies from the West such as photography and cinema.

Over time, Muslims also began to show interest in this new medium. Fuat Uzkınay, the internal director of Istanbul Sultanisi (Istanbul High School), became highly interested in cinema and sought to learn how to use this new medium from Sigmund Weinberg. After learning the trade, Fuat Uzkınay held film screenings together with Şakir Seden at the school in 1910, marking the entrance of cinema into Ottoman educational spaces.[55]

Ottoman Muslims not only were attracted to cinema out of pure interest but also saw considerable profit potential in the new invention. In March 1914, Murat and Cevat Boyer opened a movie theatre called Emperyal Sineması in Şehzadebaşı. It was the first movie theatre run by Ottoman Muslims of Turkish origin. After the outbreak of the First World War and in the heyday of nationalism, they significantly renamed it Millî Sinema (National Cinema). Following this, Ali Muhsin Bey opened a movie theatre called Türk Sineması (Turkish Cinema) in Sirkeci in June 1914. In its promotions, the movie theatre emphasized that the films would be screened with Turkish intertitles.[56] Another Turkish entrepreneur, Ali Efendi, opened a movie theatre called Ali Efendi Sineması in Sirkeci in July 1914.

Despite all the developments, the number of movie theatres was still limited in the Ottoman Empire and, as mentioned before, cinema did not reach the vast majority of the population, especially those living outside the major cities. Even in urban centres like Istanbul, Izmir, Trabzon, Adana, Konya and Bursa, the medium did not reach all inhabitants. In Istanbul, for instance, there were only about thirty-two permanent movie theatres in 1921.[57] In contrast, according to one estimate, there were already more than 10,000 movie theatres in the United States, and more than three hundred in France by the end of 1909.[58]

Nevertheless, while cinema was available for entertainment in Istanbul's Pera, Mustafa Kemal was a young cadet in Istanbul.[59] On his days off, he went with his friends to the cafés, restaurants and beerhouses of Istanbul, including those in Pera.[60] He spent time in public spaces run and frequented by non-Muslims and foreigners in Istanbul and in his hometown Salonica.[61] It is likely that Mustafa Kemal first became acquainted with cinema in one of these places. Yet not everyone was as lucky as Mustafa Kemal. Being a modern, young Turkish man and a member of the Ottoman army, a privileged class in Ottoman society, he could visit the places where cinema was screened, while many others could not.

In the early years of cinema, Muslim women were excluded from this form of public entertainment to a great extent. Only a few privileged Muslim women had the opportunity to become acquainted with the new medium through private film screenings organized in mansions.[62] Although there were mixed-gender film screenings in Pera, a respectable Muslim woman would not have put her reputation at risk by going there.[63]

Until the Young Turk Revolution of 1908, the attendance of Muslim women at public screenings was limited.[64] Exclusive 'women-only' film screenings were organized for the first time in the movie theatre owned by a non-Muslim Ottoman entrepreneur, Asaduryan (of Armenian origin), in Pangaltı, Istanbul.[65] These special daytime screenings, which became popular among middle-class women, were limited to certain days of the week. In Ramadan months, on the Anatolian side of Istanbul, in Anadoluhisarı and Kadıköy, there were open-air film screenings, where a curtain separated male and female audiences.[66]

In some theatres, women could only sit in designated zones or in special lodges, separated from men.[67] These lodges mainly attracted upper-class Muslim women.[68] Some critics perceived Muslim women's cinema visits as a threat to societal norms and values. The *Tasvir-i Efkâr* newspaper, for instance, included complaints about Muslim women's theatre and cinema visits, and their sitting together with men. According to the newspaper, this was neither compatible with Islam nor adequate for social customs.[69]

The criticism of the newspaper concerning women at the cinema theatres has a number of reasons behind it. First, by treating its audience as a homogeneous mass, cinema could easily blur gender differences and downplay their importance, and thus pose a potential threat to patriarchal social norms.

Second, by bringing men and women physically together in the same public space, cinema could provoke social interaction between them, which might eventually lead to the dissolution of the segregation of women in public spaces. It should not be forgotten that cinema is not just a public space; it is also a dark space, so who knows what may happen when the lights are switched off.

As French philosopher Michel Foucault shows, separation, especially spatial separation, can function as an instrument of power designed to keep the inferior in its position.[70] By providing a new public space where women could sit together with men, cinema allowed Muslim women – albeit, only temporarily – to overcome their segregation and feel equal to men. This, of course, entailed a subversion of traditional gender roles in a strongly patriarchal society, which was something that the conservative newspaper could not condone.

It is interesting to see how, in the first decades of cinema, similar reactions occurred almost everywhere around the world, including conservative Christian countries like the Netherlands. Dutch media historian Frank van Vree, for example, has shown how the Dutch parliament discussed taking measures against the risks of cinema. These proposed measures included banning children from public screenings, dividing cinemas into two parts and placing men on the left side and women on the right as was customary in church, prohibiting the dimming of lights during film screenings and censoring films.[71]

Returning to the Ottoman context, could the separation of male and female audiences by a curtain, by creating designated zones or by organizing exclusive film screenings for women have been compromises to assuage the moral panic? This is not likely, because the concern was not only about where and how film screenings took place but also about who executed them and what it was about. In fact, all of the film companies operating in the Ottoman Empire were initially of foreign origin. After Pathé's entrance into the Ottoman film market with their representative Sigmund Weinberg, another French film company, Gaumont, followed suit with their representative Tilemahos Spiridis, who was of Greek origin.[72] Another Ottoman businessman of Greek origin, Panayiotis Hrisos, introduced the Vitagraphe Company of America's films to the public.[73] A different film distribution company called Ciné Théatrale d'Orient represented German and Danish films.[74] Thus, the films that were screened to Ottoman audiences were foreign films that could be seen as a potential threat to the traditional values of a Muslim society.

In fact, cinema enabled audiences of all cultures to imagine other possible lifestyles. By displaying common human experience on the screen, cinema could lead audience members to perceive themselves as belonging to not only a particular local, regional or national community but also to a global one. Other media of communication might also lead to the same, but cinema, according to Italian film theorist Francesco Casetti, has one particular advantage: in being visual, it speaks a 'universal language' and therefore can speak to all.[75] Given the fact that the vast majority of people in the late-Ottoman and early-Republican periods were illiterate, cinema could be a very convenient medium to speak to everyone. This feature might have made it dangerous in the eyes of some and beneficial in the eyes of others, who wanted to break with the old and create a new culture.

Casetti also argues that by basing itself on the idea of the allegedly universal values of 'love, duty, and revenge', cinema can promote a 'universal taste'.[76] This purported universality can contradict traditional values, because the way a Hollywood or a French movie approaches certain issues can contradict the way traditional Ottoman culture would approach them. Lastly, through the collective and simultaneous viewing of the same films, film stars and spectacles by millions of people from different countries and backgrounds, cinema can cultivate a feeling of 'universal synchrony' in its audiences.[77] It can help to imagine new forms of communities, including national and global ones, by making people aware of their fellow viewers.[78]

In comparison to many other private or individual media of communication, cinema provides a more communal experience; it encourages 'broader access', delivers a 'common idiom' and allows 'collective participation'.[79] By screening the images, performances and moral deeds of humankind, it creates 'myths and rites of an entire community'—the one formed by cinema audiences.[80] If all these possibilities cinema offers to transform lifestyles are considered, it is not difficult to understand the moral panic of the conservative Ottoman newspaper concerning female cinema attendance.

However, it was not only foreign countries and cultures that were being shown on domestic screens; some images of Turkey were also exported. When, for instance, the Lumière cameraman Alexandre Promio visited the Ottoman Empire in 1896, he shot a number of scenes in Istanbul and Izmir showing the Turkish infantry, the Bosporus and the Golden Horn.[81] Consequently, scenes from Turkey were already featured in a Lumière catalogue published in 1897.[82]

Besides the French film-makers, the Germans, the Italians and the British also shot scenes in Turkey to be shown in their respective countries.[83] Some of these films were screened in the Ottoman Empire as well. For instance, in 1899, the scenes of the Bosporus were in the catalogue of the Odeon Theater (a.k.a. Éclair).[84] In 1908, Sigmund Weinberg's Cinémathéatre Pathé screened films on Istanbul. One year later, in 1909, the Odeon Theater showed a film concerning the Young Turk Revolution of 1908.[85] Some newspapers reported on 14 December 1910 that the Cinéma Pathé had shown a film about the manoeuvers of the Ottoman army, including scenes of Sultan Mehmed V Reşad, his visit to Edirne, a public *selamlık* procession of the sultan and his return to Istanbul.[86]

Another cinema, the Star American Bioscope, featured a film called *Türkiye'de Meşrutiyet* (The Constitutional Monarchy in Turkey) and another one featuring the Serbian king's visit to Istanbul.[87] Provided that the vast majority of these films were produced by foreign film companies, it is not amiss to talk about a 'foreign gaze' dominating film-making regarding the Ottoman Empire from the beginning. Despite a growing popular demand for films in the empire, it was only foreign film companies and non-Muslims that could satisfy the demand. Muslims did not produce films until a particular occasion necessitated their participation in the industry.

Wartime cinema

As the Ottoman government officially declared war against the Entente powers on 10 November 1914, it also increased propaganda activities, or, in the words of the Minister of the Interior Talat Pasha,[88] 'the activities that would render the war popular.'[89] As part of these activities, a meeting was organized at the Fatih Mosque on 14 November 1914, at which Ottoman Sultan Mehmed V's jihad proclamation against the Entente powers was read aloud to the public. The Ottoman sultan, who was at the same time the caliph of all Sunni Muslims in the world, called for them to unite under the Ottoman flag to fight the Allies.

On the same day, another furious crowd went to Ayastefanos (San Stefano), a suburb of Istanbul, in order to demolish the Russian Monument. The Russians had erected this monument after the war of 1877–8 against the Ottoman Empire in order to commemorate their fallen soldiers. When war was declared on the Allies, the statue reminded the Ottomans of their humiliation and therefore it had to be demolished. The demolition of the monument was not spontaneous but planned.[90] To film this important event for propaganda purposes, according to Özön, a Vienna-based Austro-Hungarian film company called Sascha Film was employed.[91]

According to some historians, although the foreign operators were on location to film the event, it was decided at the very last moment that the one to film such an important national event should be a Turk.[92] Fuat Uzkınay, who already had some experience in film screening but not in filming, was chosen for the job, in order to increase the propaganda value of the event. He learned how to use the camera on site from the foreign film crew and shot the film, titled *Ayastefanos'taki Rus Abidesinin Yıkılışı* (The Demolition of the Russian Monument at San Stefano), on 14 November 1914.[93] Although the film has not survived, it is still considered by many to be the first motion picture in the history of Turkish cinema.[94]

Although little is known about the story of its production, recent research shows that the film probably existed.[95] The Ottoman newspaper *Tanin* announced the screening on 25 December 1914 as follows: 'Ayastefenos'taki Moskof Heykeli'nin Tahribi. Sirkeci'de Ali Efendi Sineması bügünden itibaren *Moskof Heykelinin Tahribi* ve *Cihâd-ı Ekber İlanı* manzaraları ile *Harb-i Umûmi* şeritleri ve zengin teferruat programı göstermektedir'.[96] (The Demolition of the Moscow Monument at San Stefano. From today, the Ali Efendi Cinema in Sirkeci shows scenes from *The Demolition of the Moscow Monument* and *The Declaration of Jihad Proclamation*, together with *World War* reels in a rich, detailed programme.)

The film does not exist in Filmarchiv Austria archives either. However, they retain another film titled *Türkei (Konstantinopel): Kriegskundgebung der Bevölkerung bei der Fatih Moschee*[97] (Turkey [Istanbul] War Demonstrations of the Public at the Fatih Mosque, 1914), which must have been shot on the day of the earlier-mentioned meeting. This fifty-five-second newsreel produced by Messter Film (Berlin) is likely to be the aforementioned film *The Declaration of Jihad Proclamation*, which was shown with a different title in Germany.

Film-making has always been a collaborative exercise. During the First World War, Sascha Film was one of the most important film production companies in the Austro-Hungarian Empire, and Oskar Messter's German film company frequently collaborated with them to create its weekly newsreel series called *Messter-Woche*. There were special film propaganda missions of the German and Austro-Hungarian Empire in Turkey. An Austrian film operator called J. Goldschmid, for instance, showed propaganda films about the Austria-Hungarian Empire throughout the Ottoman Empire in 1916 and 1917, and reported about their successful screening.[98] To influence Ottoman public opinion in favour of Germany, Germans also screened many propaganda films in cities of the Ottoman Empire such as Istanbul, Konya, Aleppo and Baghdad.[99] It is likely that, being allies, the Austro-Hungarian and German film producers collaborated with Ottoman officials to produce and screen these films. As one of the few experts on cinema in the Ottoman Empire, Fuat Uzkınay might have been involved in some of these productions or screenings. In this respect, Uzkınay was perhaps both the first Turkish film-maker and the only one who never thought of himself as one.

Rather than searching for the origins of Turkish cinema in a single event or a person and giving it an exaggerated significance, it is important to look at the general trends in Ottoman cinema around the time of the First World War. From 1914 onward, deliberate attempts were made by the ruling party, İttihat ve Terakki Cemiyeti (Committee of Union and Progress, CUP), to build a 'national economy'.[100] As a result of these economic policies, the cinema business, formerly in the hands of foreigners and local non-Muslims, began to be embraced by Muslim entrepreneurs and film-makers mostly of Turkish origin. However, the word 'national' in the CUP context does not necessarily refer to a broader Turkish nationalism, but rather to a mixture of Ottoman, Muslim and Turkish nationalism that considers the non-Muslims of the empire less and less as a constituent part of the Ottoman state and nation.[101]

The outbreak of the First World War changed the content of film programmes in Ottoman cinemas. Due to the Ottoman Empire's entrance into the war on the side of the German and Austro-Hungarian Empire, popular French films were gradually replaced by German films.[102] As the war continued, the importance of political and military propaganda in the belligerent countries grew. As a potent weapon in modern warfare, Western armies made use of photography and cinema for visual propaganda, intelligence (aerial reconnaissance),[103] and military training. Enver Pasha, the Ottoman Minister of War, was well aware of the importance of cinema for a modern army. In its issue of 26 February 1914, the *Proodos* newspaper records Enver Pasha's statement that the army needs to appropriate cinema as a tool for education and discipline.[104]

In an army in which the majority of soldiers were illiterate, film as a visual medium could provide a powerful means of conveying information regarding strategic military matters probably more effectively than written instructions. In addition, the *Tanin* newspaper stated that the army decided to organize screenings of films imported from Europe for the divisions on military manoeuvers, military competitions and strategic areas.[105]

At the beginning of war, the Ottoman Ministry of War's main film supplier was the German Empire, which had an intelligence agency in Istanbul for influencing Ottoman public opinion in favour of Germany. In 1915, the German intelligence agency sent an official called S. A. Urich to the Çanakkale front (a.k.a. Gallipoli) in order to produce propaganda films for both German and Turkish audiences.[106] The Ottoman military museum (Müze-i Askerî-i Osmânî) in Hagia Sophia, part of which was turned into a cinema theatre, was one of the popular places where German and Austro-Hungarian propaganda films were displayed. The propaganda films of the Allied countries were also screened regularly in other Ottoman cinemas, which were close to the CUP government, such as Müdafaa-i Milliye Sineması (Theatre of National Defense), Ali Efendi Sineması, Kemal Bey Sineması, Emperyal Milli Sineması, Turan Sineması and Donanma Cemiyeti Sineması.[107]

The German Empire was also actively involved in propagating Enver Pasha's image as a military hero during the First World War. His image was reproduced in posters, journals and postcards several times. He also appeared at least three times in the famous German newsreel series *Messter-Woche*: in the episode *Türkische Militäraufnahmen aus dem Weltkrieg*[108] (Turkish Military Film Records from the World War, 1915), the episode *Der türkische Kriegsminister, Vizegeneralissimus Enver Pascha besucht Se. Exzellenz General von Winkler, Führer einer Armee an der mazedonischen Front*[109] (The Turkish Minister of War, Vice General Enver Pasha visits his Excellency General von Winkler, Leader of an Army at the Macedonian Front, 1916), and the episode *Der Kaiser bei unseren türkischen Verbündeten*[110] (The Emperor with our Turkish Allies, 1917). Mustafa Kemal also fought during the First World War and was well aware of how Enver Pasha used the media, including film, to facilitate his rise in a meteoric manner to receive the German designation of 'Enverland'.

Besides using foreign sources, the Ottoman Ministry of War cooperated with other state departments for its propaganda campaign. In 1915, the Ottoman

Ministry of Education commissioned the photography teacher Ahmet Necati Bey to produce photographs and films on the heroism of the fighting Ottoman soldiers at the Çanakkale front so as to provide inspiration to students.[111] In May 1916, the Ministry of Education commissioned Ahmet Necati Bey again, this time to take photographs and shoot films in Baghdad, which would be lost to the British one year later.[112]

Since the Ottoman army did not have its own cinematography office at the beginning of the war, the Ottoman Ministry of War also cooperated with a local organization called Müdafaa-i Milliye Cemiyeti (Society of National Defense) in order to produce propaganda films. Founded in 1903, the Society of National Defense was a social and cultural organization that had a Turkish nationalist character and close ties with the governing party CUP. Its main aim was to support the army. To raise more money, they entered the film business, opening the aforementioned movie theatre in Şehzadebaşı called Müdafaa-i Milliye Sineması in 1914. The head of the Society's cinema branch was Kenan Erginsoy, who would later serve as a cinema expert for Atatürk's Cumhuriyet Halk Partisi (Republican People's Party). As the Society did not have any experience in film-making, it commissioned Sigmund Weinberg to produce films concerning the Battle of Çanakkale in 1915. Weinberg sent two film operators, Maksi Hardel and Arakisyan, to the front. The films they recorded were shown with the title *Çanakkale Harb Menazırı* (Scenes of the Çanakkale Battle) in Istanbul for the benefit of the Society.[113]

In the initial years of the First World War, Weinberg was perhaps the most employed film producer hired by the Ottoman Ministry of War. According to the *Proodos* newspaper, in 1915, he sent two cameramen and the necessary equipment to the headquarters of the Fourth Army, which was planning a raid on the British-protected Suez Canal under the command of Cemal Pasha.[114] To film the actions and the success of the Ottoman soldiers at the Galician front, Weinberg went to Galicia in 1916 with photographer Ibrahim Ferit Bey. When they returned to Istanbul in 1917, the films they had shot in Galicia and Romania were shown first to an elite audience at Weinberg's movie theater Cine-Palas during a special event organized by the Central Command, and later to the general public.[115]

Enver Pasha eventually decided to establish a cinematography department within the Ottoman army, taking the German army's military film and photo office as a model.[116] On 14 November 1916, Fuat Uzkınay was appointed as an officer to the Merkez Sinema Dairesi (Central Office of Cinema), which was affiliated with the Central Command in Istanbul.[117] Hüseyin Bey served as his assistant. Mazhar Yalay and Cemil Filmer also worked for the department.

Weinberg also helped to develop the cinematography department in the army. In August 1917, he was sent to Berlin in order to buy tools and equipment for the cinematograph in the Central Command in Istanbul.[118] Towards the end of 1917, the Central Command decided to establish cinema detachments within the army corps. For this purpose, on 18 December 1917, Fuat Uzkınay was sent to Berlin in order to pick up the cinematograph and technical equipment from German companies.[119] Significantly, his journey was extended until 18 January 1918 by the Ministry of War so that he could increase his knowledge of and expertise on cinema. When in Europe, Uzkınay visited the military film department of the German Army in Berlin and that of the Austro-Hungarian Army in Vienna, as well as some other film factories to observe their operations.[120]

The establishment of a film institution within the Ottoman army points to the important fact that the desire for film-making did not emerge from a simple admiration for the West, nor from a technological and artistic curiosity, but rather from a pragmatic necessity to keep up with the modern Western armies and their communication technologies. In fact, in order to keep on an equal footing with the other imperial powers, the Ottoman Empire had to pay careful attention to the modernization of the army. The establishment of a cinematography office within the army can be understood as part of this survival strategy.

Özön suggests that the Central Office of Cinema also had a programme for its own operations. According to this programme, the office had to produce films about: '1. Operations of fighting troops at the front 2. Important events 3. The functioning of the military factories 4. Instructions about new weapons sent by allied countries 5. Maneuvers'.[121] Some films produced by the office before the Ottoman Empire signed the Armistice of Mudros in 1918 were *Alman İmparatoru'nun Dersaadet'e Gelişi* (The Arrival of the German Emperor in Istanbul, 1917), *Alman İmparatoru'nun Çanakkale'yi Ziyareti* (The German Emperor's Visit to Çanakkale, 1917), *Abdülhamit'in Cenaze Merasimi* (Abdülhamit's Funeral, 1918), *Sultan Reşat'ın Cenaze Merasimi* (Sultan Reşat's Funeral, 1918), *Vahdettin'in Biat Merasimi* (Vahdettin's Ceremony of Accession, 1918) and *Cülus-ı Hümayun'da 26. Fırka Resmigeçidi ve Vahdettin'in*

Kılıç Alayı (The Pageantry of the 26th Division in the Ceremony of Accession and Vahdettin's Sword-Girding Ceremony, 1918).[122]

Besides filming important public events, the office was occasionally employed by Enver Pasha to commission his personal projects. Cameraman Cemil Filmer writes in his memoir that on the orders of Enver Pasha, he was once sent to Kozlu to film the lignite mine and the activities of the military regiment. The resulting film, whose copies were produced by Fuat Uzkınay, was shown to Enver, Talat, Sait Halim Pashas and other state dignitaries at the Sipahi Ocağı (Cavalry Club) in Istanbul.[123] Satisfied with the film, Enver Pasha ordered Cemil Filmer to come to his mansion in Ortaköy to produce photographs and films of himself, his wife Naciye Sultan and their child.[124] Later, Cemil Filmer shot films of the horse racing at the Veliefendi hippodrome in which Enver and Sait Halim Pasha's horses participated. Cemil Filmer recounts how the pashas watched the film with great pleasure at the Sipahi Ocağı.[125] Also on the orders of Enver Pasha, Cemil Filmer was commissioned to film and photograph Sheikh Ahmed al-Sennusi, who was invited to Istanbul by Sultan Mehmed Reşad in 1918. Filmer also conducted a special film screening for the sultan and the sheikh after their dinner at the Dolmabahçe Palace.[126] The production of these films shows that the Central Office of Cinema's official remit was occasionally exceeded. Nevertheless, considering that shooting films was still new to the Ottomans, the shooting of these films may have been useful for the officers to learn the craft of film-making.

During the First World War, cinema was considered one of the most convenient propaganda tools for reaching the masses. The fighting countries not only produced newsreels regarding the war but also sponsored several films encouraging the people to support the army and increasing public morale.[127] Official establishments and private companies were employed for this purpose. The propaganda thriller *Enver Pasha, predatel' Turtsii* (Enver Pasha, the Traitor of Turkey, 1914), directed by the Russian director Yakov Protazanov, is a striking example of this.[128] Fuat Uzkınay was also involved in the production of two fiction films in this period, although these were not related to the war: *Leblebici Horhor Ağa* (Roasted Chickpea Vendor Horhor Agha, 1916) and *Himmet Ağa'nın İzdivacı* (Himmet Agha's Marriage, 1916–8), an adaptation of Molière's play *Le Mariage Forcé*.[129]

Having noticed the efficacy of cinema in reaching out to ordinary people, the Society of National Defense aimed to create a 'national' cinema by representing a modernizing Turkish society in fiction and non-fiction films. In the beginning, the Society produced actuality films showing historical sites and the natural beauties of Istanbul, and films showing scenes from the Çanakkale front. Later, the Society also produced fiction films such as *Casus* (Spy, 1917), *Pençe* (Claw, 1917), *Bican Efendi Belediye Müfettişi* (Bican Efendi, the Municipality Inspector, 1917) and *Bican Efendi Tebdil-i Havada* (Bican Efendi Goes for a Change of Scenery, 1917). The Society's fiction films were introduced as 'national' films in the Ottoman press.[130]

The importance of cinema for 'national' propaganda was a widely discussed topic among Ottoman intellectuals at the time. On 15 August 1918, Muhsin Ertuğrul stated in the *Temâşâ* journal that the new development of the art of cinema in Turkey was highly important for the national prestige. In April 1919, another Ottoman intellectual, Kemal Emin, also argued in *Temâşâ* that through cinema, nations could learn about each other's customs and traditions more realistically and could consequently erase existing prejudices against each other. He suggested that through cinema, societies could influence each other and make new discoveries. Likewise, Cevdet Reşit mentioned in the journal *Yarın* in 1921 that cinema was an indispensable medium for propaganda and that Turkey should make use of it.[131] According to him, cinema could be used to change negative images of the Turks in foreign public opinion. He further stated that cinema was a more influential medium than the press and that Westerners had recently given more importance to it. Mustafa Kemal's supposed words on cinema show many similarities with contemporary intellectuals' words on cinema. Seeing parallels as close as these, it is difficult to say that Mustafa Kemal's supposed thoughts were original.

In October 1918, the Ottoman war ended. In accordance with the Armistice of Mudros, Allied troops established military administrations in Istanbul. According to the resolutions of the armistice, the Central Office of Cinema and the semi-official Society of National Defense had to be dissolved, and their equipment surrendered to the Allied forces.[132] Yet the Ottomans found a way to escape this obligation. Instead of surrendering the equipment, they handed it over to another institution called Malûlîn-i Guzât Muâvenet Heyeti (Committee of Disabled Veterans) in November 1919.[133] Similar to the Society of National Defense, the Committee of Disabled Veterans had strong ties with the CUP. It was founded in 1915 with the support of Enver Pasha by Colonel Cevdet Bey and eleven other members. Its main aim was to provide support for the war veterans and their families. For this purpose, they also established the Committee of Disabled Veterans Film Factory in 1919.[134] In the same year, Fuat Uzkınay became the director of the film factory.[135]

The Committee of Disabled Veterans Film Factory produced several films, both fiction and non-fiction. Among their fiction films, *Mürebbiye* (Governess, directed by Ahmet Fehim, 1919) stands out due to its political impact. The film is about a beautiful but immoral French woman called Anjel, who enters the service of a rich Ottoman family as a governess. More than becoming a governess to the children, Anjel becomes a governess to the men of the family, by sleeping with them and pitting them against each other. The film was essentially an adaptation of Hüseyin Rahmi's (Gürpınar) novel *Mürebbiye*, published in 1898. The novel criticized the Ottoman elite, which was fond of the *alafranga* (Western) lifestyle, by showing their tragicomic situation, as caused by Anjel.

The novel's adaptation into a film in a critical year right after the end of war could easily be interpreted as a political message or a symbolic protest against the Allies, who had occupied Istanbul. This is especially likely when one considers the public fury caused by the French general Franchet d'Espèrey's ostentatious ceremonial entrance on horseback into the city of Istanbul on 8 February 1919. Although *Mürebbiye* was screened for a short time in Istanbul, it aroused considerable interest, enough to soon be censured and banned from distribution in Anatolia by the Allied authorities.[136]

During the First World War, the military and government authorities of Britain, France and Germany were suspicious of all foreign films and newsreels, which might negatively affect public morale.[137] Therefore, all footage that came from abroad went through censorship before it ever reached the movie theatres.[138] During the years of Istanbul's occupation, the Entente authorities ordered the Ottoman Ministry of War to ban the screening of German, Austro-Hungarian and Bulgarian films in Pera.[139]

Although the Entente authorities forbade the showing of foreign powers' films, cinema was a popular form of entertainment among their own soldiers. It was used by the Allies to support troop morale. During the First World War, the French, for instance, had at least one mobile camera available for each army corps in 1916.[140] The Section Photographiques et Cinématographiques des Armées (SPCA) of the French army set up four hundred film theatres on the Western Front in 1917.[141] The British and the Americans delegated the

Young Men's Christian Association (YMCA) for the organization of film screenings for the troops in around seventy halls.[142] The films shown to the soldiers included newsreels, documentaries, feature films and comedies. Charlie Chaplin films were especially popular among the Allied soldiers. The Allied forces sometimes used the promise of distraction and entertainment to display instructional films.[143] To meet the demands of the Allied soldiers during Istanbul's occupation, the cinemas in Pera displayed films with French intertitles.[144] Film screenings for the Allied troops held in Izmir were open to public.[145]

Besides producing implicit protest films, the Committee of Disabled Veterans also filmed explicit protests during this period. The landing of the Greek army in Izmir on 15 May 1919 caused an enormous fury in the Ottoman Muslim public. Starting on Friday 19 May in Fatih, Istanbul, large demonstrations against the Greek occupation were organized. The Committee filmed parts of these demonstrations, including the prominent female novelist Halide Edip's (Adıvar) passionate speech on the Sultanahmet Square on 23 May.[146]

The occupation of Turkey by the Allied forces and their clients caused several armed resistance movements to spring up among Muslim inhabitants of Anatolia. They began to form independent irregular militia throughout the country. Although these forces, later referred to as Kuva-yı Milliye (National Forces), had some minor successes in hindering the enemy, they were not able to defeat the regular armies completely. Consequently, towards the end of 1920, the government of the Grand National Assembly decided to establish its regular army in Ankara under the leadership of Mustafa Kemal in order to fight the occupying forces.

The nationalist forces fought many bloody battles against their various enemies between 1919 and 1922. In 1922, the commanders of the National Assembly's army planned their largest military operation, a great offensive to achieve a decisive victory against the Greek forces on the Western Front. In the same year, some of the cinematographic equipment belonging to the Central Office of Cinema of the Ottoman army was transferred from Istanbul to Anatolia in order to produce films in favour of the Ankara government.[147] This shows that Mustafa Kemal did not anticipate the future potential of cinema alone or single-handedly create everything out of the ashes of the empire, but rather built the resistance movement on the remains of the Ottoman army and the existing networks of his nationalist followers, particularly the Unionists.[148]

Conclusion

By tracing the emergence of cinema in Europe, the United States and also the Ottoman Empire, it can be said that Mustafa Kemal's vision of cinema was not far ahead of his time. In fact, his supposed thoughts on cinema accorded with the way in which it was widely discussed and practiced in Europe, the United States and also parts of the Ottoman Empire. It is clear that Mustafa Kemal sided with the progressive ideas of his time, particularly in relation to modernization, and thus he was highly influenced by contemporary discourses that associated cinema with Western modernity.

As this chapter has shown, long before Mustafa Kemal's rise to power, there was already a cinema culture in the Ottoman Empire to which foreigners, non-Muslims and his predecessors made pioneering contributions. The CUP government had played a crucial role in the formation of a 'national' cinema by opening up the Ottoman cinema industry to Muslim entrepreneurs and filmmakers, establishing a department for cinematography within the Ottoman army and entering the film business with their cultural organizations such as the Society of National Defense and the Committee of Disabled Veterans.

This chapter also demonstrates that cinema did not have the same conditions in the Ottoman Empire as it did in Europe and the United States due to technical, economic and cultural factors. Significantly, at the end of the nineteenth and the beginning of the twentieth centuries, Ottoman cinema culture was limited to places with the necessary material conditions for film screenings. Access to these material conditions was largely reserved for particular ethnic groups and social classes that had a certain affinity with Western modernity. Thus, the vast majority of the Ottoman population was excluded from the opportunity of participating in the visual culture and literacy developed in cinema.

Spending his youth as a Turkish middle-class gentlemen in the leading cities of Ottoman modernization such as Salonica, Monastir and Istanbul, and being trained as an officer in the army, one of the empire's most elite institutions, Mustafa Kemal occupied a privileged position that enabled him to become aware of the social, cultural and political importance of cinema. Nevertheless, it was his ability to build on the work of his predecessors that would allow him to use this medium to his advantage. Mustafa Kemal's coming to power during the Turkish War of Independence represented a crucial moment in which he transformed his position and image into that of the undisputed national leader. The next chapter will focus on the role of cinema in this key phase of Mustafa Kemal's political career.

Notes

1. Erik Barnouw, *Documentary: A History of the Non-Fiction Film* (New York: Oxford University Press, 1993), 3.
2. Mary Ann Doane, *The Emergence of Cinematic Time: Modernity, Contingency, the Archive* (Cambridge: Harvard University Press, 2002), 190.
3. Ibid., 82–3.
4. Actuality films (*Actualités*) were short films showing real-life activities, topical events or news. See Annette Kuhn and Guy Westwell, *A Dictionary of Film Studies* (Oxford: Oxford University Press, 2012), 4–5.
5. Doane, *The Emergence of Cinematic Time*, 62–3.
6. Ibid., 23.
7. Ibid.
8. Ali Özuyar, *Babıâli'de Sinema* (İstanbul: İzdüşüm Yayınları, 2004), 13–14. The person Özuyar refers to as Diradour is most probably Istanbul's famous Armenian photographer Onnik Diraduryan. According to Özuyar, Vafiadis and Diradour already corresponded with the Lumière brothers before the public screening at the Grand Café in December 1895. Diradour sent them a letter on 30 September and Vafiadis on 3 October 1895. According to Özuyar, Diradour also published articles in different Ottoman journals to introduce the new invention, but these articles did not receive attention from either the Ottoman government or the public.
9. According to Barnouw, it was Alexandre Promio who worked in Turkey for the Lumières. See Barnouw, *Documentary*, 11. Özön also states that it was Promio who filmed Turkey. See also Nijat Özön, *Türk Sineması Tarihi 1896–1960* (Istanbul: Doruk Yayımcılık, 2010), 32–3.
10. According to Özen, another representative of the Société Antoine Lumière, Louis Janin, also experienced difficulties when trying to introduce the cinematograph in 1986. See Mustafa Özen, 'Travelling Cinema in Istanbul', in *Travelling Cinema in Europe*, ed. Martin Loiperdinger (Frankfurt am Main: Stroemfeld Verlag, 2008), 47.
11. Özön, *Türk Sineması Tarihi*, 32; Özuyar, *Babıâli'de Sinema*, 14–19.
12. Özen, 'Travelling Cinema in Istanbul', 47.

13 Istanbul suffered a number of major fires during Abdülhamid II's lifetime (1842–1918). Before Abdühamid was born, on 20 January 1839, a great fire swept through Babıâli. On 11 July 1870, another great fire occurred in Beyoğlu. During his reign (1876–1909), more fires occurred, such as the one in Babıâli on 23 August 1878 and the Çırçır fire on 23 August 1908, which affected several districts of Istanbul. On the history of fires in Istanbul in the Ottoman period, see Necdet Sakaoğlu, 'Yangınlar: Osmanlı Dönemi', in *Dünden Bugüne İstanbul Ansiklopedisi*, vol. 7 (Istanbul: Kültür Bakanlığı ve Tarih Vakfı, 1994), 427–38.

14 Özön, *Türk Sineması Tarihi*, 32, 33, 37, 39, 45. For Sultan Abdülhamid II's suspicious attitude towards devices that had a crank or functioned with electricity, see also Ali Özuyar, 'II. Meşrutiyet'in Modernleşmede Önemli Bir Araç Olan Sinema Üzerindeki Etkileri', in *100. Yılında II. Meşrutiyet Gelenek ve Değişim Ekseninde Türk Modernleşmesi Uluslararası Sempozyumu: Bildiriler*, ed. Zekeriya Kurşun et al. (Istanbul: Ebru Matbaacılık, 2009), 488.

15 Mustafa Özen, 'Visual representation and propaganda: Early films and postcards in the Ottoman Empire, 1895–1914', *Early Popular Visual Culture*, 6, no. 2 (2009): 147–51, doi: 10.1080/17460650802150408.

16 Selim Deringil, *The Well Protected Domains: Ideology and the Legitimation of Power in the Ottoman Empire 1876–1909* (London and New York: I.B. Tauris, 2011), 151.

17 Ibid., 152.

18 Muhammad Isa Waley, 'Images of the Ottoman Empire: The Photograph Albums Presented by Sultan Abdülhamid II', *The British Library Journal*, 17, no. 2 (Autumn, 1991): 111, accessed 23 June 2015, http://www.jstor.org/stable/42554325.

19 Özen, 'Visual representation and propaganda', 147.

20 Physiognomy was a popular science in the late nineteenth century according to which it was possible to deduce a person's character from his physical appearance.

21 Waley, 'Images of the Ottoman Empire', 114.

22 Ibid., 117.

23 Ayşe Osmanoğlu, *Babam Sultan Abdülhamid* (Istanbul: Timaş Yayınları, 2013), 76.

24 Giovanni Scognamillo, *Türk Sinema Tarihi* (Istanbul: Kabalcı Yayınevi, 2010), 15. According to Scognamillo, cinema most probably entered to the Ottoman Empire through the palace by the end of 1896 or in the beginning of 1897.

25 Stephen Bottomore, 'Don Ramirez: Spanish showman active in Turkey', *Who's Who of Victorian Cinema*, accessed on 2 February 2016, http://www.victorian-cinema.net/ramirez.

26 Ibid.
27 Özen, 'Travelling Cinema in Istanbul', 52. See also Özde Çeliktemel-Thomen, 'Denetimden Sansüre Osmanlı'da Sinema', *Toplumsal Tarih*, 255 (2015): 76, 78.
28 Özuyar, 'II. Meşrutiyet'in Modernleşmede Önemli Bir Araç Olan Sinema Üzerindeki Etkileri', 449.
29 Mustafa Özen, 'De opkomst van het moderne medium cinema in de Ottomaanse hoofdstad Istanbul, 1896–1914' (PhD diss., Universiteit Utrecht, 2007), 127.
30 According to Bottomore, it is not certain whether these films were made or publicly shown. See Bottomore, 'Don Ramirez: Spanish showman active in Turkey'.
31 In my email correspondence with film scholar Özde Çeliktemel-Thomen, she suggested that the privilege was signed and stamped by two people: Makrıköy'den İbrahim bin Yunus and Ahmed. According to her, it is likely that they were entrepreneurs. Özde Çeliktemel-Thomen, email message to author, 12 July 2016. For a detailed analysis of the Cinematography privilege, see Özde Çeliktemel-Thomen, '1903 Sinematograf İmtiyazı', *Toplumsal Tarih* 229 (2013): 26–32. See also Özuyar, 'II. Meşrutiyet'in Modernleşmede Önemli Bir Araç Olan Sinema Üzerindeki Etkileri', 450.
32 Çeliktemel-Thomen, '1903 Sinematograf İmtiyazı', 26–32.
33 Deringil, *The Well Protected Domains*, 22.
34 Selamlık was the weekly ceremony of the Ottoman sultan, in which he went to perform Friday prayers at a mosque.
35 İbrahim Yıldıran, 'Selim Sırrı Tarcan ve Türk Sinemasının Erken Dönem Tartışmalarına Katkı', *Kebikeç* 27 (2009): 225.
36 Özen, 'Visual representation and propaganda', 150.
37 Ibid.
38 Murat Bardakçı, 'Beyaz enerji krizimiz bir yangınla başladı', *Hürriyet*, last modified 12 May 2001, http://arama.hurriyet.com.tr/arsivnewsmobile.aspx?id=-242952.
39 Emine Öztaner, 'Technology as a Multidirectional Construction: Electrification of Istanbul in the Late Nineteenth and Early Twentieth Centuries' (Master's thesis, İstanbul Şehir University, 2014), 52.
40 Özen, 'Travelling Cinema in Istanbul', 47.
41 Scognamillo, *Türk Sinema Tarihi*, 16; Özön, *Türk Sineması Tarihi*, 36–37.
42 Doane, *The Emergence of Cinematic Time*, 103.
43 See Özön, *Türk Sineması Tarihi*, 37.
44 Leo Charney and Vanessa R. Schwartz, eds., *Cinema and the Invention of Modern Life* (Berkeley: University of California Press, 1995), 10.

45 The *ortaoyunu* was a type of traditional theatre performed in the middle of a public square or in a coffee house in Turkey. The plot was insubstantial and provided a frame for the dialogue, which was commonly improvized by the two main characters of the play, called 'Kavuklu' and 'Pişekâr'. See *Encyclopaedia Britannica Online*, 'Ortaoyunu', accessed 3 May 2014, http://www.britannica.com/EBchecked/topic/295642/Islamic-arts/13827/Ortaoyunu.

46 Doane, *The Emergence of Cinematic Time*, 24.

47 Ibid., 11.

48 Ibid., 12.

49 Özön, *Türk Sineması Tarihi*, 39.

50 Scognamillo, *Türk Sinema Tarihi*, 17.

51 Ibid., 18.

52 Özen, 'De opkomst van het moderne medium cinema', 150–62. See also Özön, *Türk Sineması Tarihi*, 39.

53 Young Mustafa began his primary education in Hafız Mehmet Efendi's school in 1886, which offered a traditional, religious education. Later he was transferred to Şemsi Efendi School, which offered a modern European-style education. Due to his father Ali Rıza Efendi's death, his family moved to his uncle's farm at Rapla, near Langaza. There, he briefly attended a Greek village school nearby and was taught some basic subjects by an Albanian farm clerk. His mother soon sent him back to Salonica, where he continued his education in a civilian preparatory school (Mülki Rüştiye). Because of a quarrel with another boy in class, his teacher Kaymak Imam beat him severely, which made him leave the school. In 1893, he entered military preparatory school (Askeri Rüştiye) in Salonica. Upon graduation, he enrolled in the military high school in Monastir (Manastır Askeri İdadisi) in 1896. In 1899, at the age of 18, Mustafa Kemal entered the War College (Harbiye Mektebi) in Istanbul, and in 1902 he was admitted to the Staff Academy (Harb Akademisi) in Istanbul. In 1905, he completed his course at the Staff Academy, staying in Istanbul until he was posted for unit training (stage) to Syria in 1905.

54 It was Yanaki Manaki who went to London and bought a Bioscope 300, produced by the Charles Urban Trading Company. See Christos K. Christodoulou, *The Manakis Brothers: The Greek Pioneers of the Balkanic Cinema* (Thessaloniki: Organization for the Cultural Capital of Europe Thessaloniki, 1997), 59.

55 Özön, *Türk Sineması Tarihi*, 39.

56 Ali Özuyar, *Sessiz Dönem Türk Sineması Tarihi (1895–1922)* (Istanbul: Yapı Kredi Yayınları, 2016), 105–6.

57 Özde Çeliktemel-Thomen, 'The Curtain of Dreams: Early Cinema in Istanbul (1896–1923)' (master's thesis, Central European University, 2009), 65. According to Nezih Erdoğan, in 1922, the number of movie theaters in Istanbul reached about eighteen, while there were fourteen shops selling films and technical devices for cinema. See Nezih Erdoğan, 'The Spectator in the Making of Modernity and Cinema in Istanbul, 1896–1928', in *Orienting Istanbul: Cultural Capital of Europe?*, eds. Deniz Göktürk et al. (New York: Routledge, 2010), 134.

58 Yorgo Bozis and Sula Bozis, *Paris'ten Pera'ya Sinema ve Rum Sinemacılar* (Istanbul: Yapı Kredi Yayınları, 2013), 78.

59 Andrew Mango, *Atatürk* (London: John Murray, 2004), 43, 50, 54. For Mustafa Kemal's leisure time, see ibid., 52–53. See also Şevket Süreyya Aydemir, *Tek Adam: Mustafa Kemal*, vol. 1 (Istanbul: Remzi Kitabevi, 2011), 106–7.

60 Mango, *Atatürk*, 52.

61 Ibid., 53.

62 Özön, *Türk Sineması Tarihi*, 41.

63 Özen, 'Travelling Cinema in Istanbul', 51.

64 Özön, *Türk Sineması Tarihi*, 41; Scognamillo, *Türk Sinema Tarihi*, 20.

65 Scognamillo, *Türk Sinema Tarihi*, 20.

66 Özön, *Türk Sineması Tarihi*, 41.

67 Özen, 'De opkomst van het moderne medium cinema', 131. See also Erdoğan, 'The Spectator in the Making of Modernity and Cinema in Istanbul, 1896–1928', 133.

68 Özen, 'De opkomst van het moderne medium cinema', 131.

69 Özuyar, *Sessiz Dönem Türk Sineması Tarihi*, 306.

70 Michel Foucault, 'The Great Confinement', in *The Foucault Reader: An Introduction to Foucault's Thought*, ed. Paul Rabinow (London: Penguin, 1991), 124–40.

71 Frank van Vree, 'Media Morality and Popular Culture. The Case of the Netherlands 1870–1965', in *Twentieth-Century Mass Society Britain and Netherlands*, ed. Bob Moore and Henk van Nierop (New York: Berg, 2006), 83.

72 Scognamillo, *Türk Sinema Tarihi*, 19.

73 Bozis and Bozis, *Paris'ten Pera'ya Sinema ve Rum Sinemacılar*, 101.

74 Scognamillo, *Türk Sinema Tarihi*, 19.

75 Francesco Casetti, *Eye of the Century: Film, Experience, Modernity* (New York: Columbia University Press, 2008), 15.

76 Ibid.

77 Ibid.

78 Benedict Anderson shows, for instance, the important role of newspapers in the creation of new imagined communities such as nations. See Benedict Anderson, *Imagined Communities: Reflections on the Origin and Spread of Nationalism* (London: Verso, 2006).

79 Casetti, *Eye of the Century*, 16.

80 Ibid.

81 Scognamillo, *Türk Sinema Tarihi*, 20.

82 Ibid.

83 Ibid.

84 Ibid.

85 Ibid.

86 Ibid.

87 Ibid.

88 Talat Pasha was a leader in the Committee of Union and Progress, and became the Grand Vizier in the Ottoman Empire in 1917.

89 Özön, *Türk Sineması Tarihi*, 49.

90 Nijat Özön, *İlk Türk Sinemacısı Fuat Uzkınay* (Istanbul: Türk Sinematek Derneği Yayınları, 1970), 8.

91 Özön, *Türk Sineması Tarihi*, 51. See also Scognamillo, *Türk Sinema Tarihi*, 24.

92 Özön, *Türk Sineması Tarihi*, 50–1; Şener, *Kurtuluş Savaşı ve Sinemamız*, 5–6; Scognamillo, *Türk Sinema Tarihi*, 24.

93 Özön, *Türk Sineması Tarihi*, 51.

94 Şener, *Kurtuluş Savaşı ve Sinemamız*, 9–10; Scognamillo, *Türk Sinema Tarihi*, 25.

95 Özuyar, *Sessiz Dönem Türk Sineması Tarihi*, 176.

96 Ibid.

97 The film is also available online: Der Erste Weltkrieg und das Ende der Habsburgermonarchie, *Türkei (Konstantinopel): Kriegskundgebung der Bevölkerung bei der Fatih Moschee*, Audiovisual file, 1914, 45 sec., accessed 21 March 2017. http://ww1.habsburger.net/de/medien/tuerkei-konstantinopel-kriegskundgebung-der-bevoelkerung-bei-der-fatih-moschee-film-d-1914.

98 KA, AOK, KPQ, Ktn. 60, Filmstelle 1917, 'Aktion Goldschmid', Nr. 3419, Mai 1917.

99 Özde Çeliktemel-Thomen, 'Osmanlı İmparatorluğunda Sinema ve Propaganda (1908–1922)', Online *International Journal of Communication Studies*, 2 (June 2010): 10.

100 For a detailed analysis of the policies of 'Millî İktisat' (National Economy), see Erik-Jan Zürcher, *The Young Turk Legacy and Nation Building: From the*

Ottoman Empire to Atatürk's Turkey (New York: I.B. Tauris, 2010), 219–20; Erik-Jan Zürcher, *Turkey: A Modern History* (London and New York: I.B. Tauris, 1998), 127–31.
101 Zürcher, *The Young Turk Legacy and Nation Building*, 213–35.
102 Özen, 'De opkomst van het moderne medium cinema', 180.
103 Paul Virilio, *War and Cinema: The Logistics of Perception* (London and New York: Verso, 1989).
104 Bozis and Bozis, *Paris'ten Pera'ya Sinema ve Rum Sinemacılar*, 132.
105 Ibid.
106 Özuyar, *Sessiz Dönem Türk Sineması Tarihi*, 205–6.
107 Harbi Umûmî Kurdeleleri (World War Reels) was frequently shown in these cinemas. See Özuyar, *Sessiz Dönem Türk Sineması Tarihi*, 182.
108 Das Bundesarchiv, *Türkische Militäraufnahmen aus dem Weltkrieg*, Messter-Woche, Audiovisual file, 1915, 7 minutes 18 seconds, accessed 22 September 2017. https://www.filmothek.bundesarchiv.de/video/574631?q=Enver+Pascha&xm=AND&xf%5B0%5D=_fulltext&xo%5B0%5D=CONTAINS&xv%5B0%5D=.
109 filmportal.de, *Einzelsujets*, Messter-Woche, Audiovisual file, 1916, 2 minutes 38 seconds, accessed 22 September 2017. http://www.filmportal.de/video/messter-woche-einzelsujets.
110 Das Bundesarchiv, *Der Kaiser bei unseren türkischen Verbündeten*, BUFA, Audiovisual file, 1917, 30 minutes 17 seconds, accessed 22 September 2017. https://www.filmothek.bundesarchiv.de/video/565699?q=Enver+Pascha&xm=AND&xf%5B0%5D=_fulltext&xo%5B0%5D=CONTAINS&xv%5B0%5D=.
111 Özuyar, *Sessiz Dönem Türk Sineması Tarihi*, 205–6.
112 Ibid., 210.
113 Özuyar, *Sessiz Dönem Türk Sineması Tarihi*, 202; Bozis and Bozis, *Paris'ten Pera'ya Sinema ve Rum Sinemacılar*, 132.
114 Özuyar, *Sessiz Dönem Türk Sineması Tarihi*, 207.
115 Ibid., 209.
116 Cemil Filmer, *Hatıralar: Türk Sinemasında 65 Yıl* (Istanbul: Emek Matbaacılık ve İlâncılık, 1984), 86.
117 Özuyar, *Sessiz Dönem Türk Sineması Tarihi*, 255.
118 Ali Özuyar, *Devlet-i Aliyye'de Sinema* (Ankara: De Ki Yayınları, 2007), 42–3.
119 Özuyar, *Sessiz Dönem Türk Sineması Tarihi*, 259.
120 Mustafa Çetin, 'Fuat Uzkınay Ailesi Tarafından Hazırlanan Özgeçmiş 2', mustafacetin.org, accessed 22 September 2017, http://www.mustafacetin.org/tr/fuat-uzkinay-ailesi-tarafindan-hazirlanan-ozgecmis-2.

121 Özön, *İlk Türk Sinemacısı Fuat Uzkınay*, 11.
122 Özuyar, *Sessiz Dönem Türk Sineması Tarihi*, 256–7.
123 Filmer, *Hatıralar*, 88–9.
124 Ibid., 89–90.
125 The film was also shown at the Anfi Sineması in Tepebaşı, Istanbul. See ibid., 90.
126 Ibid.
127 Nicholas Pronay and Peter Wenham, *The News and the Newsreel* (London: Macmillan Education Ltd, 1976), 7.
128 Hubertus Jahn, *Patriotic Culture in Russia during World War I* (Ithaca and London: Cornell University Press, 1998), 162. According to Peter Rollberg, the director of this film is Vladimir Gardin. See Peter Rollberg, *Historical Dictionary of Russian and Soviet Cinema* (Lanham: Scarecrow Press, 2009), 96, 244.
129 Özön, *Türk Sineması Tarihi,* 52–54.
130 Özuyar, *Sessiz Dönem Türk Sineması Tarihi*, 266. The Society's fiction film *Pençe* (Claw, 1917) was described as the first 'national film reel' by the journal *Temâşâ*. See Feyza Kurnaz Şahin, 'Cumhuriyetin Kuruluşuna Kadar Türkiye'de Yardım Cemiyetlerinin Sinema Faaliyetleri ve Kamuoyunda Sinema Algısı (1910–1923)', *Atatürk Araştırma Merkezi Dergisi* 88 (2014): 7.
131 Ali Özuyar, *Sessiz Dönem Türk Sineması Antolojisi (1895–1928)* (Istanbul: Küre Yayınları, 2015), 61.
132 Özön, *Türk Sineması Tarihi,* 59–61.
133 Ibid., 60.
134 Şahin, 'Cumhuriyetin Kuruluşuna Kadar Türkiye'de Yardım Cemiyetlerinin Sinema Faaliyetleri', 10.
135 Özuyar, *Sessiz Dönem Türk Sineması Tarihi*, 320.
136 Özön, *Türk Sineması Tarihi,* 62; Scognamillo, *Türk Sinema Tarihi*, 30; Özuyar, *Babıâli'de Sinema*, 74.
137 Raymond Fielding, *The American Newsreel, 1911–1967* (Norman: University of Oklahoma Press, 1980), 115–16.
138 Ibid.
139 Çeliktemel-Thomen, 'Osmanlı İmparatorluğunda Sinema ve Propaganda (1908–1922)', 9; Özuyar, *Sessiz Dönem Türk Sineması Tarihi*, 286, 306.
140 Laurent Véray, 'Cinema', in *The Cambridge History of the First World War Volume 3. Civil Society*, ed. Jay Winter (Cambridge: Cambridge University Press, 2014), 486.
141 Ibid., 487.

142 Ibid.
143 Ibid.
144 Erman Şener, *Sinema Seyircisinin El Kitabı* (Istanbul: Koza Yayınları, 1976), 59.
145 Serdar Öztürk, *Erken Cumhuriyet Döneminde Sinema, Seyir, Siyaset* (Ankara: Elips Kitap, 2005), 27.
146 Özön, *Türk Sineması Tarihi*, 61; Özön, *İlk Türk Sinemacısı Fuat Uzkınay*, 17. According to Özön, this film was sent with an American warship to the United States. The Committee of Disabled Veterans may have sent this film to the United States for propaganda purposes because among the nationalists – including the Unionists – in Istanbul in 1919 there were still many supporters of the idea of an American mandate for Turkey. With this film, they may have tried to influence American public opinion in favour of Turkey.
147 According to Özön, the cinematography equipment of the Merkez Ordu Sinema Dairesi (MOSD, Central Army Office of Cinema) was transferred to the Malûl Gaziler Cemiyeti (The Committee of Disabled Veterans) in 1919, which then rented it to the Seden brothers' private film company Kemal Film. Özön suggests that around the time when the Grand National Assembly's army was bringing the war to an end (this must have been around 1922), the Disabled Veterans Association took their cinema equipment back from Kemal Film and gave it to the Ordu Film Çekme Merkezi (Army Film Shooting Center), which was supposedly founded within the Grand National Assembly's army. This means that the cinema equipment that was used by the National Assembly's Army Film Shooting Center must have originally belonged to the Ottoman army's Central Army Office of Cinema. See Özön, *İlk Türk Sinemacısı Fuat Uzkınay*, 37.
148 On the continuities between the nationalist movement of Mustafa Kemal and the Young Turk movement, in particular the role of Committee of Union and Progress (CUP) in the National Struggle, see Erik-Jan Zürcher, *The Unionist Factor: The Role of the Committee of Union and Progress in the Turkish National Movement 1905–1926* (Leiden: Brill, 1984); Erik Jan Zürcher, *The Young Turk Legacy and Nation Building: From the Ottoman Empire to Atatürk's Turkey* (New York: I.B. Tauris, 2010).

2

Filming the struggle for independence (1919–23)

On 10 September 1922, after a great victory over the Greek army, Mustafa Kemal Pasha, the commander of the National Forces, entered Izmir. The war was won, but due to the continuous warfare since the beginning of the First World War, Turkey was depopulated, impoverished and left in ruins. In western Anatolia, the retreating Greek army had set fire to several villages and towns, and committed large-scale atrocities among the Muslim population. Similarly, the advancing troops of the National Forces had, in some cases, acted with brutality against Greek soldiers and civilians. On 13 September 1922, a fire of unknown origin broke out in the Armenian quarter and quickly spread to the Greek and Levantine neighbourhoods. The fire, which was only extinguished on 22 September, destroyed both Izmir's city centre and its cosmopolitan past, turning them to ashes.

According to the Turkish author Erman Şener, a film screening was organized for Mustafa Kemal sometime after the unfortunate event.[1] This film was known as the film that introduced him to the Western world. Mustafa Kemal, too, heard much about this film's great success. After watching the film, he expressed his satisfaction to its producers and reportedly stated: 'This is a document of great value for generations to come, who will not have seen these days.'[2] Later, he ordered the film to be screened for the public gathered in front of the hotel at which he was staying.[3] His confirmation of the historical value of this film motivated film-makers to begin collecting film fragments concerning the War of Independence.[4] But why did Mustafa Kemal want this film to be seen by generations to come? What was the role of the film-makers in the National Movement? And, most importantly, what could film do for the struggle for independence?

During the struggle for independence, films were not only produced for artistic purposes but were also weapons of war. Mustafa Kemal and his followers knew that film was one of the most powerful ways to influence the masses and counter enemy propaganda. For this purpose, they collaborated with domestic and foreign film producers. This chapter discusses the specific importance of film in Mustafa Kemal and his followers' political agenda for the War of Independence and its aftermath. The first part analyses the role of domestic film producers in the propaganda campaign of the National Movement, emphasizing the continuity between the CUP era, when a 'national' cinema industry was born, and the national resistance movement led by Mustafa Kemal.[5] The analysis attempts to demonstrate that Mustafa Kemal's vision of cinema was not ahead of its time, but rather it belonged to the culture of the late Ottoman Empire. The second part observes foreign film producers' interest in the National Movement, and their filmic activities. The third part explores 'orphan' films, the films whose actual producers have not been identified. The cultural symbols employed in the orphan films are specifically analysed in order to understand the messages they carried. The last part discovers Mustafa Kemal's relation to film through his experience as a viewer of films, in the home and at the cinema.

Domestic film producers

During the struggle for independence, the National Movement led by Mustafa Kemal benefited mainly from three domestic institutions, all of which were established in the late Ottoman period: the private company Kemal Film, the film factory of the Committee of Disabled Veterans, and the remains of the Central Army Office of Cinema (COC). Significantly, these institutions upon which the nationalists would build their major filmic propaganda campaign were linked by their nationalist ideologies, technical equipment and common personnel. They also played an important role in the creation of a 'national' cinema industry in Turkey. Among these institutions, however, Kemal Film was perhaps the most productive one.

Kemal Film was founded in 1922 as the first private film company owned by Ottoman Muslims of Turkish origin. The owners of Kemal Film, the brothers

Kemal and Şakir Seden, had entered the film business by opening Ali Efendi Sineması in 1914 when the CUP government was proceeding to create a 'national' bourgeoisie among the Muslim traders. The Seden brothers were sympathetic to the national resistance movement in Anatolia for ideological and economic reasons. After all, the nationalists offered a great opportunity for many Muslim entrepreneurs to break the hegemony of foreigners and non-Muslims in many sectors of the economy.

Kemal Film was the most productive domestic institution in this period, making several documentary films concerning the National Struggle. When the COC was closed after the First World War, Kemal Film employed most of its former officers, including Fuat Uzkınay and Cezmi Ar. The Seden brothers also employed Cemil Filmer to work in the Kemal Bey Sineması in Sirkeci as an operator.[6] Like the Seden brothers, Uzkınay, Ar and Filmer were sympathetic to the national resistance movement and supported it through their cinematic activities.

According to Özuyar, Kemal Film commissioned Fuat Uzkınay to shoot documentary films in Anatolia towards the end of the Greco-Turkish War (1919–22).[7] Kemal Film produced forty-six short documentary films about the war. The *Tasvir-i Efkar* newspaper lists these films as follows:

- *Bursa Fatihi Şükrü Paşa ve Maiyeti* (The Conqueror of Bursa, Şükrü Pasha and His Retinue)
- *Bir Fırkanın İleri Harekâtı* (The Forward Operation of a Division)
- *Kuvâ Kumandanlığının Alaylara Emir ve Tebliği* (The Order and Communiqué of the National Forces Commandership to the Regiments)
- Avcı Hattının İlerlemesi (The Advancement of the Skirmish Line)
- *Düşman Mevziine Hücum Eden Kahraman Piyadelerimiz* (Our Heroic Infantry Attacking the Enemy Position)
- *Dörtnala Mevzie Giren Bataryalar* (Rapid Position-taking Artillery Batteries)
- *Topçu Atışı* (Artillery Shooting)
- *Mudanya Sırtlarında Kolordu Tarassud Mevkii* (The Army Corps' Surveillance Position at the Outskirts of Mudanya)
- *Kolordu Erkân-ı Harbiyesi* (General Staff of the Army Corps)
- *Hücum Borusu* (Charge)
- *Hücum* (Attack)

- *Keşif Kolu* (Reconnaissance Patrol)
- *Mevzi İntihabına Gelen Topçu Tabur Kumandanı* (The Battalion Commander Who Came to Elect the Emplacement)
- *Kolordu Kumandanı ve Fırka Kumandanı* (The Army Corps Commander and the Division Commander)
- *Bir Tarafın Taaruzu* (The Attack of One Side)
- *Makineli Tüfek Bölüğü Ateşi* (The Fire of the Machine-Gun Troop)
- *Topçu Ateşi* (Artillery Fire)
- *Düşman Üzerinde Bataryaların Tesirli Endahtı* (The Effective Shot of the Artillery Batteries on the Enemy)
- *Tebdil-i Mevzi Eden Bir Cebel Bataryası* (A Position-changing Mountain Battery)
- *Süngü Hücumu* (Bayonet Attack)
- *Mitralyöz Bölüklerinin Düşmana Tesirli Atışı* (The Effective Shot of the Machine Gun Troops on the Enemy)
- *Yaralılarımızın Geriye Nakli* (The Transfer of Our Injured Soldiers to the Back)
- *Düşmanı Takip* (Chasing the Enemy)
- *Süvari Hücumu* (Cavalry Attack)
- *Yalın Kılıç Hücum Eden Süvari Alayının Düşmandan Bir Sahra Bataryasının Suret-i Zaptı* (The Exemplary Seizure of Field Artillery from the Enemy by the Cavalry Regiment Attacking with Their Swords Drawn)
- *Yunanlılardan İğtinâm Edilen Sahra Bataryaları* (Captured Field Artillery from the Greeks)
- *Yunanlıların Teslimi* (The Surrender of the Greeks)
- *Alınan Esirler* (Taken Prisoners)
- *Yaralılarımız Sargı Mahallinde* (Our Wounded People at the First Aid Site)
- *Esir Yunanlıların Yaralılarının Sıhhiye Bölüğü Tarafından Sargı Mahalline Sevki* (The Dispatch of the Wounded Captive Greeks to the First Aid Site by the Medical Brigade)
- *İğtinâm Edilen Bataryanın Tekrar Düşmana İstimali* (The Reuse of Captured Artillery against the Enemy)
- *Düşmandan Zapt Edilen Siperler* (Captured Enemy Trenches)

- *Siperler Dahilindeki Yunan Erleri ve Yaralıları* (Greek Soldiers and the Wounded in the Trenches)
- *Alay Kumandanlarının Fırka Kumandanlarından Emir Telakkisi* (The Division Commander's Acceptance of the Regiment Commander's Orders)
- *Nöbetçi Neferi* (Soldier Watchman)
- *Tarassud Mevkiinde Kolordu Kumandanı ve Maiyetinin Muharebeyi Tarassudu* (The Spotting of the Battle by the Army Corps Commander and his Retinue at the Surveillance Position)
- *İzmir Fatihi Nurettin Paşa Hazretlerinin Kolorduyu Teftişi* (The Inspection of the Army Corps by His Highness Nurettin Pasha, the Conqueror of Izmir)
- *Teftişaddan Sonra Kıtanın Hal-i İstirahatı* (The Rest and Relaxation of the Corps after the Inspection)
- *Şükrü Nailli Paşa Hazretlerinin İzmit'e Muvasalatı* (The Arrival of His Highness Şükrü Nailli Pasha in Izmit)
- *Şanlı Alayımızın Şanlı Bir Sancağı* (The Glorious Banner of Our Glorious Regiment)
- *Düşmandan İğtinam Edilen Ağır Topların Bir Kısmı* (A Part of the Heavy Artillery Captured from the Enemy)
- *Alınan Ağır Topların Efrada Teslim Ettirilmesi* (The Surrender of the Captured Heavy Artillery to the Soldiers)
- *Kendilerine Medeniyet Süsü Veren Çapulcu Alayının Anadolu'daki Tahribatı* (The Destruction of the Looter Regiment in Anatolia that Pretends to be Civilized)
- *Tahrip Edilen Bedbaht Alaşehir, Manisa, Aydın ve Civarı* (The Destroyed Unfortunate Alaşehir, Manisa, Aydın and Their Vicinity)
- *Yunanlılar Tarafından Tahrip ve Berheva Edilen Bir Köprü* (A Bridge Destroyed and Blown Up by the Greeks)
- *Düşman Tarafından Tahrip Edilen Yüzlerce Vagon ve Lokomotif* (Hundreds of Wagons and Locomotives Destroyed by the Enemy).[8]

As the list suggests, Kemal Film's productions allowed the nationalists to show not only their heroic deeds but also the alleged brutalities of their enemies. The films were screened in various Istanbul cinemas after the war. On 17 November 1922, for instance, they were shown at Yeni Millî Sinema (New National Cinema) in Şehzadebaşı, and on 29 November 1922 at Elektra

Sineması in Beyoğlu.⁹ The film screening at Elektra Sineması included some other film titles such as the following:

> *Gazi Mustafa Kemal Paşa Hazretleri ve Millet Meclisi Azaları ile Heyet-i Vekile Ankara'da* (His Highness Ghazi Mustafa Kemal Pasha and the Members of the National Assembly together with the Council of Ministers), *Mustafa Kemal Paşa Hazretleri'nin Bursa'ya Seyahatleri* (His Highness Mustafa Kemal Pasha's Trip to Bursa), and *Esir Yunan Başkumandanı Trikopis ve Yunan Generallerinin Garnizonlara Sevki* (Prisoner of War the Greek Commander-in-chief Trikoupis and the Greek Generals' Transfer to the Garrisons).¹⁰

In the following months, many Istanbul cinemas extended their programmes with additional film titles such as the following:

> *Mübeccel Başkumandanımız Mustafa Kemal Paşa Hazretlerinin Huzurunda Alınmış Bin Kişilik Milli Resmigeçit* (The National Pageantry in the Presence of Our Honored Commander-in-Chief, His Highness Mustafa Kemal Pasha), *Bursa'da Hain Yunan Tahribatı* (The Treacherous Greek Destruction in Bursa), and *Binlerce Yunan Üserası* (Thousands of Greek Captives) and *Refet Paşa Hazretlerinin İstanbul'a Teşrifleri* (The Arrival of His Highness Refet Pasha in Istanbul).¹¹

Fuat Uzkınay was not the only cameraman who recorded important events on behalf of Kemal Film in this period. While he was shooting films in Anatolia, Cezmi Ar, the other cameraman of Kemal Film, was recording events in Istanbul. By the order of Kemal Seden, the owner of Kemal Film, Ar recorded Refet Pasha's arrival in Istanbul.¹² This film was shown as a Kemal Film production in the Kemal Bey, Ali Efendi and Elektra cinemas.¹³ The *Tasvir-i Efkar* newspaper announced the film's screening at the Kemal Bey Sineması as a 'national Turkish film reel'.¹⁴

However, the most spectacular event for Kemal Film was yet to come. Having achieved victory against the Greek army, Mustafa Kemal had moved his troops to the north, to the 'neutral zone' of the Straits, with the objective of taking the Eastern Thrace, Istanbul and the Straits back from the Allies. If the Allies would not leave the area peacefully, this could mean war. The majority of the Allied countries, however, were not willing to go to war with the nationalists; only Britain was. Finally, the Allies decided to call the nationalists to a conference in order to solve the crisis through diplomacy. Both sides signed the Armistice of Mudanya on 11 October 1922, leaving the Eastern

Thrace to the Turks. Nevertheless, the Straits and Istanbul still remained under the control of the Allies or, to be precise, Britain. To resolve the conflict, on 28 October 1922, the Allies invited the nationalists to establish a peace treaty. The negotiations, which had started on 20 November 1922 in Lausanne, led to a deadlock. Meanwhile, Mustafa Kemal ordered the army to be ready for the worst-case scenario, a possible war with the Allies.

On 14 January 1923, Mustafa Kemal left Ankara in order to inspect the army units in Izmit and Bursa, which was a great story for all news reporters. Cezmi Ar and Şakir Seden from Kemal Film went to Izmit to film the event.[15] When they arrived, Ar first filmed Mustafa Kemal getting off the train. The next day, Ar and Seden received permission to accompany Mustafa Kemal's convoy going from Izmit to Gebze. There, Ar shot several more scenes, including close-ups of Mustafa Kemal. After leaving the convoy in Gebze, the Kemal Film crew went to Istanbul where the film was immediately developed and edited in the Kemal Film laboratory and distributed across the country.[16]

The film also went beyond the country's contested borders. Although little is known about the version of the film screened in Turkey by Kemal Film, there is a silent cinema newsreel called *Mustapha Kemal*[17] in the British Pathé film archives showing scenes from his inspection of the Izmit front on 18 January 1923. It is likely that British Pathé used Kemal Film's footage for the newsreel.

The Pathé newsreel starts with the title *Angora* (Ankara) written at the top of the screen and continues by announcing: 'Mustapha Kemal. Turkey's "Strong Man" on whose action peace or war depends in the Near East'. At the bottom of the announcement 'Pathé Gazette' is written. In the first scene of the film, Mustafa Kemal in his military uniform – an overcoat and his kalpak (a lamb's-fur cap) – salutes a row of soldiers and then walks with some other commanders of the War of Independence following him, of whom Fevzi Pasha (on his right) and Bearded Nureddin Pasha (on his left) can be recognized.

In the next scene, the commanders of the War of Independence in military uniforms and wearing kalpaks line up and pose for the camera. During the war, the nationalists made symbolic use of hats more than any other piece of clothing. By wearing kalpaks they distinguished themselves from agents of the sultan's government in Istanbul, who were associated with the traditional fez.[18] Thus, specific types of hats gradually acquired political meaning, distinguishing between two opposing political powers: one based in Istanbul and represented by the sultan, the other based in Ankara and represented by Mustafa Kemal.[19] In the film, all commanders of the National Movement, including Mustafa Kemal, are clean-shaven except for their moustaches; only Bearded Nureddin Pasha, as his name suggests, sports a beard.

As the camera pans across the commanders, one can identify Bearded Nureddin Pasha standing on Mustafa Kemal's right, Kâzım Pasha on his left and Fevzi Pasha standing next to Kâzım Pasha. There is an interesting detail in this film. Unlike the other officials shown, Mustafa Kemal has his right hand in the overcoat of his uniform in a Napoleonic gesture. The camera stops on Mustafa Kemal and moves in closely; he continues to pose in the Napoleonic manner and looks very briefly at the camera. In this way, the film draws attention to the uniqueness and superiority of Mustafa Kemal over the other military officers. Mustafa Kemal's 'hand-in-overcoat' gesture was not very common among Ottoman officials, so it is imbued with political significance.

Significantly, this gesture was rather common for European or American gentlemen in this period and earlier. In fact, it frequently appears in eighteenth- and nineteenth-century Western portraiture.[20] One can also see this gesture in photographs of military men, businessmen and politicians from Europe and the United States in the late nineteenth and early twentieth centuries. In her article on the 'hand-in-waistcoat' portrait type, Arline Meyer suggests that the gesture was recognized as indicating, 'manly boldness tempered with modesty' in François Nivelon's *Book of Genteel Behaviour*, published in 1738.[21]

Although it was a common convention in Western portraiture, particularly in the English and French contexts, the gesture became closely associated with Napoleon.[22] This was partly because of the French painter Jacques-Louis David, who turned his patron's gesture into an indelible military emblem in his famous portrait of 1812, *The Emperor Napoleon in His Study at the Tuileries*.[23] After Napoleon, many generals and rulers in the Western world adopted this gesture, and were portrayed in paintings and photographs making it.[24] It is likely that Mustafa Kemal saw this gesture many times in these works. During his military career, he frequently rubbed shoulders with Western military officers and must have observed their gestures both in Turkey and in Europe.

By adopting this gesture on film, Mustafa Kemal sought to communicate his self-representation not only to a Turkish audience but also to a Western one, showing that he was just like the Western leaders. Whether or not foreign audiences were convinced by the strong military image Mustafa Kemal presents in this newsreel, Pathé Gazette's announcement 'Mustapha Kemal. Turkey's "Strong Man" on whose action peace or war depends in the Near East' does suggest some success in impressing foreign news agencies.

In his book *Kurtuluş Savaşı ve Sinemamız* (The Independence War and Our Cinema), Erman Şener mentions an interesting anecdote concerning Mustafa Kemal's filming by Kemal Film. He states that Mustafa Kemal Pasha's inspection of the Izmit front coincided with the stay of some American film-makers at the Pera Palace Hotel in Istanbul, who wanted to make a documentary about the War of Independence.[25] Although the inspection was open to all journalists wanting to interview Mustafa Kemal, its occurrence was hidden from the Americans and, instead, Cezmi Ar and Şakir Seden from Kemal Film went to Izmit in order to film the event.[26]

Şener's anecdote points to an important detail about the fierce journalistic competition that characterized the early twentieth century. In this period, such competition already went beyond the domestic level, so that journalists of one country sometimes had to compete not only with their local colleagues but also with foreign journalists for news stories. One of the most important reasons for this fierce competition was a significant force in modern politics: public opinion. In fact, at the beginning of the twentieth century, there was already an audience in Europe and the United States that was fascinated with domestic and international public affairs. The news agencies tried to satisfy this demand by sending correspondents to remote parts of the world or buying news from local correspondents.[27] Therefore, filming an important event such as Mustafa Kemal's inspection of troops at the Izmit front, which had the potential to cause a crucial change in international politics, was interesting both for the domestic and international news markets.

The invention of cinema added a new dimension to the conventional journalistic competition. Although the newspaper was still the most popular medium for news reporting at the beginning of the twentieth century, cinema gradually became a real competitor. In cinema's initial years, the newspaper still had an important advantage over film. Since news could be transmitted very quickly by the 'Victorian Internet' of the telegraph, newspapers were more up to date. Furthermore, producing films was very complicated in the early years, demanding much time, effort and money. Therefore, newsreels played only a supporting role in conveying news to the public, overshadowed by newspapers.

As the French film historian Pierre Sorlin states, in Europe and the United States, the newsreels projected onto the cinema screens in major cities at the beginning of the month reached small towns only at the end of the month.[28] In other words, by the time audiences saw the newsreels, the presented information was already old news. Thus, newsreels did not convey new information, but rather visualized events that were already known through other media. What made newsreels so important was not their informative value but their perceived capacity to project the world in a direct and sensible way.

Another important advantage of cinema over other media was that by speaking a visual language, that is to say, the language of images, it allowed ordinary people to see distant events and famous men with their own eyes; by the end of the 1920s, also to hear them with their own ears. It was much easier for many people who were illiterate, semi-literate or did not have time to read to simply watch the news passing before their eyes in images. Thus, the newsreels increasingly contributed to the participation of ordinary people in politics.[29]

In fact, present-day televised news can be seen as the successor to a long line of film genres, going back to newsreels, news films and actualities. Just as televised news enjoys great popularity today, newsreels at the beginning of the twentieth century gradually became popular among ordinary people.[30] From 1910 onward, newsreels were displayed in cinemas weekly in Western Europe and the United States.[31] In the 1930s, for instance in Britain, 'newsreels already reached about half of the population, and were regularly seen by most working-class people under 30'.[32] Thus, it is imaginable that the 1922 newsreel regarding Mustafa Kemal's inspection of the Izmit front was watched by hundreds, thousands or even millions of people in Britain and elsewhere.

Besides Kemal Film, Malûl Gaziler Cemiyeti (The Committee of Disabled Veterans) was another domestic institution that produced newsreels regarding Mustafa Kemal and the national resistance movement in this period. The Committee of Disabled Veterans was a social organization that had close ties with the CUP government. It was founded with the support of Enver Pasha by Colonel Cevat Bey in 1915. To support disabled veterans and their families, the Committee collected donations and engaged in various commercial activities during the First World War. For this purpose, they also opened a cinema theatre called Malûl Gaziler Sineması in Şehzadebaşı, Istanbul.

When the Ottoman army was demobilized, the Committee of Disabled Veterans took over the film equipment of the COC. With this equipment, they established a film factory, appointed Fuat Uzkınay, the former chief of the COC, as its director (for a period of three years)[33] and began to produce films. Uzkınay employed Cemil Filmer, another former officer of the COC, at the film factory as well. During the years of Istanbul's occupation, the Committee produced several films, both fiction and non-fiction. Filmer shot the demonstrations against the Greek occupation of Izmir at Sultanahmet Square on 23 May 1919 on behalf of the Committee.[34] Towards the end of 1921, the Committee suspended its film production and began to concentrate on offering studio services, such as writing intertitles for foreign films and renting out its cinema and projection equipment.[35]

The Committee became active after the nationalists achieved victory against the Greek army. In 1922, a cameraman was sent to Ankara in order to record significant events. According to an announcement of the *İleri* newspaper on 9 December 1922, the Committee produced the following news films for the movie theatres:

- *Mustafa Kemal Paşa Hazretlerine İzmir Muzafferiyetlerinden Avdetlerinde Yapılan İstikbal* (The Reception of His Highness Mustafa Kemal Pasha after His Return from the Izmir Victory)
- *Büyük Millet Meclisi Önünde İhtifâl* (The Commemoration Ceremony in Front of the Grand National Assembly)
- *Büyük Gazi'nin Bursa Seyahati* (Great Gazi's Bursa Trip)
- *Bursa Menazırı* (Scenes from Bursa)
- *Esir Yunan Askerlerinin Ankara'dan Şimendiferle İçlere Sevki* (Captured Greek Soldiers' Transfer from Ankara to the Inland by train)[36]

The film director of the Committee, Fazlı Necip Bey, wrote to Hilal-i Ahmer Cemiyeti (Red Crescent Society) on 30 November 1922 with a proposal to shoot films of the alleged 'destructions' and 'crimes' of the Greeks in the Aydın province.[37] He offered to make filmic records of at least twenty-one destroyed places.[38] To make the films more watchable, he suggested that he would simulate what happened in most places using background actors (children and inhabitants), and he would stage the events in an affective and artistic way.[39] The Red Crescent Society, however, rejected Fazlı Necip Bey's offer.

According to Turkish authors such as Nijat Özön and Erman Şener, there was a third domestic institution called Ordu Film Çekme Merkezi (The Army Film Shooting Center), established within the Grand National Assembly towards the end of the War of Independence.[40] They also state that the Army Film Shooting Center made a number of short films such as *İzmir Zaferi* (The Victory of Izmir, 1922), *Dumlupınar Vekayi'i* (The Incidents of Dumlupınar, 1922), *İzmir Nasıl İstirdat Edildi* (How Was Izmir Taken Back? 1922), *İzmir'in İşgali* (The Occupation of Izmir, 1922), *İzmir'deki Yunan Fecayii* (The Disasters Caused by Greeks in Izmir, 1922), *İzmir Yanıyor* (Izmir in Flames, 1922) and *Gazi'nin İzmir'e Gelişi ve Karşılanışı* (The Arrival and Reception of the Ghazi in Izmir, 1922).[41]

Although Özön and Şener briefly mention the establishment of the Army Film Shooting Center and its productions, they do not say much about its staff. In my research, I was not able to find any information concerning the staff of the so-called Army Film Shooting Center. Moreover, I could not find any official document attesting to its establishment within the Grand National Assembly in 1922. Thus, I suspect that the centre was never officially founded.

It is likely that the Grand National Assembly cooperated with domestic institutions to produce some documentary films during the War of Independence and its aftermath. In fact, in the assembly meeting of 7 November 1921, the head of the General Staff Fevzi Çakmak Pasha had answered a question from the deputy of Balıkesir, Mehmet Bolak Bey, concerning the 'Greek atrocities' as follows: 'Sir, let me give an answer on that subject. As particularly these [Greek] disasters continue, a photo camera is sent to each division; they are taking photographs everywhere. As Vehbi Bey said, we ordered a cinematograph from Istanbul. We will locate these scenes and publish them'.[42]

Although it is not known which cinematograph they ordered, it is known that two domestic film production studios in Istanbul, the Committee of Disabled Veterans and Kemal Film, were sympathetic to the national resistance movement in Ankara. Uzkınay, for instance, went to Anatolia in 1922 in order to produce a documentary film called *Zafer Yolları* (Roads to Victory) in the name of Kemal Film.[43] The Committee of Disabled Veterans had already taken over the Ottoman army's cinematography equipment in 1919. Thus, they may have provided a cinematograph or even a cameraman to the nationalists in Ankara.

It does not greatly matter who the original producers of these films were because, according to Özön, when Uzkınay was reappointed as the director to the cinematography department of the Turkish army in 1924, he used most of the films produced through the cooperation of Kemal Film and the Committee of Disabled Veterans during the years of armistice to create a new documentary film called *İstiklâl* (Independence).[44]

Özön also states that the Army Film Shooting Center of the Grand National Assembly had already started to produce a documentary film titled *İzmir Zaferi* in 1922.[45] From 1930 on, Uzkınay extended this film by adding the most important events of each year.[46] In this way, by 1933, he had turned it into a film consisting of three parts.[47] When Reza Shah Pahlavi, the shah of Iran, visited Mustafa Kemal Atatürk in 1934, this version was shown to him in a private film screening.[48] Özön claims that after the screening, Atatürk ordered its further extension.[49] Consequently, a committee led by Erden – the commander of the war colleges – and other members including Nurettin Baransel, Fahri Belen and Isfendiyar Uzberk, the director of the army's Photo and Film Center at the time, extended the film from three to twelve parts between 1934 and 1936.[50] Later, another part was added to the film concerning Atatürk's death.[51] Özön states that 'today [in 1970] the 144-min. film titled *İstiklâl Harbinin Başlangıcı, Devamı, Netayici* (The Beginning, Continuation and Consequences of the Independence War) that exists in the archive of the Photo and Film Center is this film and the majority of the parts that were added after 1930 were shot by Uzkınay'.[52]

Although it might seem strange to a contemporary reader, the staging of scenes was a common practice in this period.[53] As Jay Winter and Samual Hynes state, 'most visual and literary accounts of the First World War were produced more than ten years after the Armistice'.[54] An important reason for this was the novelty of the medium. The film camera was a new medium of war that attracted enemy fire.[55] Therefore, cameramen were mostly not allowed to be on the front lines by military authorities. In addition, unlike contemporary film technologies, the cinematography equipment of the time was heavy and cumbersome and was not suitable for the conditions of war. Even if a cameraman managed to record a few pictures of warfare after putting his life at risk, the images tended to be poor in quality. As a result, the coverage that does exist was mostly produced after the war.[56] In a few cases, it was produced during the war, but in a staged setting behind the front lines or elsewhere, sometimes in the same week or month as the portrayed events. Thus, the First World War was not captured directly on film. The situation was the same in the case of the Turkish War of Independence, with most of the scenes staged after it ended.

Nevertheless, the deliberate efforts made to produce films of the War of Independence indicate that the nationalists did not use film only to document, but also to create a hegemonic story of what happened. By selectively adding original war scenes and cutting others, and by filming extra war scenes after the fact, they retrospectively constructed a cinematic narrative based on how they wanted the war to be seen and remembered.

It is not only historical films that are constructed in this way but also historical writings in general. The French philosopher Paul Ricoeur suggests that all historical writings, including those that criticize narrative history, are constructed in some way in narrative form.[57] Similarly, Hayden White in his work *Metahistory: The Historical Imagination in Nineteenth Century Europe* shows that historians do not simply represent events as they really were ('*wie es eigentlich gewesen*'),[58] but instead create a narrative form by organizing them in a certain order, including and excluding events, and emphasizing some and downplaying others.[59] According to White, in constructing their narratives, historians are often unconsciously influenced by literary tropes such as irony, synecdoche, metaphor and metonymy. For instance, the historical writings of four great historians in the nineteenth century – Michelet, Ranke, Tocqueville and Burckhardt – follow four basic plots: romance, comedy, tragedy and satire, respectively.[60]

In line with White's argument, it is a fact that at some point after their original recording, audiovisual documents get edited and organized by a director in order to create a meaningful historical narrative. Consequently, the films on the War of Independence are important to look at not so much for their documentary value (although they do offer some valuable insights into what this particular period looked like) but primarily for the way in which they construct a narrative and communicate a particular view of the past.

Thus the nationalists' efforts to document the war on film were not neutral. Significantly, in his discussion on the archive, Jacques Derrida argues that archiving does not consist of the act of preserving the past, but serves to create it. The way in which what is archived is selected, stored, preserved or excluded by those in power determines the content of the past and how it will be remembered in the future. Derrida states:

> the archive [...] is not only the place for stocking and for conserving an achievable content *of the past* which would exist in any case, such as, without the archive, one still believes it was or will have been. No, the technical structure of the *archiving* archive also determines the structure of the *achievable* content even in its very coming into existence and in its relationship to the future. The archivization produces as much as it records the event.[61]

Similarly, in his book *The Archeology of Knowledge*, Foucault conceptualizes the term 'archive' not as a physical institution where official documents are kept, but rather as the set of all statements that limits, governs and determines what can be said, including about the past.[62] He writes:

> The archive is first the law of what can be said, the system that governs the appearance of statements as unique events. But the archive is also that which determines that all these things said do not accumulate endlessly in an amorphous mass, nor are they inscribed in an unbroken linearity, nor do they disappear at the mercy of chance external accidents; but they are grouped together in distinct figures, composed together in accordance with multiple relations, maintained or blurred in accordance with specific regularities.[63]

For Foucault, the archive can never provide a neutral, unmediated view of the past, but is always constituted by certain power structures, which order, construct, limit and delimit our knowledge about the past. He states:

> It is obvious that the archive of a society, a culture, or a civilization cannot be described exhaustively; or even, no doubt, the archive of a whole period. On the other hand, it is not possible for us to describe our own archive, since it is from within these rules that we speak [...] It emerges in fragments, regions, and levels, more fully, no doubt, and with greater sharpness, the greater the time that separates us from it: at most, were it not for the rarity of the documents, the greater chronological distance would be necessary to analyze it.[64]

According to Foucault, by analysing the archive of a society, a culture or a civilization, one can still deduce what could be said, by whom and with what authority at a particular moment in history.[65] Thus, by looking at the films produced by the nationalists in the 1920s and the 1930s, one cannot obtain an objective picture of what happened at that time, but can deduce the statements and discourses that governed this period. The nationalists' archiving activities at this time indicate that they assigned considerable attention to producing visual evidence with the potential to influence public opinion about the present and the future. By constructing a visual archive of the War of Independence, they created a particular story that they wanted audiences to believe.

Foreign film producers

The archiving activities during the 1920s and the 1930s were not limited to the nationalists, as there was also foreign interest in filming the war. As mentioned before, some American film-makers came to shoot the war, but it is not known whether they were able to actually do so. However, footage by the American film-maker Louis de Rochemont while he was still an officer in the US Navy remains in which he filmed Mustafa Kemal's recapture of Izmir and the great fire of Izmir in 1922.[66] According to American communications scholar Raymond Fielding, Rochemont's newsreel material on Mustafa Kemal was commercially released.[67]

In addition to Fielding's statement, Turkish cinema historian Ali Özuyar mentions a cameraman called J. Ercol representing the American Patenior Cinematograph Company who was a correspondent of the French *Illustration* magazine and who came to shoot films in Turkey right before the Great Offensive.[68] According to Özuyar, Ercol officially applied to the Grand National Assembly in order to shoot films at the headquarters of the National Movement in Ankara. As the Ankara government was suspicious of any intelligence operations in those days, his application was delayed for some time. Nevertheless, Ercol still managed to shoot films of the Great Fire of Izmir and the Armistice of Mudanya. Eventually, the representative of the Ankara government in Istanbul, Adnan Bey, provided him access to Ankara by stating to the Ministry of Foreign Affairs: 'As the Lausanne Conference continues, the films Ercol will produce in Ankara concerning our national life and government will make a positive impact on European and American public opinion.'[69]

Fielding confirms Özuyar's claim that there was a Frenchman named 'Ercole' who came to Turkey after the Greco-Turkish War of 1922.[70] However, according to Fielding, Ercole, who was part of the European staff of Pathé News, was sent to Turkey by its managing editor Emanuel 'Jack' Cohen. Based on Cohen's account, Fielding further claims that the Turks did not allow Ercole to enter Izmir, but he somehow managed to get an airplane to fly over Izmir and take pictures from the air.[71] Ercole also found a way to board an Allied warship in the harbour to shoot the tragic scenes on the seaside.[72] Afterwards, he shipped the films by a special boat to the nearest European port and then by airplane to Paris. The local Pathé staff in Paris sent the films by airplane to New York, where they were brought to motion picture screens.[73]

Similar to Pathé News, the French film company Gaumont wanted to make newsreels regarding the Greco-Turkish War of 1922. They applied to the Ankara government to record destruction in the cities of western Anatolia (Salihli, Alaşehir, Uşak and Afyon) after the war.[74] Having received permission on 9 November 1922, they sent a film crew to western Anatolia.[75] Another noteworthy initiative came from the famous French banker and philanthropist Albert-Kahn who ran the ambitious *Les Archives de la Planète* project, collecting photographs and films from all around the world. In 1922, he sent his photographer Gadmer and his cameraman Camille Sauvegeot to Turkey. Gadmer and Sauvegeot produced several photographs and films, including a film showing Mustafa Kemal talking with Rauf Bey in Ankara.[76]

Orphan films

Besides the domestic and international films regarding the struggle for independence, there is a third category of films, those whose producers have not been identified. One can call them 'orphan' films. This part discusses two such specimens featuring Mustafa Kemal, trying to understand the messages they carried and the reality they constructed.

The first film footage is titled *Mustapha Kemel* (1920-9)[77] and was distributed by British Pathé. Although there is not much information concerning its production and reception, it is likely that the footage was used as part of a Pathé newsreel because between two scenes, an intertitle appears briefly with 'Pathé News' written at the top and 'Some Anatolian Warriors of the Nationalist Army' in the middle. In the footage, Mustafa Kemal is in military uniform and wearing a kalpak while walking and saluting a row of Turkish men as a Turkish flag waves in the background. He is followed by a group of men which includes eminent commanders of the War of Independence, such as Fevzi Pasha (Çakmak), Nureddin İbrahim Pasha (a.k.a. Sakallı [Bearded] Nureddin) and Kâzım Pasha (Karabekir), all in military uniform and donning kalpaks. Adnan (Adıvar) Bey also walks with them.

Although the footage is assigned to the period between 1920 and 1929 in the British Pathé film archives, it must have been shot between 1920 and 1923 because Mustafa Kemal is in military uniform, which he is known to have worn until he became the president of the Turkish Republic on 29 September 1923.[78] When the footage is compared to photographs of the time, it can be seen from the uniforms Mustafa Kemal and his retinue wear that this scene was probably shot when Mustafa Kemal visited the troops at the Izmit front (18–19 January 1923). It is likely that this scene was shot by Kemal Film's cameraman Cezmi Ar.

After the intertitle, the film continues by showing black-clad soldiers wearing ammunition belts over their shoulders and dark turbans tied at the side. To understand this film better, we first need to explore who these soldiers were and what their relationship was to Mustafa Kemal. The soldiers in the footage are part of the regiment of Topal (Lame) Osman, who served as Mustafa Kemal's personal bodyguard during the War of Independence. Lame Osman was a veteran of the Balkan Wars (1912–3) and the leader of a Muslim band (çete) in Giresun, which was notorious for its brutality. He was called Lame Osman due to an injury to his knee sustained during the Balkan War in which he participated as a volunteer. He also fought against the Russians during the First World War and was deployed to capture runaways from the Ottoman army.

With the loss of the First World War, the political tension between the local Muslim and non-Muslim communities had mounted, particularly in the coastal towns of the Black Sea such as Samsun and Giresun where there were substantial Greek populations. The Giresun branch of the Trabzon Society for the Defense of National Rights employed Lame Osman and his Laz irregulars against the local Greek bands that aimed to separate the 'Pontic Coast' from the Ottoman Empire.[79] Lame Osman repeatedly exceeded his orders to terrorize the Greeks and the Armenian communities, but also the local Muslim population, who tried to oppose him.

When armed resistance began against the Allied forces on the Western Front and elsewhere, the commanders of the National Movement collaborated with local Muslim bands in order to disrupt the advance of the Allied forces through guerrilla warfare. Mustafa Kemal attached great importance to incorporating these scattered irregular bands, which would later be called the Kuvâ-yı Milliye (National Forces), into the regular army that he was establishing in Ankara.

Osman's band fought fiercely against the local Greek bands of the Black Sea coast until Mustafa Kemal called them to Ankara, where they would serve as his personal bodyguards. This did not appease Osman. When, for instance, the Alewite Kurdish Koçgiri tribe rebelled against the Ankara government and demanded an autonomous province in Dersim, the government sent a force led by Bearded Nureddin Pasha to suppress the insurrection. It included Lame Osman's Laz irregulars, who brutally crushed the rebels on 24 April 1921.

Lame Osman was also implicated in another controversy, which began with an angry debate between Mustafa Kemal and Ali Şükrü at the assembly on 6 March 1923. Opposition politicians led by Ali Şükrü had sharply criticized Mustafa Kemal and Ismet Pasha's politics during the Lausanne negotiations and accused them of betraying national interests. The angry debate almost ended in a shooting duel between Mustafa Kemal's followers and the opponents. On 26 March, Ali Şükrü was seen for the last time in the assembly; after that, he disappeared.

Ali Şükrü's disappearance worried his friends, who brought the issue to the assembly three days later, demanding a government inquiry, to which Mustafa Kemal assented. The inquiry led to the discovery of Ali Şükrü's body in a grave near Lame Osman's house, and concluded that Osman and his men had murdered and buried him there. A warrant for their arrest was issued by Mustafa Kemal on 31 March 1923. When Lame Osman heard that a government battalion was searching for him, he knew that this was not possible without Mustafa Kemal's knowledge.

Meanwhile, to ensure his own security, Mustafa Kemal had to leave his villa in Çankaya. The question of how this happened has become a matter of huge controversy in Turkey in recent years due to a claim made by the Turkish author İpek Çalışlar. In her national bestseller *Latife Hanım* (2006),[80] Çalışlar claims that Lame Osman and his men had already surrounded the villa when Mustafa Kemal wanted to escape. Based on Latife's sister Vehice İlmen's grandson Mehmet Sadık Öke's account, Çalışlar tells the story as follows:

> Surrounded by Lame Osman's band, Mustafa Kemal's life was in danger. Hostage negotiations between the band and those inside the villa had

started. As was customary, women and children were the first to be allowed to leave. The plan was for Mustafa Kemal to disguise himself in order to leave with them. But someone had to stay at the villa in his place, so as not to arouse suspicion.[81]

Çalışlar asserts that Latife offered to stay at the house in order to distract the band outside.[82] Although Mustafa Kemal rejected Latife's offer in strong terms, she did not listen, putting on his kalpak and a military cloak. In the meantime, Latife's sister Vehice brought Mustafa Kemal a chador to enable him to get past Lame Osman's men. Latife then stood in front of a window, mimicking Mustafa Kemal's silhouette and giving the impression that he was still in the villa. According to Çalışlar, Mustafa Kemal managed to escape death thanks to Latife's brilliant idea and courage. When Lame Osman and his men entered the villa, they saw that Mustafa Kemal had escaped. They ransacked the place and manhandled Latife. Meanwhile, the government battalion surrounded Lame Osman's band.[83]

Although Çalışlar is convinced of the truthfulness of the story of Vehice İlmen, who was present in the villa, her account was not acceptable to the Turkish state as the defender of official historiography. In fact, because of the passage in which she describes Atatürk escaping in the guise of a woman, she was made to stand trial for 'insulting the memory of Atatürk through the press' (Law 5816) in 2006.[84] Although she was acquitted, the discussion about the passage in her book continued. Based on her story, a film called *Latife Hanım* was produced in 2006, which also included this highly controversial scene. Like the book, the film challenged the myth of Atatürk by attacking several of its components, including his masculinity, authority and bravery, as well as his intelligence, foresight and secularity.

Whether Çalışlar's story is true or not, the search for Lame Osman and his men ended in a shootout in which most of them were killed; Osman himself was mortally wounded and a few survivors were taken in for questioning. The official explanation for Ali Şükrü's murder that emerged from the questioning was that Lame Osman had killed him at his own initiative because he was standing in his patron's way by opposing his policies. For many, however, this was hard to believe. At the same time, it was also hard to believe that, despite his dislike for Ali Şükrü and being Lame Osman's patron, Mustafa Kemal was behind the plot. If Mustafa Kemal was indeed guilty and his role in the affair were to have been exposed, he would have lost all credibility as the president of the National Assembly.

According to Andrew Mango, a biographer of Atatürk, the plot was most probably planned by junior officers who joined the ranks of Mustafa Kemal's party and 'were ready to advance his cause and their own interests by eliminating those who stood in their way'.[85] In doing so, they had killed two birds with one stone. The pre-eminent speaker of the opposition had been silenced, and the opposition intimidated. Furthermore, the last unit of the irregulars who had taken part in brutal killings of Greeks, Armenians and Muslim opponents had been eliminated, conveying the message that there was no longer a place for such unruly men in the new order. According to Mango, it would not have been necessary to inform Mustafa Kemal of the plot, as he would benefit from it most if he did not know about it.[86]

However, it is certain that Mustafa Kemal did not mourn Ali Şükrü's death. What worried him more than the murder was the possible exploitation of this issue by the opposition.[87] To refresh the assembly's confidence in himself, he held new elections. Even after the murder issue had been resolved, he and his supporters did their best to keep it under wraps. Years after the incident, in his famous six-day speech (*Nutuk*) held between 15 and 20 October 1927 at the General Congress of the Republican Party, Mustafa Kemal did not say anything about the murder of Ali Şükrü, nor did he mention Lame Osman as the murderer.[88] Despite these efforts, this unfortunate incident has never been entirely forgotten; Lame Osman is still commemorated as a national hero by the nationalists, with a statue erected in his hometown Giresun in 2008, while Ali Şükrü was given a humble memorial in his hometown of Trabzon.[89] Both are also remembered in films such as *Latife Hanım* (2006) and *Atatürk'ün Fedaisi Topal Osman* (Lame Osman the Bodyguard of Atatürk, 2013).

Returning to the film at hand, since most of the black-clad warriors shown in it were killed in the shootout, the scene could not have been shot any later than March 1923. This year also marked an important change in Mustafa Kemal's image, as reflected in his dress style. After being elected president of the Turkish Republic, he would not wear his military uniform anymore, but dress only in civilian, Western-style clothes. Hence, his heroic warrior image would turn into the image of a progressive civilian leader.

Another documentary film from the period, whose producers have not been identified, is called *Lozan Sulh Heyetinin Karşılanması* (The Reception of the Lausanne Peace Committee, 1923).[90] When the Turkish delegation returned home from Lausanne, high-ranking officials and the public convened at the Çatalca (Chataldja) railway station to welcome them. The film shows what the reception looked like: the public awaits the Committee in front of the railway station. A group of children dressed in folkloric costumes and soldier uniforms carry small signs on their chests. Some of the signs are written in Arabic letters, indicating the names of cities in Turkey: Izmir, Kars, Erzurum.[91] Through their attire, each of the children represents the respective city. Together, they constitute an interesting mise en scène for the camera.

Interestingly, the children in folkloric costumes surround a girl who is standing above the others and is dressed differently. She is in a white, winged costume and wears a laurel wreath on her head with an upside down crescent in the middle, a symbol of Islam.[92] She holds a big flower bouquet in her hand, probably to be given to the leader of the victorious Lausanne Peace delegation, Ismet Pasha. A white ribbon is hanging from the flower bouquet with 'Mekatib-i İptidaiye Muallimleri Cemiyeti' (Primary School Teachers' Association) written on it.[93] The camera pays particular attention to this girl in white, distinguished from the others. Her symbolism is overt, and the message she conveys serves the nationalists' interests.

The use of little girls or women as allegorical figures in public festivals in the Ottoman context goes back to the Young Turk Revolution of 1908. In order to restore the constitution of 1876, the Young Turks revolted against Sultan Abdulhamid II's 'despotic' regime, and they began to use new symbols to represent their 'liberal' regime, which was highly influenced by the French Revolution (1789). Inspired by the French Revolutionary figure of Marianne, standing for reason and liberty, the Young Turks and their supporters created their own 'Ottoman Marianne' to represent the same.[94]

In contrast to the old 'despotic' male sultan, 'liberty' was depicted as a little girl or young woman in most printed matter at the time so as to indicate a break with the old regime.[95] At the same time, by using this figure in the Ottoman press and in public festivals, the Young Turks showed that the new regime was following the liberal tradition of the French Revolution. In the parade held in Monastir's Shirok Street after the Young Turk Revolution of 1908, the freedom coach carried five girls dressed in white costumes symbolizing liberty.[96] The girls were also filmed and photographed by the Manaki brothers, showing that this was a staged spectacle designed to convey a message to the Western world.[97] As the representation of the female liberty figure changed in the Ottoman press and the figure appeared under different names such as Turkey,

Vatan (Motherland), Efkar-ı Umumiye (Public Opinion) and Meşrutiyet (Constitutionalism),[98] its reception by the public also changed. In some cases, especially when the figure had wings, it was interpreted as an angel or even a fairy.

According to the Turkish academic Cemal Avcı, the girl who appears in the welcoming ceremony of the Lausanne Committee represents *sulh perisi* (The Fairy of Peace).[99] Nevertheless, looking at her costume closely, there is something that is very familiar: a figure from Greco-Roman mythology. In fact, the little girl's dress is similar to the Roman goddess Victoria's (the Greek equivalent being Nike). In ancient Greece and Rome, victory was personified as a winged, female figure. Victoria was the messenger of the gods, an angel or a goddess, depending on the myth, 'who descended to earth to crown the victor in a contest of arms, athletics or poetry'.[100] The winged Roman image of Victoria was commonly represented during the Renaissance as granting a laurel crown or a palm branch to the victorious.[101] Victoria inspired several works of art in the Western context, including the Siegessäule (The Victory Column) in Berlin and the Victoria Memorial in London. As the film shows, she also inspired the little girl figure in the welcoming ceremony. But the transmission of a goddess of victory derived from Western culture to an Ottoman context needs more elucidation.

To understand this, we should go back to the final years of the Ottoman Empire. The nationalists had won the war; the Grand National Assembly of Turkey had decided to abolish the sultanate on 1 November 1922 and on 17 November, the last Ottoman sultan Mehmed VI was compelled to leave the country. With the abolition of the sultanate, the nationalist government in Ankara stood as the supreme and sole representative of Turkey in the international arena. Although the Grand Turkish National Assembly had not yet declared the new regime, backstage, it was already being discussed that the new state form would be a republic.

On 20 November 1922, negotiations started at the Conference of Lausanne between Turkey and the Allies. Due to disagreements, the parties resigned on 4 February 1923, but continued again on 23 April 1923. The negotiations would end on 24 July 1923, and the new republic declared on 29 October 1923. In the meantime, the nationalists began to convey implicit messages about the upcoming changes to Turkish cultural identity that would be propagated by the new regime. The fedora and top hat worn by Ismet Pasha during the conference can be interpreted as early signs of these imminent changes. And so can the Turkish goddess of victory shown in *The Reception of the Lausanne Peace Committee*.

At the first and most obvious level of representation, the little girl garbed as the goddess of victory signifies the victory won by the nationalist government in Lausanne and the peace they brought to their country after a long and brutal war. Going further into other connotations of this symbol, the allegory of the goddess of victory was probably not understood by much of the public gathered at the Çatalca railway station, so it was clearly not meant for their eyes alone.

With the allegory of the goddess of victory, the nationalists were aiming to convey a message to Western audiences. They were showing that the new government of Turkey, under the leadership of Mustafa Kemal, shared similar cultural values with the Western world. To transmit this message, there could not be a more appropriate medium than film; not only because film itself was a sign of modernity that could easily appeal to Western audiences but also because it was widely believed at the time that film was a transparent medium that could not lie and displayed what was actually happening. Thus, the Western symbol captured on film conveyed the reality of its message, confirming that this was not just an ideological manoeuvre.

Unlike the Ottoman government, which represented 'Islamic civilization', and therefore frequently employed and promoted Islamic symbols in governing its subjects, Mustafa Kemal and his followers were gradually shifting the cultural axis of Turkey from Islamic to common symbols of 'Western civilization', which claimed to have its roots in ancient Greco-Roman civilization. Hence, by including a Turkish goddess of victory in their welcome ceremony, the nationalists were taking a step towards bridging the cultural gap between Turkey and Western civilization – at least at the level of the image.

As the film also shows, in the initial years of the new regime, Islamic symbols were not immediately banished, but entered a transitional phase. Similarly, the cultural symbols of 'Western civilization' were not adopted outright without changes, but rather were adapted to suit Turkish conditions. Many of the symbols used by the new regime were cultural hybrids:[102] Turkish in some ways, but Western in others. Hence, it would be more appropriate to speak about cultural hybridization than about a mere imitation of 'Western civilization'.

In another scene, Mustafa Kemal, his wife Latife, Ismet Pasha and a retinue consisting of politicians, soldiers and an imam are walking towards the camera. Although this scene might seem quite normal, Latife's presence among the male leaders and the retinue was fairly extraordinary for the time and place in which *The Reception of the Lausanne Peace Committee* was filmed. After all, affairs of the state were considered a man's business in traditional Ottoman society; so what was a woman doing at the centre of it all? To understand this, it is important to know who Latife was and what her significance was at the time.

Latife was born in 1898 in Izmir as the daughter of one of the richest Turkish merchants in the city, Uşakizâde Muammer Bey, who was influenced by Western culture and provided all his children with an exceptional education. Latife was educated through private lessons at home before going to the American College for Girls in Istanbul for a year.[103] She continued her training at the girls' boarding school Tudor Hall in London for one more year and then went to Paris in order to study law at the Sorbonne.[104] When the Greek forces occupied Izmir, her father moved the family to France to wait out the end of the war. While in France, Latife followed the news about the national resistance through newspapers. She even carried a picture of Mustafa Kemal Pasha, cut from a newspaper, in a locket around her neck, believing that only he would save Izmir from the occupation.[105] After the Turkish victory at Sakarya, Latife interrupted her legal studies to return to Izmir in the autumn of 1921.[106]

When Mustafa Kemal was looking for safe lodging in Izmir, the Uşakizâde mansion was offered to him, which is where he would meet Latife for the first time on 11 September 1922.[107] According to her biographer, Mustafa Kemal was highly impressed by this confident young woman who hosted him warmly.[108] In fact, it was hard not to be impressed by Latife's qualities. Born to a wealthy and respectable family in Izmir, one of the most modern and cosmopolitan cities of the Ottoman Empire, she was educated in Europe at a time when it was exceptional for a Muslim girl to study abroad. She had also travelled around Europe and spoke several languages including Arabic, Persian, Greek, Latin, Italian, English, German and French.[109] Furthermore, like many daughters of bourgeois families in nineteenth-century Europe, Latife could play the piano excellently.[110] She could also ride a horse. Aside from her physical attractiveness, she was a modern young woman, deeply engaged in the struggle for women's rights.

During Mustafa Kemal's stay at the Uşakizâde mansion, Latife demonstrated all her qualities including her ability to organize the household, in order to impress him. She also served as his translator and secretary during the ceasefire negotiations with the Allied forces.[111] Latife and Mustafa Kemal fell in love and they married on 29 January 1923 at the Uşakizâde mansion.[112] For Mustafa Kemal, Latife was more than a wife; beautiful, smart and highly educated, she could play a crucial role in the creation of modern Turkey by representing the new face of the Turkish woman, domestically and internationally.

Latife would be one of the important driving forces behind Mustafa Kemal's campaign to build a modern country, with the emancipation of women at the top of the agenda. After their marriage, Mustafa Kemal and Latife went on a tour of Anatolia for their honeymoon. Dressed modestly in European clothes, Latife charmed the people wherever she went. As *The New York Times* reported: 'MME. KEMAL'S CLOTHES ARE PLEDGE OF REFORM: Her Riding Breeches Indicate Her Intention of Sweeping Away the Harem Conventions.'[113] For foreign correspondents in particular, Latife was more than Mustafa Kemal's wife; she was 'the harbinger of Turkey's transformation'.[114]

Latife fulfils a similar symbolic function in *The Reception of the Lausanne Peace Committee*, where she stands besides Ismet Pasha and Mustafa Kemal among the men. She appears self-assured as she walks in the forefront of the image. She wears a long dark dress with white gloves and carries a walking stick. Most significantly, although she wears a headscarf, her face is bare. By allowing his wife to walk together with other state dignitaries, Mustafa Kemal shows that he is a modern statesman.

In the next scene, the camera moves in closely on Latife, Ismet Pasha and Mustafa Kemal, enabling audiences to see her face clearly. Mustafa Kemal and Ismet Pasha are dressed in Western-style suits with ties, but they still keep their kalpaks on, as do the other men in the scene.[115] The film shows how neither Latife nor Mustafa Kemal and his followers abandoned traditional-style dress completely. This may have been partly due to the need to please two separate audiences: the Turkish-Muslim population, which would likely resist overly radical changes, and the international community, which was eager to accept a Turkey with more commonalities to it than differences. Latife's appearance in the film underlines how Mustafa Kemal consciously employed the moving image to communicate his message of cultural change (including women's emancipation) and rapprochement to the Western world, while remaining careful not to alienate the national Turkish-Muslim public.

Mustafa Kemal's relation to film in this period cannot be understood by textual analysis alone; to achieve a deeper understanding, it is necessary to know what his cinema experience looked like. In his memoirs, Cemal Filmer mentions two interesting anecdotes concerning this subject, which will now be discussed.

Mustafa Kemal at the cinema

Cemil Filmer was one of the pioneers of Turkish cinema. As mentioned before, he worked as an officer at the COC as a cameraman for the Committee of Disabled Veterans' film factory, and as an operator at Kemal Bey Sineması in Istanbul. After the war, he saw great opportunities for himself in Izmir. As the majority of the cinema owners were Greek in the city, many cinema theatres stayed empty when they left.[116] Thus, Filmer decided to leave Istanbul in order to run movie theatres in Izmir. There, he would not only find an enthusiastic Turkish audience but also meet Mustafa Kemal on two interesting occasions, which he cherished in his memoirs.

Filmer states that, when Mustafa Kemal was staying at the Uşakizâde mansion in the early days of his marriage, he called Filmer to screen films for him, Latife and their guests in the garden.[117] Filmer writes that once, without waiting for Mustafa Kemal's conversation with some high officials to finish, Latife angrily ordered Filmer to start screening. Mustafa Kemal responded by stating that he would let Filmer know when the films could start and that Filmer could take a little rest.[118] This anecdote shows that, although the couple agreed ideologically on the need for women's emancipation in Turkey, masculine dominance at home was not always easy to abolish.

Filmer recalls another significant event regarding cinema that occurred in the early days of Mustafa Kemal and Latife's marriage in Izmir.[119] On one of his visits to the Uşakizâde mansion, Filmer wanted to screen the last parts of the films presenting the war fronts, but complained about the poor quality of the fabricated screen in the garden. Instead, he invited Mustafa Kemal to his cinema theatre, Ankara Sineması, where he could offer him a much better visual quality and some other films. After cancelling some tasks from his programme, Mustafa Kemal accepted the offer to go to the cinema, stating that he would be there at three o'clock on that day.[120]

As can be imagined, a cinema visit by the nation's hero was something out of the ordinary.[121] For the visit, the balcony box of the cinema was prepared with silver tea sets and cookies. The streets were full of people who had heard about Mustafa Kemal Pasha's cinema visit. When he arrived in his car, people were shouting, crying, applauding and even sacrificing animals. Men and women were pushing each other in order to see Mustafa Kemal. Finally, when he left the car, Filmer led him to the box prepared for him. When the pasha arrived, he looked down at the audience and asked: 'Why are there no women among the audience?' Filmer answered: 'My pasha, we have an exclusive film screening for women only on Tuesdays; on other days it is forbidden.' Mustafa Kemal turned to his aide-de-camp Muzaffer and said: 'Go down and bring the women inside.' Soon, the cinema was full of women.[122] Apparently, the women applauded Mustafa Kemal for so long that Filmer could not start the film screening on time.[123]

The cinema programme started with the film *Şarlo İdama Mahkum* (Charlie is Sentenced to Death).[124] After watching the film, Mustafa Kemal called Filmer over and said: 'Cemil, I do not remember laughing so much ever before in my life, can we watch the film again?' So the film was screened again, and the programme continued with documentary films showing Mustafa Kemal at the fronts. After the screening, Mustafa Kemal left Ankara Sineması to a standing ovation from the public.[125]

What does this anecdote tell us about Mustafa Kemal's approach to film and cinema at the time? It can be said that Mustafa Kemal knew that the films made of him at the fronts would be screened, and that he therefore used film for propagandistic purposes. This is certainly true, but not sufficient. To fully understand Mustafa Kemal's attitude towards cinema, we should pay attention to the details of the cinema visit. When Mustafa Kemal arrived at his lodge on the balcony, he asked about the lack of women in the audience. As a member of Ottoman society, he would have known that separate film screenings were organized for Muslim men and women, so this was actually a rhetorical question indicating his wish to abolish gender segregation in the cinema and, potentially, elsewhere. Moreover, he was implicitly heralding upcoming measures for the emancipation of women in Turkey. Thus, Mustafa Kemal not only considered film as a modern propaganda tool through which he could effectively influence public opinion, but also saw the cinema as a public space that could help him transform culture and society.

Conclusion

Between 1919 and 1923, Mustafa Kemal and his followers used film as an effective tool of communication to produce a positive public opinion in favour of their political ambitions for the country on both domestic and international stages. They documented the War of Independence, stressing their own efforts and carefully recording alleged atrocities against the Turkish-Muslim people. Their selective use of film footage, which was mostly staged after the fact, served as propaganda for the Ankara government. On the one hand, these efforts were aimed at gaining international recognition for the nationalist government by garnering sympathy for their cause, displaying their power and intimidating adversaries. On the other hand, they appealed to a burgeoning sense of 'national' pride among former Turkish-Muslim Ottomans by projecting a heroic image of those fighting for freedom and independence.

The adoption of the remains of the Ottoman COC and the extensive use of other civilian sources for film footage together confirm the level and scope of the nationalists' investment in this medium and, by extension, illustrate the centrality of film to the political agenda of Mustafa Kemal. At a time of battle, Mustafa Kemal appeared in front of the cameras in his kalpak and military uniform, projecting the image of a strong military leader. He was well aware of cinema's potential to produce historical evidence for the future in order to build a new community based on common memory and national consciousness.

Although mainstream Turkish historiography has viewed Mustafa Kemal's vision of cinema as far ahead of his time, a close analysis of this period makes clear that Mustafa Kemal and his followers' approach to cinema demonstrates strong continuities with the CUP era. The seeds of a 'national' cinema industry had already been sown by the CUP government in the late Ottoman period, but the harvest would be reaped by Mustafa Kemal's government during the national resistance movement and its aftermath. Perhaps it would be more appropriate to say that the war won by Mustafa Kemal and his followers accelerated the rise of a 'national' film industry by changing the cosmopolitan structure of the society (since many Greeks, Armenians and foreigners left the country) and by transferring the ownership of the cinema industry from non-Muslims to Muslims (mostly Turks).

At the same time, the technical limitations of the time and the political conditions of war limited the use of cinema as a popular mass medium by the nationalists. Despite these limitations, the nationalists aimed to win the struggle over the visual representation of the war by filming their version of events and preventing the display of enemy propaganda films in their domains. In addition, the nationalists also initiated a film 'archive' in the Foucauldian and Derridean sense, which would shape the narrative of the war not only for their lifetime but also for the future.

The archive of this period is relevant not only for what it reveals but also for what it conceals. While the nationalists consistently used cinematic images to remember the atrocities committed by their enemies, they neglected to use them to portray unfortunate events that happened on their own side. More importantly, the established archive does not offer multiple perspectives on the events, or reveal the deaths of innocent civilians or the miseries suffered by the war's refugees.

In the early twentieth century, many European nations and the United States used film as a popular and efficient means of transmitting news. While it is not clear to what extent Turkey was included in Euro-American newsreels, it is known that Mustafa Kemal appeared in some of them during the War of Independence. These international appearances and the certain interest of the Ankara government in producing its own film footage of the war together suggest that the nationalists were well aware of the political uses of cinema. During the war and its aftermath, they consciously mobilized film in order to change public opinion around the world. Unfortunately, as of today, there is no conclusive evidence of the extent to which Mustafa Kemal and the War of Independence appeared in international cinemas or of the impact this had on foreign audiences. Further research in this area is therefore necessary.

This chapter demonstrates that for Mustafa Kemal, cinema was more than just a medium for political propaganda; it was a means of social transformation both through the cinema space and the film content. By providing a public space in which gender segregation could be abolished and women emancipated, cinema assisted Mustafa Kemal in transforming culture and society. What was shown on the screen had a strongly symbolic dimension, illustrating the transformations taking place in the image politics of the Ankara government.

By including unusual scenes or characters, such as Mustafa Kemal adopting a Napoleonic gesture, the Turkish goddess of victory in the welcome ceremony or Latife walking beside the country's leaders, film – considered the most modern and 'realistic' medium of the time – was used to convey a message of cultural change and rapprochement to 'contemporary civilization'. The next chapter explores its further use in the construction of the Republic of Turkey and Atatürk's public image.

Notes

1. Erman Şener, *Kurtuluş Savaşı ve Sinemamız* (Dizi Yayınları, 1970), 27.
2. In Turkish: 'Bu, bugünleri görmeyen nesiller için büyük değeri olan bir belgedir'. See ibid.
3. Ibid.
4. Ibid., 27–8.
5. In the context of the National Struggle, the term 'national' refers to Ottoman Muslim nationalism. For a detailed analysis of the term, see Erik-Jan Zürcher, 'Young Turks, Ottoman Muslims and Turkish Nationalists: Identity Politics 1908-38', in *The Young Turk Legacy and Nation Building: From the Ottoman Empire to Atatürk's Turkey* (New York: I. B. Tauris, 2010), 213–35.
6. Cemil Filmer, *Hatıralar: Türk Sinemasında 65 Yıl* (Istanbul: Emek Matbaacılık ve İlâncılık, 1984), 107.
7. Ali Özuyar, *Sessiz Dönem Türk Sineması Tarihi (1895–1922)* (Istanbul: Yapı Kredi Yayınları, 2016), 364.
8. *Tasvir-i Efkar*, 12 Teşrinisani 1338 (Kasım 1922).
9. Özuyar, *Sessiz Dönem Türk Sineması Tarihi*, 367.
10. Ibid., 368.
11. Ibid.
12. Filmer, *Hatıralar*, 110–11.
13. Özuyar, *Sessiz Dönem Türk Sineması Tarihi*, 369.
14. Ibid.
15. Ibid., 23.
16. Ibid., 23–5.
17. British Pathé, *Mustapha Kemal* (1923), Pathé Gazette, Audiovisual file, 1923, 29 sec., accessed 3 May 2014. http://www.britishpathe.com/video/mustapha-ke mal/query/Mustapha+Kemal.

18 Since 1909, the Ottoman military had donned the kalpak instead of the red fez, especially on ceremonial occasions. The kalpak would function as a sign of recognition for Ottoman officials until the end of the Turkish War of Independence. See Klaus Kreiser, *Atatürk: Eine Biographie* (München: Verlag C. H. Beck, 2008), 62, 239.

19 During the war, Mustafa Kemal wore a kalpak even when he was in civilian dress. Other irregular militia (Kuvâ-yı Milliye) in Anatolia followed Mustafa Kemal's example, so the kalpak became a symbol for those who supported the nationalist government in Ankara. It should be mentioned that although the kalpak increasingly became a symbol of the nationalists during the War of Independence, not everyone followed this fashion. In the first Grand National Assembly, the fez was still widespread among the members. See Toktamış Ateş, *Türk Devrim Tarihi* (İstanbul: Istanbul Bilgi Üniversitesi Yayınları, 2010), 255.

20 Arline Meyer, 'Re-dressing Classical Statuary: The Eighteenth-Century "Hand-in-Waistcoat" Portrait', *The Art Bulletin*, 77, no. 1 (1995): 45–63, accessed 20 January 2016, doi 10.2307/3046079.

21 Ibid., 53.

22 Peter Burke, *Eyewitnessing: The Uses of Images as Historical Evidence* (Ithaca: Cornell University Press, 2008), 70, 71, 73.

23 Burke, *Eyewitnessing*, 70; Meyer, 'Re-dressing Classical Statuary', 63.

24 Burke, *Eyewitnessing*, 73.

25 Şener, *Kurtuluş Savaşı ve Sinemamız*, 23–4.

26 Ibid., 23.

27 Oliver Boyd-Barrett and Terhi Rantanen, eds., *The Globalization of News* (London: Sage Publications, 1998).

28 Pierre Sorlin, 'War and Cinema: Interpreting the Relationship', *Historical Journal of Film, Radio & Television* 14 (1994): 358.

29 Nicholas Pronay and Peter Wenham, *The News and the Newsreel* (London: Macmillan Education Ltd, 1976), 1.

30 Raymond Fielding, *The American Newsreel, 1911–1967* (Norman: University of Oklahoma Press, 1980), 4.

31 Betsy A. McLane, *A New History of Documentary Film* (London: Continuum, 2012), 8.

32 Pronay and Wenham, *The News and the Newsreel*, 1.

33 Özuyar, *Sessiz Dönem Türk Sineması Tarihi*, 320.

34 Filmer, *Hatıralar*, 99–100.

35 Özuyar, *Sessiz Dönem Türk Sineması Tarihi*, 370.

36 The announcement stated that movie theatres willing to show these films had to apply to the Committee of Disabled Veterans by Saturday three o'clock. See Özuyar, *Sessiz Dönem Türk Sineması Tarihi*, 370.
37 Ibid., 372.
38 Ibid., 373.
39 Ibid.
40 Nijat Özön, *İlk Türk Sinemacısı Fuat Uzkınay* (Istanbul: Türk Sinematek Derneği Yayınları, 1970), 37; Nijat Özön, *Türk Sineması Tarihi, 1896–1960* (Istanbul: Doruk Yayımcılık, 2010), 69–70; Şener, *Kurtuluş Savaşı ve Sinemamız*, 22, 25, 26. See also Özuyar, *Sessiz Dönem Türk Sineması Tarihi*, 372.
41 Genelkurmay Başkanlığı, letter to author, 16 July 2012. See also Şener, *Kurtuluş Savaşı ve Sinemamız*, 26; Özuyar, *Sessiz Dönem Türk Sineması Tarihi*, 371–2; Özön, *İlk Türk Sinemacısı Fuat Uzkınay*, 37–9.
42 Özuyar, *Sessiz Dönem Türk Sineması Tarihi*, 371.
43 Özön, *İlk Türk Sinemacısı Fuat Uzkınay*, 37.
44 Based on Kemal Film's owner Şakir Seden's account, Özön also claims that the army's cinema department confiscated many films that were produced by Kemal Film alone during the armistice years, when there was a short cooperation between the Committee of Disabled Veterans and Kemal Film, on the grounds that the films belonged to the Committee of Disabled Veterans. He further states that it is plausible that these documentary films were used to extend the *İstiklâl* film. Özön states that the extended version of *İstiklâl* was shown to the public for the first time in the summer of 1959, as part of the 'Spring and Flower Festival' in Istanbul, featuring the exhibition of the army. According to Özön, Colonel Nusret Eraslan, director of the Photo Film Center, used and edited the footage of this film in his 1966 film *Atatürk*. See Özön, *İlk Türk Sinemacısı Fuat Uzkınay*, 38–9.
45 According to Özön, the film *İzmir Zaferi*, which would be retitled *İstiklâl* after its extension, initially consisted of short parts, such as *Dumlupınar Vekayi'i*, *İzmir Nasıl İstirdat Edildi* and *Gazi'nin İzmir'e Gelişi ve Karşılanışı*, that were shot in 1922. See ibid., 38.
46 Ibid.
47 Ibid., 39.
48 Ibid.
49 Ibid.
50 Ibid.
51 Ibid.
52 Ibid.

53 Frank Van Vree, 'The Imagery of War: Screening the Battlefield in the Twentieth Century' (Paper presented, Cultures of War and Peace, Peace Palace, The Hague, 15 June 2013).
54 Sorlin, 'War and Cinema', 361.
55 Fielding, *The American Newsreel*, 115, 125.
56 Ibid., 116.
57 Paul Ricoeur, *Time and Narrative*, vol. 1, trans. K. McLaughlin and D. Dellauer (Chicago: University of Chicago Press, 1990), 91–174.
58 This was a maxim proposed by the famous German historian Leopold von Ranke.
59 Hayden White, *Metahistory: The Historical Imagination in Nineteenth-Century Europe* (Baltimore: The Johns Hopkins University Press, 1975).
60 Ibid., 135–264.
61 Jacques Derrida, 'Archive Fever: A Freudian Impression', trans. Eric Prenowitz, *Diacritics*, 25, no. 2 (1995): 17, accessed 28 September 2014, doi: 10.2307/465144.
62 Michel Foucault, *Archaeology of Knowledge*, trans. A. M. Sheridan Smith (New York: Routledge, 2002), 145.
63 Ibid., 145–6.
64 Ibid., 146–7.
65 Ibid., 142–8.
66 Raymond Fielding, *The March of Time, 1935–1951* (New York: Oxford University Press, 1978), 30.
67 Ibid.
68 Özuyar, *Sessiz Dönem Türk Sineması Tarihi*, 374.
69 Ibid.
70 Fielding, *The American Newsreel*, 128–9.
71 Ibid.
72 Ibid.
73 Ibid.
74 Özuyar, *Sessiz Dönem Türk Sineması Tarihi*, 375.
75 Ibid.
76 During her research on Ankara, Turkish researcher Saadet Özen discovered these films and photographs in the Musée Albert-Kahn in Paris.
77 British Pathé, *Mustapha Kemel*, Pathé News, Audiovisual file, 1920–1929, 20 sec., accessed 3 May 2014, http://www.britishpathe.com/video/mustapha-kemel.
78 After 1923, Mustafa Kemal wore his military uniform only for very special occasions, such as when directing military manoeuvers in Ankara in 1926,

when posing for a photographer and on a couple of other occasions. See Metin Toker, 'Atatürk ve Barış', *Atam.gov.tr*, accessed 3 May 2014, http://www.atam.gov.tr/dergi/sayi-09/ataturk-ve-baris-2.

79 The Laz are an ethnic group and one of the native populations of the coastal Black Sea regions of Turkey and Georgia. They used to be Christians, but the majority converted to Islam under Ottoman rule in the sixteenth century. See also Kreiser, *Atatürk*, 137–8.

80 İpek Çalışlar, *Latife Hanım* (Istanbul: Everest Yayınları, 2011).

81 Ibid., 155.

82 Ibid.

83 Ibid.

84 Ibid., IX–X. See also Radikal.com.tr, 'İpek Çalışlar'a 'Latife' davası', last modified 19 August 2006, http://www.radikal.com.tr/haber.php?haberno=196265.

85 Ibid., 383.

86 Ibid.

87 Ibid.

88 Ibid.

89 Ibid., 384. See for the erection of Lame Osman's statue in Giresun: Ufuk Kekül, 'Topal Osman'ın heykeli dikildi', *Kentselhaber.com*, last modified 8 August 2004, http://www.kentselhaber.com/V2/News/90518/Topal-Osman-in-heykeli-dikildi.

90 *Lozan Sulh Heyetinin Karşılanması*, Turkish Film & TV Institute, Mimar Sinan Fine Arts University, 35 mm. Nitrate Film, 1923, 4 minutes 30 seconds.

91 Although the film does not reveal all the names, Avcı states that other place names were also written on the signs worn by the boys and girls in the welcoming ceremony, including 'Birinci İnönü', 'İkinci İnönü', 'İstanbul', 'Sivas', 'Bursa', 'Trakya', 'Ankara', 'Sakarya', 'Afyonkarahisar', 'Dumlupınar' and 'Eskişehir'. 'Zafer-i Milli' (National Victory) was also on the signs. See Cemal Avcı, 'İsmet İnönü'nün Lozan Dönüşü ve Demeçleri (10 Ağustos 1923—23 Ağustos 1923)', *Ankara Üniversitesi Türk İnkılâp Tarihi Enstitüsü Atatürk Yolu Dergisi*, 3, no. 12 (1993): 344.

92 The crescent was used as a religious symbol by ancient civilizations in the Middle East. The Byzantine Empire also employed it as a political, military and religious symbol. It was long believed that the Ottoman Turks adopted the crescent for their own flags after the conquest of Constantinople in 1453, but they were already using the crescent a century before, during the reign of Sultan Orhan (1326–62). Although it is hard to determine its precise origin, the symbol became increasingly associated with the Ottoman Empire and the

Islamic world. Today, the crescent is used as a symbol on national flags by many countries where Islam is the major religion, including Turkey, Azerbaijan, Algeria, Malaysia, Pakistan and Tunisia. See *Encyclopaedia Britannica Online*, 'Crescent', accessed 3 May 2014, http://www.britannica.com/EBchecked/topic/142628/crescent.

93 The welcome ceremony was probably organized by the Primary School Teachers' Association.
94 Günhan Börekçi, 'The Ottomans and the French Revolution: Popular images of "Liberty-Equality-Fraternity" in the late Ottoman Iconography, 1908–1912' (master's thesis, Boğaziçi University, 1999), 45.
95 Ibid., 42.
96 Saadet Özen, 'Rethinking the Young Turk Revolution: Manaki Brothers' Still and Moving Images' (master's thesis, Boğaziçi University, 2010), 95.
97 Ibid., 94–6.
98 Börekçi, 'The Ottomans and the French Revolution', 42–3.
99 Avcı, 'İsmet İnönü'nün Lozan Dönüşü ve Demeçleri', 344.
100 James A. Hall, *Hall's Dictionary of Subjects and Symbols in Art* (London: John Murray, 1991), 321.
101 Ibid.
102 For the term 'cultural hybridity', see Peter Burke, *Cultural Hybridity* (Cambridge: Polity Press, 2009).
103 Çalışlar, *Latife Hanım*, 21.
104 Ibid., 34–5. See also Utkan Kocatürk, *Doğumundan Ölümüne Kadar Kaynakçalı Atatürk Günlüğü* (Ankara: Atatürk Araştırma Merkezi, 2007), 322.
105 Çalışlar, *Latife Hanım*, 3.
106 Mango, *Atatürk,* 350.
107 Kocatürk, *Doğumundan Ölümüne Kadar Kaynakçalı Atatürk Günlüğü*, 297.
108 Çalışlar, *Latife Hanım*, 44–5; See also Mango, *Atatürk,* 350.
109 Çalışlar, *Latife Hanım*, 24.
110 According to Çalışlar, Latife took piano lessons from the Austro-German poet Rainer Maria Rilke's relative, the pianist Anna-Grosser Rilke, for three years. See Çalışlar, *Latife Hanım*, 22–3.
111 Ibid, 48.
112 Kocatürk, *Doğumundan Ölümüne Kadar Kaynakçalı Atatürk Günlüğü*, 322.
113 Çalışlar, *Latife Hanım*, Albüm.
114 Çalışlar, *Latife Hanım*, xii.
115 The kalpak fashion continued among the nationalists even after the war, until Mustafa Kemal introduced the hat reform in 1925. When the armed struggle for

independence ended and the diplomatic struggle began, the Turkish delegation led by Ismet Pasha went to the Conference of Lausanne (1922–1923) wearing kalpaks. However, after signing the Treaty of Lausanne on 24 July 1923, which certified the birth of a new independent Turkish state at an international level, Ismet Pasha left the conference wearing a top hat. Although this change did not attract much attention at the time, it can retrospectively be interpreted as an early sign of the changes that would take place in the newly founded, modern Turkish Republic.

116 Filmer, *Hatıralar*, 111.
117 Filmer mentions that he wanted to show Mustafa Kemal a film depicting the latter's inspection of a front together with the famous female writer Halide Edip (Adıvar). Ibid., 122.
118 Ibid., 122–3.
119 Filmer does not give an exact date for the anecdote, but mentions that it happened in the early days of Mustafa Kemal's marriage, when they were trying to organize the first Izmir Economic Congress, which took place between 17 February and 4 March 1923. See ibid., 123.
120 During his lifetime, Mustafa Kemal frequently visited cinemas in Izmir, Istanbul and Ankara. In Izmir, he visited Ankara Sineması and Sinema Palas. In Istanbul, he watched films in high-class cinemas such as the Elhamra, the Opera and the Glorya. In Elhamra, he watched Mushin Ertugrul's film *Istanbul Sokaklarında* (1931) and *Bir Millet Uyanıyor* (1932). In Ankara, he visited Yeni Sinema. For Atatürk's cinema visits see also Özuyar, *Babıâli'de Sinema*, 69.
121 Filmer, *Hatıralar*, 124.
122 According to Filmer, this was the first time in Turkey that men and women, along with Mustafa Kemal, watched a film together in Ankara Sineması. However, Filmer's argument cannot be true. As mentioned in the first chapter, Mustafa Kemal probably watched cinema in Istanbul and elsewhere before this date, where mix-gender film screenings were being made.
123 Ibid., 126.
124 At the time, the famous Hollywood actor Charlie Chaplin was known in Turkey as Şarlo, probably because Turks preferred to pronounce his name 'Charlot' like the French, instead of 'Charlie' like the Americans or British. This can also be read as another indication of the strong French influence on the cinema culture of Turkey in the late Ottoman and early Republican periods. In my research, however, I could not find a Charlie Chaplin film called 'Charlie is Sentenced to Death', so I suspect that instead of translating the film's original title directly into Turkish, a new name was given to it. Changing a foreign movie title was

common practice in those days. It was done in order to convey the movie's theme more clearly to domestic audiences or if the foreign title did not translate well. To find the film, I went through the Charlie Chaplin filmography and found that Chaplin played the role of a convict three times before Mustafa Kemal's cinema visit, in 1916, 1917 and 1923. He played an ex-convict in *Police*, released on 27 May 1916, and an escaped convict in *The Adventurer*, released on 22 October 1917, and *The Pilgrim*, released on 26 February 1923. Given that Chaplin played an ex-convict in *Police*, this film could not have been the film Mustafa Kemal watched. Since Filmer mentions that the cinema visit took place when 'Mustafa Kemal and Latife Hanım were newly married and trying to organize the first İzmir Economic Congress', *The Pilgrim* could not have been released in Turkey yet, so the film they most likely would have watched was *The Adventurer*.

125 Filmer, *Hatıralar*, 126.

3

Performing modernity:
The film of Mustafa Kemal Atatürk on his Forest Farm

The Republic of Turkey was not the natural product of democratic growth within the country; 'therefore we must look for the growth and development of this republic not in the psychology of the masses, as we should do in studying the French and American democracies, but in the policies of its few leaders'.[1]

Joseph Clark Grew quoting Arnold J. Toynbee and Kenneth P. Kirkwood

The end of the war was a new beginning for Mustafa Kemal and his followers. They had won against the Allies, forcing them to sign a peace treaty in Lausanne on 24 July 1923. However, a new struggle was about to begin: to rebuild Turkey on the ruins of the Ottoman Empire. The Kemalists began by forcing the sultan to leave the country (1922) and replacing the old monarchic regime with a new republic, appointing Mustafa Kemal its first president (1923). They declared its capital city Ankara in place of Istanbul (1923) and abolished the caliphate (1924). Finally, they undertook various modernization projects ranging from civil law (1926) to changing the alphabet (1928) in order to establish a new society based on the principles of science, secularism and nationalism, modelled on what they referred to as 'contemporary civilization'.[2]

Despite their commitment to radical modernizing reforms, it proved difficult to change everything overnight. After all, when Mustafa Kemal came to power, he took over a country with a population of which the vast majority was illiterate (90 per cent),[3] lived in the countryside (80 per cent) and had little access to electricity. Moreover, despite the new regime's rejection of the Ottoman heritage and the promise of a new beginning with the West, the image of the Turks in Western public opinion, inherited from the days of the Ottoman Empire, was not easy to replace. This image was buttressed by a Western Orientalist discourse that had represented Turks in a stereotypical manner for hundreds of years. Consequently, building a modern country that could match the advancements of 'contemporary civilization' required not only radical infrastructural but also cultural, reforms that would refashion the image of Turks abroad. As I have shown in the previous chapter, the nationalists started to signal such a change towards the end of the Lausanne conference, but this was not sufficient. To take its place among the 'civilized nations' of the world, it had to be made clear that what was happening was not just a one-time ideological manoeuvre, but a real, lasting transformation.

The aim of this chapter is to examine Mustafa Kemal's attempts to represent himself and the 'Turkish nation' on film as modern and civilized, and thus as belonging to the community of 'civilized nations'. I suggest that between 1923 and 1938, Mustafa Kemal performed his own vision of himself and of the Turkish nation, contradicting the established visual representations of the Ottoman Empire projected in part by the empire itself and in part formed in Western Orientalist discourses. By using film, he tried to demonstrate to both domestic and international audiences that Turkey was a rapidly developing country, and that the Turks were a 'modern', 'democratic' and 'civilized' people capable of change and progress.

Film was a convenient tool to convey this message, not only because it was the most modern visual medium of the time, which could easily speak to Western audiences, but also because it was believed to be the most realistic medium, providing a 'direct' view of events.[4] By performing his reforms on film for both domestic and foreign audiences, Mustafa Kemal sought to convey that his modernization efforts were sincere and successful. However, film also carried some potential risks. Because moving images were open to contingency, they did not allow full control over the representation as a whole. Moreover, once a film was shown outside Turkey, it escaped Turkish state control and could be reproduced and used for different purposes. What if a film depicting Atatürk Mustafa Kemal fell into the hands of people with bad intentions, who could reframe his image and that of Turkey for foreign crowds?

In what follows, I will analyse the story of Mustafa Kemal's filming on his Forest Farm, alongside some other footage from Turkey by Fox Films. By looking closely at the film's production, content and reception, I approach the following questions: What were the potential risks and benefits for Mustafa Kemal in using film to create the new image of Turkey? How did he seek to represent himself and the Turkish nation in this film? And, in Lasswell's terms, what did he want to convey with this film, to whom and with what purpose?

The making of Mustafa Kemal's film

On 12 November 1930, the US ambassador to Turkey, Joseph C. Grew, wrote a letter from Ankara addressed to the Secretary of State in Washington, joyfully stating that Fox Films supported his efforts and that he had achieved a victory in convincing the president of the Turkish Republic, Gazi Mustafa Kemal, to let himself be filmed and movietoned for the first time.[5] For four hours the Fox Films crew had photographed Mustafa Kemal and gave him instructions about where to stand and what to do, all of which he had followed.[6] Ambassador Grew continued by explaining that he had divided the film into nine separate acts: 1. *Preliminary Speeches: The Ambassador presents the President to the American public and the President responds*; 2. *The Fountain*; 3. *The Garden*; 4. *The Cows*; 5. *The Poultry*; 6. *The Sheep*; 7. *The Tractors*; 8. *Machine Shop*; 9. *Woman, Lovely Woman*. He concluded the letter as follows: 'In order to present a true picture of this epoch-making event I venture, most deprecatingly, to enclose a somewhat more intimate statement than customarily included in the body of dispatches to the Department.'[7]

Before analysing the film footage, it is necessary to account for its various versions.[8] There are at least three versions of the film: the first is the one the ambassador describes in his letter to the Secretary of State; the second can be found in the Turkish Film Archives and is titled *Atatürk'ün Amerikan Büyükelçisi Joseph C. Grew'u Orman Çiftliğinde Kabulü* (The Reception of the American Ambassador Joseph C. Grew by Atatürk on the Forest Farm, 1930);[9] and the third, called *Ataturk Entertains Grew on His Private Estate*,[10] I discovered in the University of South Carolina, Moving Image Research Collections (MIRC).

When comparing the three versions, I noticed that the order of the scenes was different in each. For instance, according to Grew's letter, the film originally started with a scene called 'Preliminary Speeches' and continued with 'The Fountain'. However, in the Turkish Film Archives version, which I had the opportunity to see for myself, the footage starts with 'The Fountain', while the 'Preliminary Speeches' appear much later, while some other scenes are missing altogether This version lacks the scene the ambassador calls 'Woman, Lovely Woman', in which Mustafa Kemal's adopted daughter, Âfet Hanım, expressed her opinion of American women and their success in gaining the right to vote, which does exist in the newly located MIRC version.[11] This scene, as well as other missing scenes, might have been damaged over time or cut from the original version.

In order to understand the film and its portrayal of Mustafa Kemal in relation to the cultural context of Turkey in 1930, my analysis will follow the version described in the ambassador's letter, as it most comprehensively reflects the intentions behind its making.

Preliminary Speeches (Scene I)

The film starts with Mustafa Kemal walking among the flowerbeds and chatting with the ambassador in French.[12] Although it is hard to hear what they are saying, it is clear that they are speaking in French. Why is this? We could answer that he did so because French was still the language of international diplomacy at the beginning of the twentieth century. Yet Mustafa Kemal could also have easily used a translator. Thus, we should try to understand the cultural significance of French for Mustafa Kemal as well as for 'contemporary civilization' at the time.

During the eighteenth century, France was widely recognized as the leading Western nation, setting the standard in Europe and the rest of the world.[13] In this century, French became the *lingua franca* among European elites. Many Europeans saw French as the language of *politesse*, enlightenment, civilization, cosmopolitanism and modernity. From the eighteenth century onwards, French cultural influence also became obvious in the Ottoman Empire, and proficiency in the French language became increasingly important among Ottoman elites.[14]

The Ottoman interest in Western culture started after they suffered a series of military defeats against modern Western armies, whose military techniques, skills and training were superior to those of the Ottoman army.[15] To modernize the army, the Ottoman Empire carried out several reforms, taking guidance mainly from the French government.[16] Modernization began under the supervision of French instructors, who, of course, spoke French. As part of the modernization reforms, French was also made the compulsory language for the newly established military and naval schools,[17] one of which Mustafa Kemal would attend a few decades later.

The modernization of the empire continued with educational reforms, introducing modern schools based on European, primarily French, models.[18] This led to the establishment of a new Ottoman elite consisting of military officers, diplomats and civil servants who could usually speak French and were thus more open to Western intellectual influences. Most of them admired the social, cultural and political achievements of 'Western civilization', in particular, France.[19] Since it was the *lingua franca* among European elites, proficiency in French enabled the Ottoman elite to follow contemporary philosophical and political discussions as well as scientific, technical and cultural developments in Europe. The writings of Enlightenment *philosophes* such as Jean-Jacques Rousseau and Baron de Montesquieu influenced the Ottoman reception of concepts such as 'liberty' and 'democracy'.[20] Mustafa Kemal also read Rousseau and Montesquieu, and was inspired by their political notions.[21] He had great sympathy for the principles of the French Revolution as well as for the idea of 'republicanism'.[22] French was also a means for the Westernized Ottoman elite to display their education and cultural sophistication. Thus, by speaking French to the ambassador in the film, Mustafa Kemal was showing the ambassador, as well as the American audience, that he was not an ordinary person, but a sophisticated gentleman sharing 'universal' values and tastes with a Western elite.

As mentioned in the previous chapter, Mustafa Kemal paid great attention to the value of film in documenting events and representing reality. Nevertheless, the ambassador's letter tells us that this particular film did not represent reality directly, at least not fully. Instead, it selected, ordered and crafted reality carefully in order to give a good impression of Mustafa Kemal and the new Turkey. For instance, while the ambassador and Mustafa Kemal were chatting in French and walking in the flower garden, the Fox Film cameraman, Mike, was reposing among the rose bushes[23] in order to create an impression of naturalness. Moreover, a line had been marked on the path for Mustafa Kemal and the ambassador, a few yards away from the camera, indicating where they should stop.[24]

As Mustafa Kemal and the ambassador halt at the marked line, the ambassador politely asks Mustafa Kemal's permission to present him to his compatriots. Before analysing the ambassador's speech in the film, we should consider an important detail in his letter. The ambassador states that he had already given his speech in Ankara and had received positive feedback.[25] This shows that although Mustafa Kemal and the ambassador maintained an appearance of spontaneity in the film, the ambassador and, in all likelihood, Mustafa Kemal had rehearsed their speeches in order to deliver them 'naturally' when the scene was shot. Paradoxically, to present a favourable image of the president and the new Turkey, the film had to present them, in an artificial way, as natural, because only in this way could they convince American audiences that the reforms happening in Turkey were real and not staged.

The ambassador introduces Mustafa Kemal to the American audience with the following words:

> In times of crisis, happy is the nation, which can produce a leader worthy of the task and of the opportunity. Such a crisis, not yet a decade ago, confronted the Turkish State. Like the tree whose branches are withered from disease but in whose stalwart trunk the healthy sap still runs strong, so the former Ottoman Empire had become moribund from the disease of age-long maladministration and retarding traditions. There was one possible cure: the withered branches of those retarding traditions, methods and institutions must be ruthlessly severed from the trunk, from which by judicious pruning new and healthy shoots could be led to spring. This has been accomplished. Today, freed by the wise and courageous action of her leader from those retarding trammels, the Turkish State is steadily progressing along the road of modern political and social development and progress, independent, idealistic, efficient, proud of her achievements and certain of her future happy destiny. For this revolution and high accomplishment one man is primarily responsible. The name of Gazi Mustafa Kemal will forever be associated with the development, founding of the Turkish [sic], the new modern Turkish state and will forever be inscribed indelibly upon the rolls of history. I have the great honor and the great privilege and pleasure, to present to you His Excellency the President of the Turkish Republic.[26]

The ambassador's speech, in presenting Mustafa Kemal as the leader who saved the Turkish state, follows an interesting rhetorical structure based on the decline narrative: the Ottoman Empire was declining, but then a hero arose among the Turkish people who freed them from oppression through his wise and courageous actions, bringing them back onto the path of development and progress or, in other words, the path to modernity. The ambassador diagnoses the decline as a result of the 'disease of age-long maladministration and retarding traditions' in the Ottoman Empire. He also diagnoses the creation of the modern Turkey as the result of the extraordinary accomplishments of one man: Gazi Mustafa Kemal. Clearly, the ambassador was trying to emphasize that Mustafa Kemal was not just a political leader, but a modern and progressive one who brought his people happiness and who shared the values and ideals of contemporary Western civilization. The underlying message can be read as follows: Mustafa Kemal is one of us, and the new modern Turkish State he is building is increasingly catching up to our modern Western nation states.

To make sense of the way the ambassador's speech presents the Ottoman Empire as lagging behind modernity, we need to understand how Western Europe and North America understood themselves as central and leading in modernity during the twentieth century. In the early twentieth century, the so-called modernization theory was hegemonic in sociology. According to this theory, societies developed progressively from a 'pre-modern' or 'traditional' stage to a 'modern' stage through transitions in social, cultural and economic structures. However, this modernization theory was Western-centric; it viewed Western European countries and the United States as having arrived at the final stage of modernity, and assumed other countries to be lagging behind. According to this view, traditional societies could make the transition to becoming advanced industrial societies by following the Western programme of modernity, which was characterized by a number of features such as industrialization, urbanization, secularization, rationalization, professionalization, individualism, faith in progress through human action, mass politics, the emergence of the nation-state and its essential institutions (public education, modern bureaucracy and representative democracy), a market economy, and so on.

Strongly influenced by the Enlightenment, as well as by late-nineteenth and early-twentieth-century scientism,[27] Mustafa Kemal also believed that progress was indeed possible, and that the Turkish nation had to catch up with Western modernity in order to participate in the 'universal civilization' and 'onward march of humanity'.[28] This is clear from Mustafa Kemal's reply to the ambassador and, by extension, the American audience, in the film. After the ambassador's introduction, Mustafa Kemal politely greets him and states the following: 'Excellence, vous me permettez que je parle quelques mots'.[29] After the ambassador has responded 'Je vous en prie, Excellence',[30] Mustafa Kemal addresses the American audience with the following speech, which is worth citing in full.

Honorable Americans,

I am very happy for having found the possibility of addressing you, face to face [directly], for the first time. I thank particularly Mr. Grew, your distinguished Ambassador, for the kind and sincere words he used in speaking about the Turkish Nation and, on that occasion about myself. I am sure, these words correspond entirely to the feelings of affection which the Turkish Nation and I cherish for the great American People.

Honorable Americans,

I would like to say a few words about the true origin of the affection and cordiality which exists between the Turkish and American Peoples and which, I am sure is reciprocal. The Turkish people is [sic] by nature democratic. If this truth is not sufficiently known all over the civilized world, the reason for it has been very well explained by your esteemed Ambassador when he made an allusion to the later epochs of the former Ottoman Empire. On the other hand, at the moment when the American people was [sic] conscious of her existence, it was democracy that she upheld and it was democracy she exalted. With this gift in their hands, Americans have joined the human community as an esteemed people and they founded a great unity. It is from this point that the Turkish people, whose essential characteristic [nature] is democracy, nourishes a sentiment of profound and strong affection for the Americans who have proved themselves to be democracy itself. I hope that this observation will strengthen the affection between the two Peoples. It will not only remain there but will perhaps help the whole humanity to love each other, to wipe away the traditional obstacles to this mutual love, to place the world into [sic] the path of peace and tranquility. Honorable Americans, this is the humanitarian aim of the young Turkish Republic and of the Turkish Nation, which I have the honor to represent. I have no doubt that the American People who are far ahead already in pursuit of this aim are together with the Turkish Nation in this respect. At any rate, this civilized and humane and peaceful ideal must be made a reality.[31]

Despite Mustafa Kemal's radical attempts to Westernize Turkey at the beginning of the twentieth century, there was already an Orientalist image that was deeply ingrained in Western attitudes towards the Turks. Representations of the Turks by Europeans had shown a great variety in the sixteenth and seventeenth centuries, when Europe was militarily lagging behind the Ottoman Empire. However, this started to change radically during the eighteenth century, when Europe became militarily and technologically superior to the Ottomans.[32] The Western representations of the Turks in arts or literature that emerged at this time were constant and coherent, forming a discourse in the Foucauldian sense.[33]

As the ambassador's speech also shows, one of the most well-known representations of the Ottoman Empire in the European Orientalist discourse was as the 'sick man of Europe'.[34] The description of the Ottoman Empire as 'sick' or 'in decline' was not innocent or objective; rather, it implied a strong European self-image associated with progress. Discursively, the Ottoman Empire served as the ideal 'other' for Europe, enabling Europe to define its own identity based on a supposed dichotomy between the 'Occident' and the 'Orient'. Furthermore, this dichotomy allowed European powers to establish a hegemonic relationship to the Ottoman Empire, in which Europeans were represented as superior, progressive, liberal, civilized, rational and familiar, and the Ottomans or Turks as inferior, static, backward, oppressive, uncivilized, barbarian, irrational and exotic. Representing the Ottoman Empire and Turks in this way in literature and paintings, the Orientalist discourse provided a justification for and legitimization of European imperialism within the Ottoman territory.[35]

Another popular representation in the Orientalist repertoire was 'Oriental despotism'. In eighteenth-century political discourse, despotism became synonymous with an Oriental system of regime.[36] The Ottoman Empire leaders were classified as despotic rulers and the Turks were described as having a 'slavish' national character.[37] For many European observers, the Ottomans were a 'stagnant', 'backward' and 'corrupt people', ruled by a despotic government.[38] This, of course, was not compatible with the Enlightenment ideals of a good government that provided its citizens with the rule of law, freedom and liberty.[39]

These representations of Turks within the Orientalist discourse circulated despite the Westernizing reforms undertaken by the Ottoman Empire from the eighteenth century onwards. Turks were still mostly perceived as a people lagging far behind Western civilization in terms of science, technology and culture.⁴⁰ For many European authors, they were a lazy and ignorant people who lived an inactive life. In fact, they were portrayed as so lazy that they did not even cultivate their own land, but left Turkey as a desolate country. Instead of working, they were portrayed spending their time in coffee houses or harems.⁴¹ In other words, the Europeans projected onto the Turks everything they scorned.

Mustafa Kemal was aware of these well-established stereotypes and prejudices about the Ottoman Empire and Turks in the Western world. He tried to counter them by projecting a modern image of the new Turkish state and the Turkish people in front of the camera. It is interesting to see however that in his own speech, although he separates the Ottoman Empire from the Turkish people, he agrees with the ambassador's negative description of the later epochs of the Ottoman Empire. By emphasizing that 'the Turkish people [*sic*] is by nature democratic', Mustafa Kemal was countering the essentialist clichés of the Western Orientalist discourse that had represented the Turks as a 'despotic' or 'obedient' people. Nevertheless, his own formulation uses similar essentialist logic to suggest the opposite. According to Mustafa Kemal, there is indeed a 'nature' to the Turkish people, but it is a democratic one, equal to that of any other 'civilized nation'.

In Mustafa Kemal's view, there was a single civilization in the world, which was the 'universal civilization'.⁴² Every nation could demonstrate its value by its contribution to this common universal civilization of mankind,⁴³ and all nations were on the same path of progress towards a single goal: modernity. In line with this, he believed that some nations were lagging behind or were ahead of others in the march of human progress. Americans, for instance, 'who have proved themselves to be democracy itself' in Mustafa Kemal's words, were ahead of the Turkish nation in terms of their democratic achievements. This did not mean, however, that the Turkish nation was not a natural member of the community of civilized nations, only that it had some catching up to do after its progress had been suspended by the maladministration of the Ottoman government in its later epochs. That it was indeed catching up and taking up its rightful place at the forefront of universal civilization under his leadership was the main message he sought to communicate by appearing in the film under discussion.

But why did Mustafa Kemal associate America with democracy itself and how did he understand the link between modernity and democracy?

Before the modern state was born in Europe, the main type of government was feudalism, a political system built on land tenure and relations between social orders.[44] The principal form of political identity in this system was the 'subject', who was under the political control of a sovereign, usually a monarch. The rise of the idea of civil society in Europe from the early modern period onwards started to change this. The French and American Revolutions in particular, which also deeply inspired Mustafa Kemal, introduced new types of governments and marked the beginning of modern democracy.[45]

The United States Declaration of Independence (1776), for instance, proclaimed: 'We hold these truths to be self-evident, that all men are created equal, that they are endowed by their Creator with certain unalienable Rights, that among these are Life, Liberty and the pursuit of Happiness.'[46] This implies that a government could not bestow upon its people their natural human rights, because these rights already belonged to them by birth.[47] Consequently, the American government could only rule its citizens by their consent, within the framework of a democracy.[48] The modern nation, not the sovereign, was seen as the main guarantor of democracy. Mustafa Kemal, who was a follower of the Enlightenment, and the American and French Revolutions, as well as the philosophy of positivism,[49] agreed with these principles, at least in theory.

Accordingly, in his filmed speech, Mustafa Kemal praises America, associating it, in its very inception, with democracy itself. What was Mustafa Kemal implying by this? Most European philosophers considered the United States as an important experiment in freedom and democracy.[50] This was because, unlike Europe, where civil society and democratic forces had to defeat traditional feudalism, the United States was seen as having been born in democracy.[51] In the nineteenth century, for instance, many European intellectuals, pre-eminently Alexis de Tocqueville (1805–59) and Harriet Martineau (1802–76), visited the United States to study American democracy as a model.[52] Mustafa Kemal's speech shows that he was well aware of the image of America as a natural-born democracy. Nevertheless, he does not take this feature of America for granted, but gives credit to the American people, who were not only born into democracy but also managed to uphold and exalt it. Because of this, he argues they joined the human community as an 'esteemed people' and 'founded a great unity'.

Mustafa Kemal continues his speech by emphasizing that the Turkish people's nature is also democratic and that they have a strong affection for the American people. In this way, he sought to demonstrate that both nations shared the same values and ideals. The message of the first scene of the film, then, is that: the 'West' should no longer perceive Turkey as an 'other', but rather as an ally and as a natural member of contemporary civilization, pursuing the same ideals.

In the film, Mustafa Kemal establishes a connection between himself and the American audience not only through his words but also through his body language. When the ambassador is giving his speech, Mustafa Kemal's hands occasionally grab the lapels of his jacket, giving him an air of gentlemanly confidence. Although this was not a very common posture for Turkish-Ottoman gentlemen, it frequently appeared in late-nineteenth-century and early-twentieth-century American or Western European movies.

In the MIRC version of the film, we see that Mustafa Kemal first observes the body language of the ambassador addressing the American audience. Later, when delivering his own speech, he copies the ambassador's gesture of holding the lapels of his jacket with both hands. As Mustafa Kemal continues his speech, it is the ambassador who starts to mirror his body language. When Mustafa Kemal holds his lapels, the ambassador also holds them, and when Mustafa Kemal drops one of his hands – leaving only the left one touching his lapel – the ambassador drops both of his hands. The visual harmony between Mustafa Kemal and the ambassador is striking, emphasizing that they are not only thinking along the same lines but also looking and acting alike. Moreover, both are dressed in Western bourgeois fashion and act in accordance with modern Western gentlemanly etiquette. In this way, the scene indicates that, in addition to seeking to abolish the perceived intellectual difference between himself and the American ambassador, Mustafa Kemal also tries to erase any visual differences between them. In this way, he delivers a subtle message to the American audience: there is virtually no difference between you and me; I am not unlike you.

The Fountain (Scene II)

In the second scene of the film, Mustafa Kemal, his adopted daughter Âfet Hanım and the ambassador are at a table beside a fountain on the terrace. According to the ambassador's letter, Mustafa Kemal is speaking French to the ambassador, stating that 'much has been done on his farm during the past two years,'[53] to which the ambassador answers that he can see enormous progress has been made since his first visit to the farm three years ago.[54] Mustafa Kemal also tells the ambassador that one million trees have been planted.[55] The MIRC version of the film shows part of this conversation:

> Mustafa Kemal: Excellency, are you happy with what you see here this year?
> The Ambassador: Now, I notice great progress since I saw the farm three years ago.
> Mustafa Kemal: It was only five years ago that we started working here. Before, the land was a complete swamp. It was especially Tahsin Bey who has worked her, who supervised, surveilled, isn't it? Do you want me to introduce him to you?
> The Ambassador: Please, Excellency.
> Mustafa Kemal: Tahsin Bey![56]

Mustafa Kemal then presents Tahsin Bey (Coşkan), the director of the Forest Farm, to the ambassador.[57] Tahsin Bey proceeds to summarize what has been done at the farm so far:

> My Pasha, the first year when we started, all of these places with trees that you see now, there was no single tree, it was a desert [...] we bought Fordson American tractors and with these we began our work [...] we gave importance to agriculture with machinery, animals to a great extent [...] and within five years we planted around one million trees, created fruit gardens and vineyards, and raised around seven thousand sheep.

To understand the importance of the Forest Farm for Mustafa Kemal and to answer the question of what he wanted to convey to American audiences by showing it to them, some background information is needed. While the Soviet Union was seeking rapid industrialization at the expense of its peasants in the beginning of the twentieth century, the young Turkish Republic was making reforms to improve the conditions of its peasants and to modernize agriculture. The Kemalists believed that augmenting agricultural production was the most realistic way for Turkey to develop economically.

After all, when Mustafa Kemal came to power, Turkey was predominantly an agrarian society. Eighty per cent of Turks lived in the countryside. The economy was largely based on agriculture, which provided more than half of the gross national product (GNP) and was the livelihood of more than seventy per cent of the population.[58] Peasants were the driving force behind

Turkey's economy. Nevertheless, their productivity was quite low due to a lack of mechanization and industrialization.[59] Mustafa Kemal was determined to change this by merging agricultural society with the scientific methods and techniques of modern farming. He believed that a farm that could combine agriculture with industry could serve as a model for other farms.

For this project, Mustafa Kemal chose Ankara – the city he envisioned as the modern capital of new Turkey. For him, this small city, which had been the headquarters of the national resistance, symbolized a new beginning, the ground upon which he could build a modern civilization. For Mustafa Kemal's opponents, however, Ankara was nothing more than a remote, unattractive provincial town in the middle of the Anatolian steppes. For them, it was hard to imagine a tree growing here, let alone a new civilization.[60] In fact, they had a point. Ankara, now the second largest city of Turkey with around five million inhabitants, harboured only thirty thousand people in the 1920s.[61] Situated on a rocky hill, it was an arid, bleak and monotonous city. It had cold, snowy winters and hot, dry summers. Its main products were grapes, grain and wool, obtained from the famous Angora goats and rabbits.

When the Allies occupied the empire's capital Istanbul, however, Ankara's geographical location had provided Mustafa Kemal and the nationalists with a strategic advantage. Situated in the middle of Anatolia, it was a secure place to establish the headquarters of the national resistance movement. In fact, the city's destiny changed rapidly after Mustafa Kemal's arrival in 1919, first serving nationalists as their headquarters and then becoming Turkey's new capital in place of Istanbul on 13 October 1923.[62]

Mustafa Kemal won National Independence, making Ankara the capital, and then set out to secure Turkey's economic independence by building a model farm near the same city. This project, the Gazi's Forest Farm (*Gazi Orman Çiftliği*), would be a model for the young republic's economy.[63] With his farm, Mustafa Kemal wanted to prove to everyone that agriculture was possible not only on fertile land but also on the barren grounds of Anatolia. Thus, he bought about twenty thousand acres[64] of partially poor, swampy and infertile land to show the 'Turkish nation' that nothing could stop them if they were determined, worked hard and employed the techniques of modern farming.

On 5 May 1925, his struggle against nature began. Over time, the swamps were drained, trees were planted, and farmhouses and shelters built. In addition to plantations, a vineyard and orchards were established. To turn the farm into a forest farm, in accordance with its name, one of the largest afforestations in Turkish history was realized by planting a million trees, as Tahsin Bey mentions in the film.[65] The farm grew rapidly from 20,000 acres to approximately 100,000 acres in Mustafa Kemal's lifetime.[66] Agricultural production, which started with basic agricultural products such as eggs, milk, yogurt and wine, would grow to include manufactured goods such as beer,[67] malt, ice, soda, carbonated beverages, leather, agricultural tools and iron. By turning agricultural raw materials into industrial products, the farm would serve as a model for the new Turkey's 'self-sufficient' and 'independent' economy.

Besides creating a space for economic production, Mustafa Kemal envisioned his farm as a space with an educational function, specifically to teach modern agricultural techniques. By educating the peasants, he aimed at turning them into farmers. The Forest Farm served as a laboratory for the Turkish Agriculture Institute – opened in 1933 – where the institute's students could do internships. To increase the use of modern farming techniques across the country, lectures and workshops were organized for farmers from all over the country. A workshop organized in the iron and pillow factory of the farm, for instance, taught young farmers – between fourteen and seventeen years old – how to use modern farm machinery.

Furthermore, with the farm, Mustafa Kemal planned to create a public space where the citizens of Ankara could socialize. To make the farm more attractive for citizens, two large ponds were built – one in the shape of the Sea of Marmara and the other in the shape of the Black Sea. These ponds were a popular place for leisure and recreation. The construction of the artificial ponds ameliorated the absence of the sea in Ankara, which had always made the city seem less attractive in comparison to Istanbul. Next to the Marmara pond, a cinema, theatre and hotel were built.[68] A restaurant, café, brewery, park and zoo were added in the following years. After all, these public spaces were an indispensable part of the Western bourgeois lifestyle. Public concerts were organized in the music hall, usually by the Presidential Orchestra (Riyaseti Cumhur Orkestrası), which performed Western classical music. All these events would make the farm a centre of social and cultural life in Ankara, which had been lacking in this respect. With all these events and attractions, the farm was more than the sum of its parts; it was an extension of Mustafa Kemal's project to transform the Turkish people into 'modern citizens'.

The farm, whose construction Mustafa Kemal supervised from the very beginning, also served as a vehicle for his self-representation. Indeed, the president embraced his new role as a farmer. When, for instance, a delegation of farmers visited him in Kastamonu on 24 August 1925, four months after the establishment of his farm, he told them: 'I too am a farmer' and 'Farming requires machinery.… Come together and buy machines!'[69] He frequently visited his farm, usually in the afternoons, to plant trees, hoe fields and drive a tractor.

Nevertheless, Mustafa Kemal was not a typical Turkish farmer. He never went to the farm in traditional farmers dress, but always dressed like a Western bourgeois gentleman, wearing a suit commonly combined with a tie.[70] He even went to the farm in a redingote, which he normally wore for special occasions. His entourage and local people visiting the farm also used to dress in formal clothes when they visited the farm. More than representing a taste in fashion, I want to suggest that the farm's dress code conveyed the message that the Forest Farm was an urban space, so citizens should dress as they would dress in the city, in a 'civilized fashion'. Moreover, Mustafa Kemal wanted to emphasize that the Forest Farm was demonstrating a new, modern type of farming that no longer needed to be accompanied by traditional farmers' clothes.

Proud of his achievement, Mustafa Kemal sometimes took friends and other guests to the farm to entertain them. When, for instance, the King of Afghanistan, Amanullah Khan and his wife Queen Soraya, visited Turkey from 20 to 27 May 1928, Mustafa Kemal gave a reception in their honour at the Marmara Mansion on the Forest Farm. The guests were taken on a tour of the farm in order to display its progress. The Forest Farm provided Mustafa Kemal with a setting to show off his success in reforming the country without being a show-off. Adapting Shakespeare's famous phrase, we can perhaps say that all the farm was a stage, and all the men and women guests merely players,[71] and Mustafa Kemal was the main character, performing modernity.

All this makes clear how, for Mustafa Kemal, there could not be a better setting for a film to display the vast improvements made in the new Turkey than the Forest Farm. Unlike the dark and gloomy chambers of official buildings, the farm provided a bright, open and informal space, much more likely to make an American audience sympathize with the Turkish president. Moreover, as part of its economic modernization and development programme, Turkey wanted to expand its trade with the United States, which could offer particular commodities as well as important markets for Turkish products.[72] After all, agricultural products were the foremost export goods of the Turkish economy. In 1929, for instance, Turkey exported cigarette leaf tobacco, liquorice root and figs as well as mohair, sheep, lamb and goat casings along with handmade rugs to the United States, while importing machinery and vehicles, metals and manufactured goods, vegetable food products and beverages from them.[73]

In opening the farm to American audiences, enabling them to see the high standards of Turkish agricultural production with their own eyes, the film constituted a valuable advertisement for Turkey's progress under Mustafa Kemal's 'modern', 'civilian' and 'democratic' leadership. In the years of the Great Depression (1929–30), the images of the farm conveyed an important message to the world: despite the severe economic crises in the world, the Turkish economy is strong and steadily growing. Neither American companies nor other foreign investors should hesitate to invest in Turkey.[74]

In the film, instead of outlining the progress himself, Mustafa Kemal prefers to have an expert, Tahsin Bey, convey it. This makes for a subtler message to the ambassador and the American audience. Tahsin Bey's explanation, which emphasizes the progress made, the advantages of American tractors and thus of Turkish-American cooperation, and the use of machinery in developing the farm must have satisfied Mustafa Kemal, who was known for paying attention to such details.

The Garden (Scene III)

According to the ambassador's letter, in the third scene, Mustafa Kemal, Âfet Hanım and the ambassador, followed by the retinue, walk through the garden while the cameraman was hidden among the flowers.[75] All the men in Mustafa Kemal's entourage are dressed in Western bourgeoisie fashion;[76] the only woman who appears in the film, Âfet Hanım, is wearing Western fashion accessories such as a fox pelt and high heels. In his letter, the ambassador gives the names of some of the people in the retinue: Numan Bey, Kadri Rıza Bey, Mr. Shaw (G. Howland), Mustafa Kemal's military *aide de camp* and 'the ever present secret service man'.[77] In the background of the scene, the camera shows the Hüseyin Gazi Mountain and the city of Ankara.

The Cows (Scene IV)

In scene four,[78] we see Mustafa Kemal, the ambassador and the retinue visiting the cowshed. The camera films Mustafa Kemal closely and shows that he is dressed fashionably in a dark morning coat with tie. The ambassador and the retinue are also all dressed formally; not a single person is dressed in traditional farmer's clothes. As it was mentioned before, Mustafa Kemal always visited the farm in formal dress usually *tenue de ville*. He did not wear a flat cap but preferred a fedora, trilby, Panama hat or being bareheaded to any kind of hat associated with a traditional farmer's outfit. For him, as noted, the Forest Farm was part of the city and thus a modern urban space.

While visiting the cowshed, Tahsin Bey gives some information on the cattle breed, a four-year-old pure Simmental. Tahsin Bey reveals that from the Simmentals they obtain 18 *okka*[79] of milk per day. This information is important because it indicates that the animals on the farm were not cultivated primarily to till the land, but for their products. In other words, by mentioning the milk, Tahsin Bey suggests that agriculture is no longer dependent on animal power but instead relies on modern machinery, as the film shows explicitly in scene seven, 'The Tractors'.

An interesting moment occurs when Tahsin Bey explains that they have breeds of cattle from Crimea, Simmental and Holland on the farm. One can see Mustafa Kemal standing very closely to the right of a Simmental's head before there is a quick cut in the scene, identifiable from Mustafa Kemal's sudden distance from the cow. It is not clear why the cut was made, but when the scene continues, the Simmental shakes its head wildly and Mustafa Kemal first moves his head back and takes a step back. This moment indicates an important feature of film, namely, that it displays contingency. Unlike other visual media such as sculpture, painting or photography, which represent fixed moments in time, film displays movement. Resisting representational wholeness more than any other visual medium, film is open to surprise. This is the allure of film and also its danger.

In the rest of the scene, Mustafa Kemal acts as if nothing has happened and asks Tahsin Bey about the other cows. Tahsin Bey answers that they are mostly from the Crimea, Switzerland and Holland, and indicates that the ones from Holland, because they give the most milk (up to forty litres a day), have been hybridized with local cattle to increase their size and milk production.

Without regard for Mustafa Kemal Pasha, the Simmental is mooing. Showing his expertise on the topic, Mustafa Kemal asks, 'Hybrid, you acclimatize them?' to which Tahsin Bey answers: 'We acclimatize them.' Mustafa Kemal notes that the Simmental is bigger than the local cows and holds its horn with his right hand, but when the Simmental shakes its head he withdraws his hand.

While Tahsin Bey explains that the calves of the Simmental are best in terms of meat and milk, Mustafa Kemal looks briefly at the man behind Tahsin Bey and then at the camera. The man says something to Mustafa Kemal. It is not possible to see whether the Fox Film team or the man behind Tahsin Bey gave a sign to indicate that Mustafa Kemal and Tahsin Bey should stop talking here, but Mustafa Kemal interrupts Tahsin Bey's words by making a move with his right hand, signalling that he should stop talking. He then turns briefly towards the camera, signalling that they are done. If this was Mustafa Kemal's own initiative, it could be suggested that he was co-directing the film with the Fox Film crew. If it was not, then it might be concluded that he was making an effort to perform in line with the film crew's instructions.

Next, we see Mustafa Kemal in a full shot, dressed in a morning coat and tie, and wearing patent leather shoes. He is passing by the herd, which has been driven out to drink water. He reviews the front row of cows, which are being carefully held by some workers to minimize the risk. Regardless of all measures, however, the cows are mooing loudly. Patting each of them warmly with his right hand, Mustafa Kemal walks towards the camera and looks into it very briefly; in his left hand, he holds a cigarette. This scene shows the audience that the cows are being treated well at the farm. By monitoring their cultivation on site and petting each of them warmly, Mustafa Kemal emphasizes his love and affection for the animals. The implicit message to the audience is that he is a civilized man who personally looks after the welfare of the animals on his farm. Despite the cows' unruliness, Mustafa Kemal remains unfazed; yet at the same time he does not leave the animals completely free. To ensure the desired outcome, the cows are held carefully, so that they are not seen to defy Mustafa Kemal's authority.

The Poultry (Scene V)

According to the ambassador's letter, the next scene is called 'The Poultry'.[80] In both the TFA and MIRC versions, this scene is placed before 'The Cows'.

We see the presidential party visiting the chicken coop. Tahsin Bey approaches the fenced yard to feed the chicken with grain, making a strange noise and shaking the fence. The hens and geese answer his call by coming towards him squawking and gaggling. The camera films them eating the grain and shows the white chicken coops which look clean and modern.

The scene shows that the hens and geese are being kept in the best hygienic conditions and raised according to the highest quality standards. Moreover, in the background of the scene, a self-regulating windmill can be seen. As farmers moved into the barren Great Plains in the United States, they used self-regulating windmills as a power source to pump water from the ground. Mustafa Kemal's modern farm seems to have adopted this agricultural technology as well. This scene, therefore, again appears to have been designed to make a statement about the modernity of the farm and its owner Mustafa Kemal.

The Sheep (Scene VI)

In the next scene, called 'The Sheep', we see the presidential party on a hill near the Forest Farm to which, as the ambassador's letter describes, they were taken.[81] On the hill, there is a large flock of sheep, numbering 800 according to the ambassador's letter.[82] He also reveals that the sheep had travelled for three days on 'forced marches' to reach the farm in time for the filming event. In the scene, a shepherd plays the flute (*kaval*) while Mustafa Kemal, the ambassador and the retinue – all in formal dress – review the flock, which passes between them and the camera. The ambassador notes that when the scene was filmed for the first time, the sheep rushed and kicked up so much dust that they had to repeat the scene with the animals passing more slowly.[83] Thus, although Mustafa Kemal turned to film for its presumed ability to represent reality directly, if reality did not conform to the image he wanted to project, it was constructed (as in the case of the sheep being marched to the hill) or reconstructed (as in the case of the reshot scene) to fit this image.

The shepherd playing the flute is identified as an Albanian and, although this is not audible in the film, the ambassador states in his letter that while observing this scene, Mustafa Kemal smiled and in *sotto voce* said to him: 'The Albanians make the best shepherds in the world but are good for nothing else.'[84] If the ambassador's statement is true, Mustafa Kemal's remark points to his adoption of a discourse that was prevalent at the end of the nineteenth and the beginning of the twentieth century in Europe and North America. This discourse thought about different nations through the lens of popular understandings of ethnicity and Darwinian sociocultural theories of evolution.[85]

According to these theories, societies progress through different stages, beginning with a primitive state, and developing over time into more complex and civilized forms. This sociocultural evolutionary discourse considered Western civilization as the pinnacle of human civilization, the standard in relation to which other civilizations could be ranked as either primitive or civilized. With his statement about the Albanian shepherd, Mustafa Kemal implicitly assigns Albanians to a lower stage of development and Turks to a more advanced one. Moreover, by sharing this ethnic stereotype quietly with the ambassador, he builds a social solidarity between Turks and Americans as civilized selves united in their view of Albanians as less civilized others, while also indicating his politeness by not expressing the ethnic joke in a way that is audible to the audience.

The Tractors (Scene VII)

In the next scene, we see the presidential party watching six tractors ploughing the fields. In his letter, the ambassador explains that the tractor drivers tried to preserve a military formation for the camera, but were unsuccessful. According to the ambassador, the tractors appeared to be German or Czechoslovakian, but the six or eight automobiles present (though not shown in either the TFA or MIRC version of the film) were American. The display of the farm's tractors to the American audience had several implications. As we saw at the beginning of the film, Tahsin Bey had told Mustafa Kemal and the ambassador that they began building the farm by buying American Fordson tractors. In this way, the success of Turkish-American economic cooperation was emphasized.

Furthermore, the tractor was more than just an agricultural tool at the beginning of the twentieth century; it was an instrument of modernity, revolutionizing farming in the early 1900s by increasing efficiency and productivity.[86] Before tractors, the principal source of power in agriculture, besides human labour, had been animal power. Draft animals such as horses, oxen and buffalo were used to cultivate fields and reap the harvest. With the invention of tractors at the end of the nineteenth century, a new form of power entered agriculture, capable of tackling almost every major task on a farm.[87] Like other industrial machines, tractors were seen as the 'great emancipators' of humanity that would allow farmers to enjoy leisure time.[88] With all its features, the tractor was an important symbol and technological component of modern agriculture in the United States and Europe. Mustafa Kemal's farm could not be imagined without it.

In fact, in 1926, one year after the farm was established, there were already thirteen Fordson tractors produced by the Ford Motor Company on Mustafa Kemal's farm. Each of these American tractors had twenty horsepower and could plough one twelve-acre plot of land daily.[89] In presenting the farm's tractors (albeit, according to the ambassador's letter, not the Fordsons) to foreign audiences, the film was not only showing US–Turkish cooperation but also pointing out that there was virtually no difference between the way agricultural tasks were performed on Mustafa Kemal's farm and on farms in nations recognized as being at the forefront of modernity.

The Machine Shop (Scene VIII)

According to the ambassador, the next scene is called 'The Machine Shop'.[90] He explains that for this scene, they visited the machine shop where ploughs and other farming tools were produced.[91] The machine workshop was established at the farm in line with Mustafa Kemal's vision of modern farming. The ambassador mentions how, when the presidential party approached the workshop, they could hear the banging of hammer and anvil. Indeed, in the MIRC version of the film, we see the presidential party visiting the machine shop and can hear the banging of hammers and anvils, and we see the great number of ploughs produced there standing outside of the machine workshop.

This scene, like most others, was not spontaneous but prearranged. It shows that not only Mustafa Kemal and the ambassador but also the farm's workers performed active roles for the camera. The workers in the machine workshop do not stop working as Mustafa Kemal and his retinue approach, but continue with great concentration as if nothing unusual is happening. This scene stood in stark contrast to Orientalist images of the Turks that represented them as a lazy, backward and stagnant people. By using its capacity to capture motion in time, the film sought to create a new image of the 'Turks' as always on the move, in action, working or busy. Moreover, the workshop scene shows that Turks are capable not only of farming but also of producing complex tools. The machine shop thus signifies Turkish people as industrious and technologically *au courant*.

The ambassador further notes that Mustafa Kemal personally took the handles of a plough, showing the easy manageability of this tool, followed by a conversation about the uses of the tools on the farm.[92] In the MIRC version of the film, Mustafa Kemal indeed takes the handles of a plough, and the ambassador follows his example. By demonstrating the user-friendly plough, which was most probably the workshop's own product, Mustafa Kemal was displaying his knowledge about the techniques of modern farming as well as his investment in the production of agricultural machinery in Turkey. The tractors, machine shop and plough, all pointed to the farm as a symbol of Turkish modernity and, by extension, to the modernizing leadership of its owner, Mustafa Kemal.

Woman, Lovely Woman (Scene IX)

According to the ambassador's letter, the Fox movie operator Harry E. Squire insisted that Âfet Hanım, Mustafa Kemal's favourite adopted daughter, deliver a message to the women of America.[93] The ambassador mentions that Mustafa Kemal was first hesitant but then gave his permission. The stage in the film is set as follows: Mustafa Kemal, Âfet Hanım and Ambassador Grew sit in three wicker chairs in the garden with flowers in the background.

For the benefit of the American public, the ambassador asks Âfet Hanım in English: 'Âfet Hanım, would you tell us your opinion of the American woman?'.[94] The film shows that before Âfet Hanım can answer, Mustafa Kemal smilingly asks the ambassador: 'Excellency, will you permit my daughter to respond in Turkish?'[95] After the ambassador's confirmation in French, 'Please, Excellency',[96] Âfet Hanım turns to the ambassador and says:

> I appreciate and congratulate the American women because they have fully won their political rights. The Turkish women are not satisfied with the

rights at present but I am sure the full right to elect and be elected deputies to the Grand National Assembly will be secured.[97]

In his letter, the ambassador gives the information that this scene had to be shot twice because Âfet Hanım at first spoke directly to the ambassador instead of the camera. He also notes that this was a lovely scene, his favourite.[98]

Mustafa Kemal's slight hesitation before permitting Âfet Hanım to speak on film makes us question the reasons behind it. Today, Mustafa Kemal is known as the great emancipator of Turkish women, so why did he hesitate to allow his daughter to deliver a message to the women of America? To understand this, we first need to understand the position of women in 1920s Turkey and how the Kemalist revolution changed it.

Although Mustafa Kemal and his followers were only a small elite in Ankara, their revolution touched everything, influenced everyone and permeated every aspect of the social life of the country. For instance, on 17 February 1926, the Ankara government voted for a new civil code, an adaptation of the Swiss civil code.[99] With this law, designed to Westernize family life in Turkey, the revolution inserted itself into the most intimate relationships of its citizens. According to the Kemalists, *Sharia* law was pre-modern and therefore not civilized for the Turkish nation, so it had to be abolished. *Sharia* law allowed divorce only at the husband's discretion, polygamy for men and unequal inheritance rights in favour of men. The new law not only gave equal rights to both parties in divorce and inheritance but also banned polygamy. Moreover, it allowed the marriage of a Muslim woman to a non-Muslim man.[100]

The new civil code was a revolutionary step for the emancipation of women in Turkey, but there were still loopholes and inconsistencies. Like most European countries of the time, a man would remain the head of the family, and women could not work outside the home or travel abroad without his approval.[101] The code also did not turn Turkey into a European country overnight. While it was enforced in cities, in rural areas, the old traditions continued side by side with the revolutionary legislation. Nevertheless, once the taboo was broken, the social status of women started to gradually improve across the country. The state increasingly opened up all trades and professions to women, including higher education, medicine, law and public services, which had formerly been largely restricted to men. Mustafa Kemal, the man behind this radical step, became the hero of women's emancipation in Turkey.[102] This reform had the further implication of bringing global attention to Turkey as the first Muslim country to provide women's rights to such an extent, as well as to Mustafa Kemal's leadership as a politician who shared a vision with modern Western democracies.

For Turkish feminists who wanted to receive full political rights, however, the code was not enough. As in the United States, where women won the right to vote in 1919,[103] they also wanted the right to elect and be elected as members of parliament.[104] In fact, five months before this film was shot, on 3 April 1930, the Turkish Grand National Assembly passed a law allowing women to vote and to be elected locally,[105] followed by a law, passed on 5 December 1934 giving women the right to vote nationwide.[106] Thus, when the film was shot in November 1930, women's enfranchisement was still being discussed, but Mustafa Kemal was already of the opinion that the time to give women their full political rights had come.[107]

Thus, when Âfet Hanım suggested in the film that Turkish women were not satisfied, her father likely shared her opinion. What may have made him hesitate, however, was Âfet Hanım's possible comparison of the rights of Turkish women with those of American women, which would create an image of Turkey as lagging behind the United States. This would contradict Mustafa Kemal's goal of representing Turkey as a natural member of modern Western civilization. Introducing an independent modern Turkish woman to the American audience, however – especially if this woman was his daughter – would fit his aim of representing the new Turkey as a modern country eager to become a member of the Western club perfectly. Furthermore, if she was not allowed to speak, the audience may have wondered who the sole woman present in the film was and what her relationship was to Mustafa Kemal. Either way, the decision was risky, also because this scene had clearly not been planned and rehearsed, so he could not be sure what Âfet Hanım would say and whether she would affirm or undermine the message he wanted to convey with the film. Nevertheless, as the MIRC version of the film shows, Mustafa Kemal took the risk and let his daughter deliver a message to the women of America.

The fortunes of the film

The ambassador notes that filming took them four hours, from eleven o'clock in the morning until three o'clock in the afternoon.[108] He calls the filming event a great triumph for Fox Films, writing: 'Nothing of the kind has ever [been] done here before.'¹⁰⁹ According to the ambassador's letter, Mustafa Kemal was so keen to see the result that he delayed his journey through Anatolia. The film was supposed to be developed in Berlin at the Fox studio and then returned for screening in Turkey within nine days.¹¹⁰ For the film's screening in the United States, Mustafa Kemal's speech needed to be translated into English, whereas for the screening in Turkey, the ambassador's speech needed to be translated into Turkish.¹¹¹

It was also necessary for Fox Films to shoot some extra scenes in Turkey that did not involve Mustafa Kemal. However, when the film crew wanted to shoot some of these scenes and take photographs of the old bazar, they ran into difficulties.¹¹² Because of a complaint, the governor (*Vali*) arrested the movie operator (Squire) and confiscated the film, since he felt it would give a false impression of the new Turkey.¹¹³ According to the ambassador, the reason behind this trouble was a certain Fuad Bey, the head of the Himaye-i Etfal (Children's Protection Society).¹¹⁴ The ambassador mentions that Fuad Bey was a self-seeker who was supposedly jealous of American enterprises setting up in Turkey and who thought the filming would damage his interests. Thus, Fuad Bey prevented Squire from filming either the Jennings playground or the orphanage for which definitive arrangements had been made.¹¹⁵ He went to the governor and accused Squire of photographing indecent and obscene scenes in the streets and the old bazaar.¹¹⁶ The crisis was only resolved through Mustafa Kemal's intervention, and the finished footage was rushed to Berlin by a special Turkish courier.¹¹⁷

The ambassador notes that what the governor and Turkish authorities failed to understand – as both he and Squire pointed out – was that pictures of the streets and buildings of a modern city are not themselves interesting, but the antithesis between the old and the new Turkey was the very thing that would appeal to the American public and would enhance Turkish prestige by showing what has been accomplished in these few recent years.¹¹⁸ The ambassador's comment is significant because it explains the motivation behind the film, which was designed to demonstrate Turkey's progress under Mustafa Kemal and to contribute its prestige in the United States. However, what is even more interesting is the story of the film's confiscation and the governor's fear that the footage of the old bazaar could give a false impression of the new Turkey. This detail tells us much about the mentality of the Kemalist elite, which was often more Kemalist than Mustafa Kemal. Being aware of the sensitivity of the Kemalist ruling elite to affirm Turkey's new image, Fuad Bey knew that his accusations of indecency and obscenity would mobilize the governor to take action against the film.

The ambassador does not give any details about Fuad Bey's motivation, except stating that there was an American enterprise that had definitive plans regarding the Jennings playground and the orphanage. The Jennings playground and orphanage were related to the American philanthropist Asa K. Jennings, the secretary of the International Young Men's Christian Association (YMCA) of the United States and Canada.[119] Since the secular Kemalist elite was not very keen on any form of missionary activity by foreign religious organizations in Turkey, Jennings established a new society called American Friends of Turkey in 1930 in order to continue his activities in Turkey. The society was particularly interested in child welfare work, and they supported the establishment of kindergartens, playgrounds, sports clubs, libraries and dental and baby clinics in Turkey.[120] Although the ambassador's letter does not give any details, Fuad Bey's supposed envy may have been related to a conflict of interest between him and the American Friends of Turkey. In fact, in the MIRC, there is footage registered as *Turks Still Smoke the Old Way*,[121] shot in 1930 by Squire, including some sequences of children at play in an orphanage. These sequences look like they were designed to be part of a story related to the American Friends of Turkey. But, leaving local intrigue aside, and concentrating on the bigger picture, what might have been wrong from the governor's and the Turkish authorities' perspective with Americans photographing scenes in the streets and in an old bazaar in Turkey?

The bazaar was an Orientalist symbol. Mustafa Kemal and the Kemalist elite did not like to be seen as Oriental, so they attempted to erase Oriental symbols from public space as much as they could in order to make Turkey look like a modern Western country. Unlike the contemporary department stores in Europe and America that signified capitalist modernity, the old bazaar stood for an outdated Oriental tradition. Moreover, the bazaar was a public space that provided a kind of archaeology of society, where people from different social classes and professions met.

Despite Mustafa Kemal's radical modernizing reforms in the 1930s, one could still witness scenes in the bazaar that could be easily associated with Orientalism, such as women in chador or men dressed in an 'uncivilized fashion' drinking coffee in coffee houses, smoking shisha or bargaining in the 'Oriental manner'. Contrary to the Kemalist's attempt to craft a Westernized image of a new Turkey that was homogenous, orderly and progressive, the bazaar projected an Oriental image that was heterogeneous, chaotic and anachronistic. From their perspective, filming scenes in the streets and in the old bazaar could easily be seen as potentially damaging to the new Turkey's image, and therefore as something that had to be prevented.

The above-mentioned film *Turks Still Smoke the Old Way* confirms the governor's concerns. It shows the traditional manufacturing process of waterpipes and wooden spoons by some workers in an old-style assembly line. The camera pays particular attention to an elderly gentleman who smokes a traditional waterpipe while doing his job. A close-up shot reveals him dressed in a traditional fashion and sitting on the ground. A small coffee table stands next to him on his left side and two coffee cups are in front of him. While smoking his waterpipe, he coughs occasionally. At some point, he complains that the coffee maker has not brought the coffee yet. Traditional Turkish carpets hang behind the workers. In its entirety, this footage offers the perfect scenery for the Fox Films crew for an Orientalist representation.

The footage also includes long-shot street scenes together with scenes filmed in an old bazaar. The men filmed in the streets are mostly dressed traditionally, with some of them donning turbans and others fezzes. The few women that can be seen in the film are wearing either the chador or the hijab. In one scene, a number of men are sitting in front of a place resembling a coffee house, observing passers-by. Consequently, it is very difficult to place the images within a Turkish context; they could have been shot anywhere in the Middle East at the time.

Other footage entitled *Turkish Market Day*,[122] also shot by the Fox Films crew, shows an ordinary market day in Ankara. Again, unlike the image of Turkey projected by Mustafa Kemal and his followers on the Forest Farm as homogenous, orderly and modern, the market day delivers a counter-image that is heterogeneous, chaotic and anachronistic. The film shows men and women from all classes of society dressed mostly in a traditional manner. In contrast to Mustafa Kemal's well-ordered farm, the market place delivers a picture of a crowd ruled by disarray. The Kemalists were positivists and as the slogan of positivism – 'ordre et progrès' – suggests, they exhibited a strong tendency towards order. Furthermore, Mustafa Kemal and his followers grew up in the late nineteenth and early twentieth century, when the ideas of the French polymath Gustave Le Bon on crowd psychology were highly popular among right-wing circles as well as Western armies. Le Bon had an elitist view, believing that the essential irrationality, impulsiveness and danger of the masses should be controlled.[123] With his ideas on crowd psychology, Le Bon influenced many political leaders and intellectuals in the Western world from Benito Mussolini and Adolf Hitler to Sigmund Freud and Edward Barneys. Influenced by Le Bon's ideas,[124] the Kemalist elite also distrusted disorderly masses such as the one at the Turkish market, which could impress a negative image on the audience. Whereas the official voices of Mustafa Kemal and the ambassador largely dominate the film produced on the Forest Farm, in the market scene, one can hear a great variety of different voices of ordinary people, male and female, high and low, none of which can be individually identified. Nevertheless, together they deliver a powerful message to the audience: as Mustafa Kemal and his followers attempt to refashion Turkey into a modern country, a large part of the country still retains its traditional nature.

To fill the visual (and social) divide between the new Turkey and contemporary civilization, Mustafa Kemal and his followers had to perform modernity for different audiences. They were keenly aware of how the staging of a scene could enhance – or disrupt – particular performances of modernity. Seen as the most realistic medium of the time, film had a particular allure for the Kemalists because it could help them project their new identity as well as convince Western audiences that Turkey had changed and should now be seen as a natural member of civilized nations. At the same time, undesirable scenes from Turkey, such as the scenes in the streets and in the old bazaar, could also convince Western audiences of the opposite: that Turkey remained an Oriental country.

To overcome this dilemma, Mustafa Kemal and his followers developed a particular relationship towards cinema. As defenders of modernity, they were open to this medium but were anxious about their ability to control its effects. It was encouraged to produce or display films in and about Kemalist Turkey, but only as long as the cinema was under state control and the films did not contradict Kemalist state ideology. Turkey's friends, such as the American ambassador, were also welcome to produce films about Turkey and the Kemalist regime, but only if the films did not give a false impression of the new Turkey and meshed well with the regimes' vision of modernity.

Conveying the message of change through film on an international level was a kind of Faustian bargain[125] for Mustafa Kemal and his followers. They had to trade Turkey's cinematic image and its potential manipulation for a more positive public opinion abroad. They wanted to control new Turkey's image as much as possible, but were not able to fully do this if they wanted foreign audiences to see it. Therefore, they followed the strategy of better the devil you know. If a film had to be produced concerning Kemalist Turkey, it should be produced either by the state or at least by someone they knew and could control to a certain extent.

Otherwise, even a short scene representing the new Turkey in a negative way could cause a loss of prestige and endanger their efforts to become (seen as) modern. Since film was believed to be the most realistic medium of the time, it could damage their public image more than any other visual medium. Moreover, once a film damaged their image, this could have a lasting impact on the audience, which would be almost impossible to erase. The fact that the Turkish Republic was a young country that was just introducing itself on the world stage made the use of cinema – also a relatively new medium – even riskier.

In fact, by creating a split between the filmed subject and its cinematic image, film made the former lose control of the latter. The Kemalist government was very successful in its attempt to control the cinematic image within the country's borders, but once a film left Turkey, they had no such control. The mechanical reproducibility of film enabled an unprecedented spread and endless unauthorized dissemination of filmic and photographic images.[126] Thus, films concerning Kemalist Turkey could easily fall into the hands of people with hidden intentions, who could manipulate, reproduce and display these films to an anonymous, foreign crowd of millions. Worse still, a voice-over could be added to these cinematic images in order to spread falsehoods about Kemalist Turkey over the whole world.

As the German philosopher Walter Benjamin suggests, film creates a kind of mirror image but unlike the ordinary image in the mirror, the filmic mirror image is 'detachable' and 'transportable'.[127] Consequently, entrusting his cinematic image to someone else, especially a foreigner, was by no means easy for Mustafa Kemal. It should be understood as a favour that created a friendly bond between him and Ambassador Grew, with a responsibility to reciprocate on the part of the ambassador.[128] The ambassador's excitement in his letter, in which he calls the filming of Mustafa Kemal 'for the first time' a 'victory' and 'epoch-making',[129] points to his awareness of the privilege given to him and to the American nation:

> Fox Films, Incorporated, supported by my own modest efforts, have achieved a signal victory in persuading the President of the Turkish Republic for the first time to be filmed and movietoned in the intimacy of that sanctum sanctorum, his much beloved farm. [...] In order to present a true picture of this epochmaking [sic] event I venture, most depreciatingly, to enclose a somewhat more intimate statement than is customarily included in the body of dispatches to the Department.[130]

By allowing the Americans to film him, on the one hand, Mustafa Kemal risked losing control over his cinematic image, but on the other hand, it could bring him and Turkey the priceless gift of influencing public opinion abroad. Film could give him what other media could not: directness, sincerity and prestige, but also a chance to wipe out the Orientalist image of the Turks in the Western world. To achieve the higher goal, he accepted the 'Faustian' bargain with the ambassador, accepting that from now on, he would no longer be able to control the cinematic image created in the film. Or would he?

Turkish scholar Utkan Kocatürk, in his book *A Documented Atatürk Diary*, writes that Mustafa Kemal watched the film made by Fox Films, including his speech to the American nation, at the Elhamra Sineması (Elhamra Movie Theater) in Istanbul on 3 December 1930.[131] This cinema visit is verified in a photo album recently published by the Turkish General Staff in Ankara.[132] One photograph in the album shows Mustafa Kemal and his entourage sitting in the cinema hall. Şükrü Kaya, the Minister of Interior, sits on his left side, while Âfet Hanım and Makbule (Atadan), his sister, sit on his right.[133]

Niyazi Ahmet Banoğlu's book *Atatürk'ün İstanbul'daki Günleri* (The Days of Mustafa Kemal in Istanbul) gives more details about this cinema visit.[134] According to Banoğlu, Mustafa Kemal was at the Elhamra Movie Theater from 14:30 to 17:10. It was a private film screening organized by Kemal Film.[135] The cinema programme began with a sound film, shot by Fox Films, including scenes showing Mustafa Kemal's Forest Farm. Then, another sound film was screened relating to Mustafa Kemal's speech to the Americans, in which the American ambassador explained and praised 'The Great Turkish Revolution' and its leader for an American audience.[136] A screening of Atatürk's speech to the Americans in Turkish followed, in which he pointed to the mutual appreciation between the two democratic nations.[137]

Then, a silent film charting Mustafa Kemal's last journey from Ankara to Istanbul was screened.[138] In this film, Atatürk was shown among students in Kayseri, then among the people in Sivas, at Turhal station reading the petition of a citizen, speaking to a peasant on a train, and also in Amasya and Samsun, conversing with citizens. Later on, the film displays a panoramic view of Trabzon with Mustafa Kemal visiting the local branch of the Republican People's Party (Cumhuriyet Halk Partisi, CHP) followed by his departure from Trabzon on the Ege steamship paired with a scene of a foggy Bosphorus and Mustafa Kemal's departure from the Dolmabahçe Palace. After this, one film showed the pageantry on Republic Day in Ankara while another featured the signing of a Turkish-Greek Friendship Treaty by the Prime Minister of Greece, Eleftherios K. Venizelos,[139] the Greek Foreign Minister Andreas Michalakopoulos, the Prime Minister of Turkey, Ismet Pasha (İnönü), and the Turkish Foreign Minister Tevfik Rüştü (Aras).[140] Finally, some war scenes from the silent film *All Quiet on the Western Front* (directed by Lewis Milestone, 1930) were shown[141] as well as the sound film *The Vagabond King* (directed by Ludwig Berger, 1930).

Turkish communications scholar Serdar Öztürk mentions an interesting letter that was sent by the Minister of Economics, Mustafa Eşref Bey, to the Prime Minister's Office in 1931, one year after the Forest Farm film was produced. The letter, dated 15 February 1931, points out the importance of using cinema films abroad in order to introduce the reforms initiated by the new regime to transform Turkey from an empire to a new state.[142] It suggests that some foreign countries, most importantly the United States, had requested films for display via the Turkish embassies.

Öztürk notes that the National Geographic Society requested a film from the Turkish embassy in Washington, DC for display at a conference concerning the new Turkey on 9 January 1931.[143] The film had to be three or four hundred meters long and demonstrate the developments in Turkey in various areas. The Turkish embassy in Washington conveyed the request to the Ministry of Education in Turkey. In 1931, only one film promoting Turkey's reforms existed: the film made by Fox Film about the Forest Farm and Mustafa Kemal's meeting with the American ambassador. Nevertheless, Öztürk explains that the film could not be screened in the United States because its reproduction had to be approved by Mustafa Kemal, which he refused.[144] Ebru Boyar and Kate Fleet's article 'Making Turkey and The Turkish Revolution Known to Foreign Nations without any Expense'[145] contests Öztürk's claim that Mustafa Kemal was against the film's reproduction. They claim that he did approve the film's screening, but that since insufficient copies were available, it could not be sent to the United States.[146]

The fact that there exists footage shot by Fox Films in the Fox Movietone News Collections at the MIRC, which I found during my research, suggests that the film did reach the United States. According to the MIRC's records, the Fox Movietone News Story *Ataturk Entertains Grew on His Private Estate* was not incorporated into a nationally released newsreel. This, however, does not preclude its use or screening in other forms, including at private screenings or in other newsreels.[147]

There is scant information about how often the film was screened or where it was shown in the United States. The only trace I have been able to find of it is in a film called *Incredible Turk* produced in 1958, which I came upon in the National Archives. It is a film originating from the Central Intelligence Agency (CIA) about Mustafa Kemal Atatürk and the modernization of the Turkish Republic, which partly shows three scenes ('The Cows', 'The Garden' and 'Preliminary Speeches') from the Forest Farm film. These scenes are juxtaposed with others showing Mustafa Kemal engaging in farming activities.

According to the officials at the National Archives, this film might have been used by the state for propaganda as well as educational purposes. For instance, the CIA may have used it to train their agents. The *Incredible Turk* is a documentary film that begins with an introduction on Turkey's strategic importance in guarding against Soviet expansion in the Middle East, followed by Mustafa Kemal Atatürk's modernizing reforms and his pro-Western attitude, and ends with Turkey's alliance with the West and NATO to defend its way of life. This film was screened nationwide in the United States on a documentary television programme called *The Twentieth Century* that ran on the CBS network between 1957 and 1966, hosted by the famous American broadcast journalist and anchorman Walter Cronkite.[148]

It is unclear how the producers of *The Incredible Turk* acquired the three scenes from the Forest Farm film, or how the film reached the archives of the CIA. However, it is certain that once Mustafa Kemal had made a pact with the American ambassador to exchange his cinematic image for international prestige, he relinquished control over it and accepted that it could wander around the world, from archive to archive and from screen to screen, without his knowing who would use it and for what purpose.

Conclusion

With the end of the War of Independence, Mustafa Kemal and his followers set out to build a modern nation-state out of the remains of the Ottoman Empire. They initiated several reforms to modernize Turkey and to raise it to the level of the 'civilized nations of the world'. Despite all their efforts to distance themselves from the Ottoman past, however, the shadow of Turkey's Oriental image haunted the new government. This image had developed over centuries as a result of Western Orientalist discourse as well as Ottoman self-representation. To become a respected member of the Western community, Mustafa Kemal and his followers had to refashion Turkey's image and convince the Western world that they were being sincere and successful in their efforts. Considered the most modern and realistic medium of the time, cinema offered the Kemalists a particularly powerful means of achieving this. Yet the same features of cinema that made it attractive also made it difficult to control and therefore a risky medium for self-representation. By analysing one specific film made for an American audience in this chapter, I have demonstrated why film might have been both the most beneficial and the most risky vehicle for Mustafa Kemal to represent himself to foreign audiences.

To raise Turkey's prestige in the United States, Mustafa Kemal accepted Ambassador Joseph C. Grew's offer of being filmed for the first time on his Forest Farm. Faced with film, the ultimate medium of contingency, he tried to leave nothing to chance. To convince American audiences of the veracity of Turkey's modernity, Mustafa Kemal, together with the ambassador and the Fox Film crew, carefully crafted the film to present himself and the Turkish people as countering Orientalist stereotypes. He performed a modern, civilized and democratic image of himself and the Turkish nation as capable of change and progress. Mustafa Kemal's choice of the Forest Farm as the film's setting was deliberate, because in combining agriculture with industry, the farm was the epitome of the republic's economic development.

Dressed like a Western bourgeois gentleman even at the farm, Mustafa Kemal presented himself as a civilian president working tirelessly to industrialize his country and increase the people's standard of living. He emphasized the importance of mutual amity and common interest between Turkey and the United States, while demonstrating in practice the importance of American industry for his economic development programme and the success of Turkish-American cooperation. In this way, he not only intended to show his pro-Western attitude but also aimed to establish an affinity between himself and the civilian political leaders of contemporary Western democracies. The directness of cinema served to convey this message to the American public more effectively than any other medium.

Both the ambassador's and Mustafa Kemal's speeches in the film stressed that the Turkish people were in essence a people of great accomplishments that had unfortunately been led astray due to the maladministration of the Ottoman Empire, causing them to lag behind the modern nations of the West. Mustafa Kemal was introduced by the ambassador and portrayed himself as the heroic leader who had restored the Turkish nation to the path of modernity, giving it back its rightful place in the community of civilized nations. In their speeches, both statesmen sought to convey the following message: Americans should no longer perceive Turkey as an uncivilized Oriental 'other', but rather as part of the civilized Western 'self'.

Nevertheless, Mustafa Kemal and his followers' attempts at controlling every aspect of the film indicate that they worried about losing control of the new Turkey's image. Mustafa Kemal tried to control the representational totality of the film by choosing the people who made the film and the settings, and by carefully performing in front of the camera. Furthermore, to shape the film's outcome, he and his followers meticulously prepared the farm and reconstructed some scenes, while preventing others from being filmed. Despite these attempts, however, a scene such as 'The Cows' as well as those shot in the streets and at the old bazaar show that they could not fully overcome the contingency of film or guarantee that it would fully and exclusively convey their vision.

The film's confiscation by the governor shows that the Kemalist bureaucrats were alert to every single detail in the film that could create a false impression of the new Turkey. This incident tells us not only about the Kemalist regime's sensitivity towards Turkey's new image but also about its belief in the power of cinema to reshape public opinion. The lack of a material base for modernization and the subsequent visual divide between the envisioned new Turkey and 'civilized nations of the world' in the early years of the republic made the regime pay close attention to public spectacles of modernity.

As purveyors of Western modernity, Mustafa Kemal and his followers embraced cinema, but only as long as they could control its outcome and ensure that it did not contradict the Kemalist state ideology. Within Turkey, the regime was successful in keeping the medium under control, but it could not do the same abroad. Despite the risk, Mustafa Kemal chose to face the challenges and handed his and Turkey's cinematic image over to the ambassador and Fox Films in order to win over US public opinion with his message stating that the Turkish nation belongs to the community of civilized nations. His continuing attempts to convey this message to the people of the 'civilized nations' through cinema, as well as his ongoing ambivalence towards the medium, will be the subject of the next chapter.

Notes

1 Joseph C. Grew, *Turbulent Era: A Diplomatic Record of Forty Years 1904–1945*, vol. 2, ed. Walter Johnson (Cambridge: The Riberside Press, 1952), 707.
2 In Mustafa Kemal's day, 'contemporary civilization' meant the modern civilization of the West; see Bernhard Lewis, *The Emergence of Modern Turkey*, 3rd ed. (New York: Oxford University Press, 2002), 292. See also Andrew Mango, *A Speech on Atatürk's Universality* (İstanbul: Aybay Yayınları, 1996), 9.
3 For a detailed discussion on the literacy rate in the Ottoman Empire, see Benjamin C. Fortna, *Learning to Read in the Late Ottoman Empire and the Early Turkish Republic* (Basingstoke: Palgrave Macmillan, 2012), 20.
4 In its early years, cinema was commonly believed to be an objective medium that represented events directly. See James Chapman, *Film and History* (Basingstoke: Palgrave Macmillan, 2013), 73.
5 RG 59 General Records of the Department of State Relating to Internal Affairs of Turkey 1930–1944, Microfilm 1224, Roll 11, Document 864.4061/Movietone/I, in *US Diplomatic Documents on Turkey II: The Turkish Cinema in the Early Republican Years*, ed. Rıfat N. Bali (Istanbul: The Isis Press, 2007), 13.
6 Ibid.

7 In the enclosure, the ambassador dated the event of filming Mustafa Kemal on his farm in Ankara as Tuesday, 11 November 1930. See ibid.
8 There is another film of Atatürk, which was shot by Ferit Ibrahim B. in 1929, on his Forest Farm in Ankara. In this film, Atatürk wears a white suit with Panama hat. He also drives a tractor. According to a newspaper's article, this film was 1,000-metre long and aimed at showing the progress achieved at the farm since it was established. Atatürk ordered the film's screening throughout Turkey. See 'Gazi Hz.', *Akşam*, 18 August 1929. See also 'Günün Haberleri', *Akşam*, 20 July 1929.
9 *Atatürk'ün Amerikan Büyükelçisi Joseph C. Grew'u Orman Çiftliğinde Kabulü*. Turkish Film & TV Institute, 35 mm. Nitrate Film, 1930, 9 minutes 40 seconds.
10 Fox Movietone News Story 8-848: *Ataturk Entertains Grew on His Private Estate*, Crew Info: Squire 14 Young, Fox Movietone News Collections, Moving Image Research Collections, University of South Carolina, B&W Sound, 1 November 1930, Ankara, Turkey, 13.53 minutes.

Although this film is dated 1 November 1930 by the Moving Image Research Collections, as I noted above, the ambassador's letter gives the date of filming as Tuesday 11 November. Utkan Kocatürk, in his book *Kaynakçalı Atatürk Günlüğü* (A Documented Atatürk Diary), also gives this date. The film *Miss Afet*, filmed on the same day, is dated 11 November 1930 by the Moving Image Research Collections, so filming most probably took place on this day. See Bali, *The Turkish Cinema in the Early Republican Years*, 14; See also Utkan Kocatürk, *Doğumundan Ölümüne Kadar Kaynakçalı Atatürk Günlüğü*, 2. Basım (Ankara: Atatürk Araştırma Merkezi, 2007), 434.
11 I discovered a scene called *Miss Afet* in the University of South Carolina Moving Image Research Collections taken from the film *Ataturk Entertains Grew on His Private Estate*. See Fox Movietone News Story 8-795-8796: *Miss Afet*, Crew Info: Squire 14 Young, Fox Movietone News Collections, Moving Image Research Collections, University of South Carolina, B&W Sound, 11 November 1930, Ankara, Turkey, 3.54 minutes. The scene shows Âfet Hanım's message to the women of America, which the ambassador mentions in his letter. This scene is not present in the version I watched at the Turkish Film & TV Institute.
12 Bali, *The Turkish Cinema in the Early Republican Years*, 14.
13 Marc Fumaroli, *When the World Spoke French*, trans. Richard Howard (New York: The New York Review of Books, 2011), XV–XXXI.
14 Lewis, *The Emergence of Modern Turkey*, 56–64; Donald Quataert, *The Ottoman Empire, 1700–1922* (Cambridge: Cambridge University Press, 2000), 81.
15 The Ottoman Empire was integrated into Europe even before the eighteenth century and there had always been military, social and cultural exchanges

between Europe and the Ottoman Empire. However, in the eighteenth-century Ottoman elites began to make conscious efforts to adopt Western modernization. See Lewis, *The Emergence of Modern Turkey,* 56.

16 Ibid.
17 Ibid., 59.
18 Emrah Safa Gürkan, 'Mutual Cultural Influences', in *Encyclopedia of the Ottoman Empire,* ed. Gábor Ágoston and Bruce Masters (New York: Facts on File, 2009), 224.
19 Lewis, *The Emergence of Modern Turkey,* 59–60.
20 Ibid.
21 M. Şükrü Hanioğlu, *Atatürk: An Intellectual Biography* (Princeton: Princeton University Press, 2011), 134.
22 Ibid.,109.
23 Bali, *The Turkish Cinema in the Early Republican Years,* 14.
24 Ibid.
25 Ibid.
26 For the ambassador's full speech, see Fox Movietone News Story 8-848: *Ataturk Entertains Grew on His Private Estate,* Crew Info: Squire 14 Young, Fox Movietone News Collections, Moving Image Research Collections, University of South Carolina, B&W Sound, 1 November 1930, Ankara, Turkey, 13. 53 minutes. See also Bali, *The Turkish Cinema in the Early Republican Years,* 19.
27 Hanioğlu, *Atatürk,* 161.
28 Andrew Mango, *Atatürk* (London: John Murray, 2004), xi.
29 English translation: Atatürk: 'Excellency, allow me to speak a few words'.
30 English translation: The Ambassador: 'You are welcome, excellency'.
31 The English translation, as included as an attachment to the Ambassador's letter, is taken from Rıfat Bali. See Bali, *The Turkish Cinema in the Early Republican Years,* 20. My transcription of the original speech in Turkish from the MIRC's version:

> 'Muhterem Amerikalılar,
>
> İlk defa doğrudan doğruya size hitap etmek imkanını bulduğumdan dolayı çok bahtiyarım. Kıymetli sefiriniz Mistır Grew'nun, Türk milletinden ve bu münasebetle şahsımdan bahsederken kullandığı samimi sözlerden dolayı, kendilerine hassaten teşekkür ederim. Eminim ki bu sözleri, Türk milletinin ve benim, büyük Amerika milleti hakkında beslemekte olduğumuz muhabbet hislerine tamamen mutabıktır'.

'Muhterem Amerikalılar,

Türk milletiyle Amerika milleti arasında mevcut olan ve karşılıklı olduğuna emin bulunduğum, muhabbet ve samimiyetin tabii menşei hakkında birkaç söz söylemek isterim. Türk milleti tab'en demokrattır. Eğer bu hakikat, şimdiye kadar medenî beşeriyet tarafından tamamıyla anlaşılmamış bulunuyorsa, bunun sebeplerini muhterem sefiriniz Osmanlı İmparatorluğu'nun son devirlerini işaret ederek çok güzel izah ettiler. Diğer taraftan Amerika milletinin, benliğini hissettiği dakikada istinad ettiği, i'la ettiği demokrasiydi. Amerikalılar bu mevhibe ile mümtaz bir millet olarak beşeriyet dünyasında arz-ı mevcudiyet eyledi. Büyük bir millet birliği kurdu. İşte bu noktadandır ki; Türk milleti Amerika milleti hakkında derin ve kuvvetli bir muhabbet hisseder. Ümit ederim ki, bu müşahede iki millet arasında mevcut olan muhabbeti kökleştirecektir. Yalnız bu kadarla kalmayacaktır, belki bütün beşeriyeti birbirini sevmeye ve bu müşterek sevgiye mani olan mazi hurafelerini silmeye, dünyayı sulh ve huzur sahasına sokmaya medar olacaktır. Muhterem Amerikalılar, temsil etmekle mübahi olduğum Türk milletinin, Türkiye Cumhuriyeti'nin insanî gayesi işte budur. Bu yüksek gayede zaten çok yükselmiş olan Amerika milletinin, Türk milleti ile beraber olduğundan şüphem yoktur. Herhalde medeni, insani, sulh perverane mefkure tecelli etmelidir'.

This scene seems to have been shot more than once, because there are two versions of the final paragraph in a single version of the film. In the second shot, which is a close-up, Mustafa Kemal repeats the last paragraph using slightly different words: 'Muhterem Amerikalılar, temsil etmekle mübahi olduğum Türk milletinin, yeni Türkiye Cumhuriyeti'nin insanî gayesi işte bundan ibarettir. Bu yüksek gayede zaten çok yükselmiş bulunan Amerika milletinin, Türk milleti ile beraber olduğundan şüphem yoktur. Herhalde medeni, insani, sulh perverane mefkure yükselmelidir'. For Mustafa Kemal's speech in both versions, see Fox Movietone News Story 8-848: *Ataturk Entertains Grew on His Private Estate*, Crew Info: Squire 14 Young, Fox Movietone News Collections, Moving Image Research Collections, University of South Carolina, B&W Sound, 1 November 1930, Ankara, Turkey, 13 minutes 55 seconds.

32 Aslı Çırakman, *From the Terror of the World to the 'Sick Man of Europe': European Images of Ottoman Empire and Society from the Sixteenth Century to the Nineteenth* (New York: Peter Lang Publishing, 2002), 50.

33 A discourse is a system of producing knowledge through language by defining what can and cannot be said (and understood as making sense) in a particular society. A discourse is never value-free or objective but always bears the imprint

of the power structures that produce it. See Michel Foucault, *Archaeology of Knowledge*, trans. A. M. Sheridan Smith (New York: Routledge, 2002).
34 Çırakman, *From the Terror of the World to the 'Sick Man of Europe'*, 1.
35 Ibid., 19. For a detailed analysis of Orientalist discourse, see also Edward W. Said, *Orientalism* (London: Penguin Books, 2003).
36 Aslı Çırakman, 'From Tyranny to Despotism: The Enlightenment's Unenlightened Image of the Turks', *International Journal of Middle East Studies* 33, no. 1 (2001): 53, accessed 1 April 2015, http://www.jstor.org/stable/259479.
37 Ibid., 57.
38 Çırakman, *From the Terror of the World to the 'Sick Man of Europe'*, 105.
39 Ibid., 108.
40 Ibid., 151.
41 Ibid., 154.
42 Mango, *A Speech on Atatürk's Universality*, 5.
43 Ibid.
44 Kenneth Allan, *A Primer in Social and Sociological Theory: Toward a Sociology of Citizenship* (California: Sage Publications, 2011), 4.
45 Ibid., 5.
46 Ibid., 4–5.
47 Ibid., 5.
48 Ibid.
49 Mango, *A Speech on Atatürk's Universality*, 11.
50 Allan, *A Primer in Social and Sociological Theory*, 8.
51 Ibid.
52 Ibid., 8–9.
53 Bali, *The Turkish Cinema in the Early Republican Years*, 14.
54 Ibid.
55 Ibid., 15.
56 The original conversation takes place in French, transcripted by the author as follows:
Mustafa Kemal: Excellence, est-ce que vous êtes content de ce que vous voyez ici dans cette année-ci?

Ambassador Grew: Maintenant, je remarque de grands progrès depuis que j'ai vu la ferme il y a trois années.

Mustafa Kemal: Il n'y a que cinq années que nous avons commencé à travailler ici. Avant il était un terrain tout à fait marécageux. C'est surtout Tahsin Bey qui travaille ici, qui survey [sic], qui surveille, n'est-ce pas? Voulez-vous que je vous lui [sic] présente?

Ambassador Grew: Je vous en prie, Excellence.
Mustafa Kemal: Tahsin Bey!
It is interesting to observe that although Mustafa Kemal speaks in French, he slips into English and says: 'survey' instead of 'surveille.' However, he notices his mistake immediately and corrects himself by saying 'surveille, n'est-ce pas?.

57 Mustafa Kemal appointed Tahsin Bey as director of his Forest Farm because of his expertise in modern farming. Having graduated from the Halkalı School of Agriculture in Istanbul, he worked as an agriculture teacher at the Bursa Agriculture School and as director of the Ankara Agriculture Office before taking up the position at the farm.

58 According to Öztoprak, 80 per cent of the population lived in the countryside. See İzzet Öztoprak, *Atatürk Orman Çiftliği'nin Tarihi* (Ankara: Atatürk Araştırma Merkezi, 2006), 5.

59 In 1924, the total number of tractors in Turkey was two hundred twenty. This number would increase to one thousand in 1929 after the modernization reforms of the Kemalist government. Ibid., 1.

60 Yalçın Memluk, 'Cephelerden Orman Çiftliğine', in *Bir Çağdaşlaşma Öyküsü: Cumhuriyet Devriminin Büyük Eseri Atatürk Orman Çiftliği*, ed. Yalçın Memluk et al. (Ankara: Koleksiyoncular Derneği Yayını, 2007), 60.

61 Ibid., 17.

62 Mango, *Atatürk*, 392.

63 For a detailed analysis of Gazi's Forest Farm, see Ayşe Duygu Kaçar, *Kültür / Mekan: Gazi Orman Çiftliği, Ankara* (Ankara: Koç Üniversitesi VEKAM Yayınları, 2015).

64 Uğurlu Tunalı, 'Atatürk Orman Çiftliği', in *Bir Çağdaşlaşma Öyküsü: Cumhuriyet Devriminin Büyük Eseri Atatürk Orman Çiftliği*, ed. Yalçın Memluk et al. (Ankara: Koleksiyoncular Derneği Yayını, 2007), 58. See also Öztoprak, *Atatürk Orman Çiftliği'nin Tarihi*, 12, 32.

65 According to Erkan, four and a half million trees were planted on the Forest Farm within a short time. See Erkan, ibid., 8.

66 Öztoprak mentions that official sources give different numbers for the size of the farm, ranging from eighty thousand to one hundred and two thousand, and twelve thousand acres. He states that a book published by the farm in 1939 lists its size as one hundred and two thousand acres. See Öztoprak, *Atatürk Orman Çiftliği'nin Tarihi*, 14. Keskinok also states that the size of the farm was one hundred and two thousand acres. See Keskinok, 'Bir özgürleşme tasarısı olarak Atatürk Orman Çiftliği', 71.

67 To make beer a popular drink in Turkey, Mustafa Kemal opened a beer factory on the Forest Farm in 1934, a radical move in a Muslim majority country.

68 Kaçar, *Kültür / Mekân, Gazi Orman Çiftliği*, 62.
69 Mango, *Atatürk*, 434.
70 Memluk, 'Atatürk Orman Çiftliği', 92.
71 'All the world's a stage, And all the men and women merely players' is the first phrase of a monologue in *As You Like It*. See William Shakespeare, *As You Like It*, ed. by George Rice Carpenter (New York: Longmans, Green and Co., 1896), 43.
72 Roger R. Trask, *The United States Response to Turkish Nationalism and Reform, 1914–1939* (Minneapolis: The University of Minnesota Press, 1971), 94.
73 Ibid., 106–7.
74 Trask states that in the mid-nineteen thirties, there were doubts about Turkey's economic capacity. An official of the US State Department, for instance, believed that Turkey was not a safe country for American firms to invest in. See ibid., 131.
75 Bali, *The Turkish Cinema in the Early Republican Years*, 15.
76 Except for Mustafa Kemal's military aide de camp, who is officially dressed in his military uniform.
77 Bali, *The Turkish Cinema in the Early Republican Years*, 15.
78 This scene is called 'The Cows' in the ambassador's letter. In the MIRC version of the film, it appears after 'The Poultry'.
79 The okka was an Ottoman measurement equal to 1,282 kg.
80 Bali, *The Turkish Cinema in the Early Republican Years*, 16. In both the TFA and MIRC versions, this scene appears after 'The Tractors'.
81 Ibid.
82 Ibid.
83 Ibid.
84 Ibid.
85 Hanioğlu, *Atatürk*, 161.
86 Sally H. Clarke, *Regulation and the Revolution in United States Farm Productivity* (New York: Cambridge University Press, 1994), 83–135.
87 Although tractors were too costly for the farmer at the beginning of the twentieth century, they became increasingly popular over time as their prices dropped. See ibid., 83.
88 Ibid., 88.
89 Öztoprak, *Atatürk Orman Çiftliği'nin Tarihi*, 69.
90 This scene does not exist in the TFA version I watched, but is in the MIRC version.
91 Bali, *The Turkish Cinema in the Early Republican Years*, 17. See also Öztoprak, *Atatürk Orman Çiftliği'nin Tarihi*, 87.

92 Bali, *The Turkish Cinema in the Early Republican Years*, 17.
93 'Woman, Lovely Woman' is another scene that does not exist in the TFA version, but is preserved in the MIRC version. The scene showing Âfet Hanım can be found in two films held in the MIRC: in Fox Movietone News Story 8-848: *Ataturk Entertains Grew on His Private Estate* and in the film Fox Movietone News Story 8-795-8796: *Miss Afet*. Crew Info: Squire 14 Young, Fox Movietone News Collections. Moving Image Research Collections, University of South Carolina. B&W Sound, 11 November 1930, Ankara, Turkey, 3 minutes 54 seconds.
94 Bali, *The Turkish Cinema in the Early Republican Years*, 18.
95 The original sentence in French is 'Excellence, voulez-vous permettre que ma fille répond [*sic*] en turc?'.
96 The original sentence in French is 'Je vous en prie, Excellence'.
97 Bali, *The Turkish Cinema in the Early Republican Years*, 18. Original speech in Turkish is transcripted by the author as 'Amerika kadınlığını takdir ederim, çünkü siyasi haklarını tamamen kazanmışlardır. Türk kadınları da şimdiye kadar aldıkları haklarıyla iktifa etmeyeceklerdir. Pek yakında mebus intihap etmek ve intihap olunmak hakkını kazanacaklarına ümidim vardır, eminim'.
98 Bali, *The Turkish Cinema in the Early Republican Years*, 18.
99 The law entered into force on 4 October 1926. See Lewis, *The Emergence of Modern Turkey*, 272.
100 Ibid., 273.
101 Mango, *Atatürk*, 437.
102 Ibid., 438.
103 '19th Amendment to the U.S. Constitution: Women's Right to Vote', *National Archives*, accessed 30 June 2015, http://www.archives.gov/historical-docs/document.html?doc=13.
104 Nuray Özdemir, 'Türk Kadınına Milletvekili Seçme ve Seçilme Hakkı Tanınması Üzerine Yapılan Kutlamalar', *History Studies* 6, no. 5 (2014): 178, accessed 21 April 2015, http://www.historystudies.net/Makaleler/2054201183_9-Nuray%20Özdemir.pdf.
105 Ibid., 179.
106 Ibid., 180.
107 Ibid., 179.
108 Bali, *The Turkish Cinema in the Early Republican Years*, 18.
109 Ibid.
110 Ibid.
111 Ibid.

112 Ibid.
113 Ibid.
114 Ibid.
115 Ibid.
116 Ibid., 18.
117 Ibid., 18–19.
118 Ibid., 19.
119 Robert L. Daniel, *American Philanthrophy in the Near East, 1820–1960* (Athens: Ohio University Press, 1970), 185.
120 John A. DeNovo, *American Interest and Policies in the Middle East, 1900–1939* (Minneapolis: The University of Minnesota Press, 1963), 271.
121 Fox Movietone News Story 8-854: *Turks Still Smoke the Old Way*, Crew Info: Squire 14 Young, Fox Movietone News Collections, Moving Image Research Collections, University of South Carolina, B&W Sound, 13 December 1930, Constantinople, Turkey, 9. 64 minutes.
122 Fox Movietone News Story 8-849: *Turkish Market Day*, Crew Info: Squire 14 Young, Fox Movietone News Collections, Moving Image Research Collections, University of South Carolina, B&W Sound, 3 November 1930, Ankara, Turkey, 9. 09 minutes.
123 Gustave Le Bon, *Psychologie des foules* (Paris: Félix Alcan, 1895).
124 For a detailed analysis of the influence of Gustave Le Bon on Atatürk's ideas see Hanioğlu, *Atatürk*, 44–5.
125 Johann Wolfgang von Goethe, *Faust: Der Tragödie erster und zweiter Teil, Urfaust,* ed. Erich Trunz (München: C.H. Beck, 1986).
126 Walter Benjamin, 'The Work of Art in the Age of Its Technological Reproducibility: Second Version', in *The Work of Art in the Age of Its Technological Reproducibility and Other Writings on Media*, ed. Michael W. Jennings, Brigid Doherty and Thomas Y. Levin (Cambridge: Harvard University Press, 2008), 19–55. See also Stefan Andriopoulos, 'The Terror of Reproduction: Early Cinema's Ghostly Doubles and the Right to One's Own Image', *New German Critique*, no. 99, (2006), 154, accessed 12 April 2015, http://www.jstor.org/stable/27669180.
127 Benjamin, 'The Work of Art in the Age of Its Technological Reproducibility', 33; Andriopoulos, 'The Terror of Reproduction', 167.
128 Marcel Mauss, *The Gift: The Form and Reason for Exchange in Archeic Societies*, trans. W.D. Halls (New York: W. W. Norton & Company, 2000).
129 Bali, *The Turkish Cinema in the Early Republican Years*, 13.
130 Ibid.

131 Kocatürk, *Doğumundan Ölümüne Kadar Kaynakçalı Atatürk Günlüğü*, 436.
132 Genelkurmay Personel Başkanlığı Askerî Tarih ve Stratejik Etüt (ATASE) Daire Başkanlığı Yayınları, *Fotoğraflarla Atatürk* (Ankara: Genelkurmay Basımevi, 2015), accessed 23 October 2015, http://www.ata.tsk.tr/content/media/07/atatur k_albumu_1.pdf.
133 Ibid., 223. According to Özuyar, Cevat Abbas (Gürer), aid-de-camp Naşit and main aid-de-camp Rüsuhi Bey were also at the screening with Atatürk on that day. See Özuyar, *Babıâli'de Sinema*, 70.
134 Niyazi Ahmet Banoğlu, *Atatürk'ün İstanbul'daki Günleri (1899–1919 / 1927–1938)* (İstanbul: Alfa Yayınları, 2012), 245.
135 Özuyar, *Babıâli'de Sinema*, 69.
136 Banoğlu, *Atatürk'ün İstanbul'daki Günleri*, 245. See also 'Gazi Hz. Dün Elhamra sinemasına giderek bazı filmleri temaşa ettiler', *Akşam*, 5 December 1930.
137 Banoğlu, *Atatürk'ün İstanbul'daki Günleri*, 245.
138 Banoğlu writes that this silent film was screened with a 'plak', which means a vinyl record. Screening a silent film synchronously with sound from a gramophone record was a common practice in the early years of cinema.
139 According to Akşam newspaper, the Orient representative of the Fox Film, M. Harley applied to the Press Association Presidency (Matbuat Cemiyeti Riyaseti) in order to shoot Venizelos' visit in Turkey. See 'Cumhuriyet Bayramı', *Akşam*, 24 October 1930. According to the newspaper, at the Republic ball and dinner given at Ankarapalas the Fox Film filmed and movietoned Atatürk's conversation with Kont Betlen that took place in French. See 'Ziyafet ve Balo', *Akşam*, 31 October 1930. Vakit newspaper states that Fox Film also recorded Atatürk and Venizelos' conversation that took place in French. See 'Foks Film Ankara'da ne gibi resimler çekti', *Akşam*, 1 November 1930.
140 Banoğlu, *Atatürk'ün İstanbul'daki Günleri*, 245.
141 Özuyar suggests that Atatürk told Şükrü Kaya, the Minister of Interior, that he appreciated Milestone's film *All Quiet on the Western Front*, which saddened him because it demonstrated the disasters caused by war so perfectly. Nevertheless, he added that it might be too early to show this film to the Turkish people as they were just recovering from the war. According to Özuyar, despite his reservations, Atatürk did not want to give an order to ban the film, so it continued to be shown in the cinemas of Istanbul. See Özuyar, *Babıâli'de Sinema*, 72.
142 Serdar Öztürk, *Erken Cumhuriyet Döneminde Sinema, Seyir, Siyaset* (Ankara: Elips Kitap, 2005), 48–9.
143 Ibid., 49.

144 Ibid.
145 Ebru Boyar and Kate Fleet, 'Making Turkey and The Turkish Revolution Known to Foreign Nations without any Expense: Propaganda Films in the Early Turkish Republic', *Oriente Moderno* 24 (85), no. 1 (2005): 117–32, accessed 24 April 2015, http://www.jstor.org/stable/25817998.
146 Ibid., 128.
147 Greg Wilsbacher, email message to author, 21 July 2015.
148 The film announces itself as 'The Twentieth Century: A Filmed Presentation of CBS News'.

4

How to impress an American: The power of the motion picture

In the 1930s, dictatorships and authoritarian regimes were in ascendance across Europe, and the dark clouds of war were hovering over the world. In the United States, these regimes were perceived as posing an increasing threat to liberal democracies as well as to universal peace. Nevertheless, there was one man who was seen as an exception to the rule. His name was Mustafa Kemal Atatürk, the president of the Republic of Turkey. Highly impressed by a movie shown at the White House in April 1937, the president of the United States, Franklin Delano Roosevelt, addressed Atatürk in a letter with the following words:

> To His Excellency Kemal Atatürk, President of the Republic of Turkey. Ankara.
>
> My Dear President:
>
> I saw a few days ago at the White House a movie reel recently taken by Julian Bryan in Turkey. I would like to express to you all the enthusiasm I felt on seeing the numerous and marvelous things you have accomplished in a space of time so relatively brief.
>
> I was particularly pleased to see on the screen pictures of your distinguished self at home, on the beach playing with your little daughter. This is why I venture to hope that some day or other we shall meet.
>
> In my rare leisure moments, I return to the examination of the Turkish postage stamps you were so kind as to send me. I trust that, some day, I shall be able to see with my own eyes the scenes which appear on these stamps.
>
> With my most sincere esteem and best wishes, I remain
>
> Ever your devoted,
> FRANKLIN D. ROOSEVELT[1]

President Atatürk, delighted to receive a personal letter from President Roosevelt, replied on 25 May 1937:

> To His Excellency Franklin D. Roosevelt, President of the United States of America. Washington.
>
> My dear President:
>
> I have received with real pleasure your friendly letter of April 6, 1937, in which you tell me of your satisfaction on seeing the films recently taken in Turkey by Julian Bryan. In it you also express the hope that we may meet some day, as soon as circumstances will permit.
>
> Pray believe me, my dear President, that I am infinitely obliged for your very sincere sentiments as well as for your just appreciation of the progress realized in modern Turkey.
>
> I take this opportunity to repeat again my admiration for the United States, all the more so because our respective countries cherish the same ideal which is that of universal peace and well being for mankind.
>
> On my side I also entertain the dearest desire to see you before long, and I impatiently await the day when I shall have the great pleasure of receiving in Turkey your charming and puissant self who has accomplished such great things.
>
> With my best esteem and most sincere wishes, I am
>
> Your very devoted,
> KEMAL ATATURK.[2]

Unlike the usual official correspondence between two state presidents, this correspondence is warm, friendly and generous. A film shown at the White House by Julien Bryan[3] seems to have impressed President Roosevelt so much that he wrote a personal letter to the president of a country thousands of miles away. Significantly, the letters expressing the two presidents' admiration for each other did not remain confidential, but were published in the *New York Times* under the headline 'Roosevelt Lauds Atatürk's Regime' on 1 August 1937. But what did President Roosevelt actually see on the movie screen that amazed him so much? Who was this Julien Bryan who shot the motion picture of Atatürk? And, most importantly, how did Atatürk project himself and Turkey on film in the face of a war that could erupt on a global scale?

In order to answer these questions, in this chapter, I will trace the journey of Julien Bryan's footage of Atatürk which fascinated not only Roosevelt but also large American audiences during the 1930s. I will show how the film played an important role in introducing Atatürk to the American public as a man of great achievements who turned his country into a strong, modern nation-state, and as a leader who shared the same ideals as the United States. Moreover, I will look at the role of the film in delivering Atatürk's message to foreign audiences in the context of global turmoil. To understand Atatürk's roles in the making of Bryan's film, both in front of the camera and behind the scenes, I will analyse specific scenes in detail. My exploration of the film performs a dialectical movement between the text (the film and its scenes) and its context to arrive at an understanding of the cultural meanings this film carried for Atatürk, Roosevelt and the American public. It begins with the story of the man behind the camera.

Who was Julien Bryan?

Julien Hequembourg Bryan (1899–1974) was a well-known American freelance photographer, documentary- and travel film-maker. He produced a great number of photographs and films all around the world during his professional career. He became particularly famous through his trips to Europe, Asia and Africa where he portrayed different cultures, important events and people, and brought them to the United States movie screen.[4] Bryan made a living by giving what were called 'travel lectures' or 'illustrated public lectures' in theatres, auditoriums and concert halls throughout the United States, during which he displayed the films and photographs of the places he had visited. These travel lectures were a popular, esteemed pastime in the era of silent movies until the late 1930s.[5] Besides getting paid for the lectures, Bryan earned money by supplying film footage to popular newsreel series such as *The March of Time* and *Pathé News*.[6] He also produced educational films for companies such as Eastman Kodak Co. and Teaching Film Division, and sold photographs to news magazines such as *LIFE*, which emphasized photojournalism.

Bryan gave illustrated travel lectures on such topics as 'Inside Nazi Germany', 'Poland Today', 'Modern Finland', 'Children of Switzerland', 'Children of Holland' and 'Turkey Reborn' in theatres throughout the United States.[7] The lectures were live presentations, lasting approximately ninety minutes, usually with just his voice-over and no music. They followed the same basic structure: first, there was a ten-minute introductory talk; second, Bryan showed the film while continuing the lecture in the form of a running commentary and explanation, ending with some still photo slides; and finally, there was a question and answer session.[8]

The travel lectures took place in several venues, such as the lecture halls of colleges and universities, concert venues including Carnegie Hall and the Brooklyn Academy of Music, clubs and film societies, institutes, town halls and the White House. According to Sam Bryan, who witnessed some of his father's performances, these travel lectures were sometimes private and performed in front of a small audience like the one for the Roosevelts in the White House, and sometimes they were public and performed in front of a larger audience averaging two to three thousand people in the case of Carnegie Hall.[9] In this way, the travel lectures reached many people throughout the United States in the 1930s.

As a traveller Bryan was curious about the world in general. However, he was particularly interested in capturing dramatic social changes in the countries he visited and in finding out who caused these changes and why. Thus, he produced several motion pictures in countries such as Germany, Poland, Finland, Italy, Soviet Russia and Japan, where drastic transformations occurred in the first half of the twentieth century. Turkey was one of the countries that interested him, particularly because it was a country in which virtually everything had changed: the script, the calendar and the dress code, as well as the legal, educational and political systems. Moreover, this radical transformation was identified with one particular person: Mustafa Kemal Atatürk, the charismatic leader of the new Turkey.

Arrival

When Bryan arrived in Istanbul in the fall of 1936, he wanted to shoot some film footage showing the recent changes that had occurred in Turkey since it became a republic.[10] This footage, of course, would have been incomplete if it did not show the man behind the reforms. Thus, Bryan wanted to do something that no journalist had ventured to do: to film Atatürk in his daily life. This was, however, not an easy task. He was told that Atatürk stayed at the Dolmabahçe Palace when he was in Istanbul. In order to gain entrance to the palace, Bryan had first of all to overcome the obstacles of the Kafkaesque bureaucracy.

Although his first attempts to reach the president proved futile, he continued relentlessly to pursue his objective. The visit of Edward VIII, the King of the United Kingdom, to Atatürk (4–6 September 1936), which coincided with Bryan's visit, made his job more difficult than ever.[11] All Turkish officials in Istanbul were excitedly waiting for the king, and nobody had time for an American journalist, so he could not get any information.[12] When Bryan finally managed to talk to a few Turkish officials, each of them appreciated his efforts to film Atatürk, but, in a traditional bureaucratic manner, passed the responsibility for making the arrangements quickly to other offices. Determined to succeed, Bryan went from one office to another, looking for somebody who would be able to offer concrete assistance. When Bryan finally met some notable Turkish bureaucrats who could provide access to the palace, they all told him that 'such intimate pictures of the President had never been taken' and that they were afraid that he would not be able to obtain official permission.[13] Instead of giving up, he asked for the help of the American embassy, hoping that they could arrange a meeting with Atatürk, but the answer was hardly encouraging.

Giving up on penetrating the enigmatic bureaucracy operating around the palace, Bryan decided to take matters into his own hands and go there directly without anyone's help, hoping to catch either someone who could lead him to the president or, even better, the president himself. When he went to the palace, the president was not there, but Bryan did manage to see his secretary, who generously devoted five minutes of his time to have Bryan state his case.[14] Sensing that this was a once-in-a-lifetime opportunity, Bryan used all of his rhetorical skills to convince the secretary that the motion picture about the 'Turkish New Deal' would be incomplete without images of its 'creator', 'leading citizen' and 'central figure' Mustafa Kemal Atatürk.[15] What Bryan said seems to have interested the secretary, because he listened and interrogated Bryan for almost an hour. Nonetheless, he responded that Bryan should not have much hope, as 'such pictures had never been taken of Atatürk, even for showing to his own countrymen'.[16] Without much hope, Bryan left the palace.

A couple of hours later, the phone in his hotel room rang; it was the palace calling to tell him that President Atatürk had not only granted him permission to take pictures of him but had also invited him to be his guest for two days at his summer residence in Florya. Bryan was told that he should ready himself and bring all his film equipment and any other necessary supplies.[17]

Bryan meets Atatürk

The next morning, when Bryan arrived at Florya, he received a warm welcome. Bryan recalled that the president used an interpreter to translate his words from Turkish into English, although they could have easily communicated in either French or German.[18] During the afternoon they spent together on the beach, Atatürk was brief and direct, asking Bryan what he wanted him to do.[19] Atatürk's openness to Bryan's directions seems to have surprised the latter, because in a report on Turkey that he wrote in 1961 he made a parenthetical note next to Atatürk's question stating: '(How do you give orders to a dictator?)'.[20] Bryan told the president that he just wanted to follow him with his camera in his daily routine for a few hours each day,[21] so he should simply relax and do what he always did: eat, play, swim and rest in the sun without paying any attention to him.[22] During the two days spent in Florya, Bryan states that Atatürk was a 'perfect subject' who neither acted and posed nor paid any attention to the camera.[23] Since Atatürk was on vacation in Florya, he did not even put on a tie for the sake of the camera, but went around in flannels and a sweater.[24] But the consent of the Turkish president, who hardly ever allowed pictures to be taken of himself in his private life, even by Turkish journalists, to allow an American journalist to film him in the fall of 1936 was significant and merits analysis. Moreover, Atatürk, who liked to control how he was portrayed in the media, and particularly in film, was suddenly so welcoming to Julien Bryan for reasons now to be explored.

We need to first understand Atatürk's foreign policy and Turkey's geopolitical situation during the interwar period in order to examine Atatürk's acquiescence to be filmed by Bryan. The 1930s were turbulent years for the world in general and Europe in particular. In Germany, Adolf Hitler and his Nazi party came to power in 1933. Not satisfied with the outcome of the First World War, they started a revengeful and aggressive campaign to redesign the map of Germany, Europe and the rest of the world. They turned Germany into a war machine by rallying the people, mobilizing industry and expanding the military. A couple of months before Bryan shot the footage of Atatürk, on 7 March 1936, German troops had entered the demilitarized Rhineland in contravention of the Treaty of Versailles and the Locarno Treaties. This unilateral action alarmed the former Allies of the First World War, including France, Great Britain, the Soviet Union and the United States, and led them to fear a new war that could erupt on a global scale. The political situation was also worrying in fascist Italy where Benito Mussolini had assumed power in 1925. Like Hitler and his Nazi party, Mussolini and his fascist party followed an aggressive expansionist foreign policy based on the dream of restoring the Roman Empire. To realize their colonial ambitions, the Italian army had invaded Ethiopia in 1935. In addition, Fascist Italy and Nazi Germany, the so-called Axis powers, supported the nationalist forces led by Francisco Franco in the Spanish Civil War that had broken out in 1936.

Thus, Axis aggression was looming over Europe, and if a large-scale war erupted between the Axis powers and the Allies, Turkey's advantageous geographical position stretching between Europe and Asia would be vital for the balance of power. This made Turkey a strategically important country, and its president a valuable ally. Moreover, unlike Germany and Italy, which were unhappy with the outcome of the Great War, Turkey was largely satisfied with the Treaty of Lausanne and did not seek comprehensive revisions.[25] After the settlement with the Allied powers in 1923, Atatürk's government focused on building a modern nation-state, developing it economically and maintaining its sovereignty. To accomplish this goal, international peace was essential because another war could slow down or ruin these efforts. Therefore, Turkey's foreign policy during the interwar era was primarily concerned with maintaining peaceful relations with other countries, following the policy of neutrality, and promoting international peace and security. In 1931, Atatürk expressed his party's foreign policy in these words: 'We work for peace at home, peace in the world.'[26]

In fact, from the Kellogg-Briand Pact in 1928 until the beginning of the Second World War, Turkey signed several international agreements that renounced war. In contrast to the aggressive totalitarian leaders of Europe, Atatürk presented himself as a constructive leader promoting world peace and security. His desire for a peaceful world during these turbulent years can also be seen in his letter to President Roosevelt where he states: 'I take this opportunity to repeat again my admiration for the United States, all the more so because our respective countries cherish the same ideal which is that of universal peace and well being for mankind.'

When Julien Bryan visited Turkey in the fall of 1936, Atatürk was already building up an image of the nation as a rapidly developing country and a constructive member of the world order. Atatürk's choice for civil rather than military dress while in front of Bryan's camera was far from random: while Axis aggression was looming in Europe, his sartorial display conveyed the message that he was on the side of the Western democracies and not on that of the fascist, militarist regimes of Germany and Italy. Film was the most convenient medium to deliver his message to Western audiences, not only because it was a medium that Western audiences were familiar with but also because it was seen as the most objective medium of the time. Such a film would be even more effective if it were produced by a film-maker from a country like America that was not directly involved in the European power struggle and, like Turkey, promoted the maintenance of world peace. Consequently, it makes sense that Atatürk took the risk and allowed Bryan to film him.

During his two-day stay, Bryan shot some 2000 stills and 1,000 to 1,200 feet of 35-mm film.[27] Significantly, he shot rare scenes of the private family life of the president, including Atatürk spending time with his little adopted daughter Ülkü, playing with her and teaching her the new Latin alphabet for the Turkish language.[28] Bryan's surviving footage shows Atatürk playing with Ülkü as she picks flowers from a flowerbed in the garden. In another scene, Atatürk is seen strolling on the porch of a building at the beach while his daughter frolics around him. When Atatürk and Ülkü are shown walking from the beach towards the summerhouse, Ülkü steals the show as she jumps off the path and sits down, posing for the camera cross-legged. She then throws herself down on the sand, pretending she fell, and Atatürk turns back and signals for her to stand up by lightly slapping his thigh, showing that he is not buying into her show. The footage also shows Atatürk in his swimsuit – a one-piece tank top and shorts – giving Ülkü safety instructions, swimming with her in the sea and sunbathing.

What is it in the images of Atatürk and Ülkü that so fascinated President Roosevelt and still fascinates millions of people? I believe the power of these images stems from the fact that they show us the human side of Atatürk. Unlike the other official visual images that depict him as an unreachable, stern-faced statesman, here we see a man of flesh and blood. By bringing him down to earth, these images demythologize Atatürk. In this film, the 'great man' is captured playing with a child and even going down to her level. These images moreover create the impression that behind his official image as a statesman, he is like everyone else, one of the people, playing, swimming and taking care of his child. By blurring the difference between his public and private image, the footage allows the public to identify with this caring father figure. The implicit message is that if Atatürk is such a doting father for his child, he must also be a good leader for the country – a leader who cares for his people and wants the best for them. Although the images of Atatürk with Ülkü seem spontaneous, their message was constructed with some care. Bryan writes in his report that Atatürk instructed his daughter not to look at the camera during filming, but he also notes how, disregarding her father's instructions, Ülkü looked at the camera 'charmingly'.[29] Making the scenes look natural, then, was not always an easy task – not even for Atatürk.

Atatürk's private secretary, Haldun Derin, recounts an interesting anecdote about Bryan's visit in his memoirs.[30] He writes that Julien Bryan, who was working for *The March of Time*, visited Turkey in September in order to produce a film showing the country's changes and development.[31] According to Derin, on the afternoon of 13 September, Atatürk had to leave the Florya summer residence to attend a meeting of the Dil Kurumu (Turkish Language Association) at the Dolmabahçe Palace.[32] Bryan wanted to shoot the scene of Atatürk leaving the summer residence and walking towards the asphalt road in order to get into the car. But the people outside, who saw the president leaving the residence, ran up to him. There were also some children in the crowd who wanted to give Atatürk flowers they had picked. This, of course, would have created a perfect spectacle for Bryan's film.

The civilian security officers, however, were highly alert to an assassination attempt and immediately jumped in front of the crowd wanting to approach the president. The security measures around Atatürk were heightened in those days because of an assassination attempt on Atatürk in 1935 planned by Ali Saip Ursavaş, deputy of Urfa. Moreover, the memory of the assassination of King Alexander of Yugoslavia in Marseille in 1934, captured on film, was still fresh.[33] All the same, Atatürk became upset with the security officers intervening between him and the people, and reprimanded them loudly: 'You made a disgraceful scene.'[34]

But why did Atatürk call this scene disgraceful? After all, the security officers were just trying to do their job. Atatürk's reaction can serve as an entry point into his understanding of film and public image. At the first level of analysis, Atatürk's secretary Haldun Derin makes clear that the intervention of the security officers upset Atatürk because they wanted to keep the public from approaching him. This explanation can be put into a simple formula: Atatürk loved the public, and the security officers annoyed him by keeping the public away from him. But we need to go deeper and try to understand the cultural significance of this scene from Atatürk's perspective. After all, he not only criticized the officers' behaviour but also called the incident a 'disgraceful scene', showing his awareness that it created the wrong type of spectacle for the camera.

To understand Atatürk's reaction, we need to know how images of leaders were being adapted to a new age of democracy in the twentieth century. According to the British historian Peter Burke, in this century it became common in the United States, Europe and the Soviet Union to see images of political leaders on walkabouts, talking to ordinary citizens on the street, shaking their hands and kissing babies.[35] Burke suggests that these images were designed to form part of a larger, new image of leadership: the so-called 'demotic' leadership image.[36] This style of public performance is reflected in different forms of visual media. Vladimir Serov's famous painting *Peasant Petitioners Visiting Lenin*, for instance, portrays Vladimir Lenin listening to three peasants carefully and taking note of their petitions.[37] There are also several photographs of President Franklin Roosevelt that show him during visits to the public, listening to them and giving them hope during the Great Depression (1929–39).[38] These images, specific to the era of visual mass media, are meant to emphasize two important aspects of democratic leadership. First, they show that the leader's right to rule is legitimated by the support of the 'people' and not by divine right, noble descent or brute power. Second, they show the leader's accessibility,[39] demonstrating that he is not a remote, distant figure but 'one of us', yet also somehow better than us.

By intervening between Atatürk and the people as Bryan was filming the scene, the security officers ruined the chance to convey the message that Atatürk is an accessible ruler and a man of the people. Since this was a spontaneous action by the people and not a staged scene, it would have looked even more natural and would thus have had a stronger impact on the audience. As noted before, by capturing movement in time, film could convey spontaneous incidents directly. However, its openness to contingency could work both to the advantage of political leaders and against them. As we have seen in the previous chapter, by staging each scene carefully, Atatürk tried to control the contingency of the filmic medium as much as possible. Yet in this case, as he seems to have realized, it could have worked to his benefit if the security officers had not spoiled it.

Derin further writes that Bryan later filmed Atatürk at the table in the Dolmabahçe Palace while chairing the meeting of the Turkish Language Association with Agop Dilaçar, a linguist of Armenian descent, at the blackboard discussing a language issue.[40] In this way, Bryan completed the part of his film concerning the president of the Turkish Republic. While filming Atatürk, Bryan also suffered some misfortunes. Since he was filming Atatürk without any assistance, he had to change the films, handle the lights and record the film entirely by himself. Once, in the middle of filming Atatürk, one of Bryan's movie cameras broke. He did not mention this to the president or the officials present but simply took a second camera to continue filming.[41] Although Bryan does not give us his reasons, it is likely that he did not want to look unprofessional and also did not want to interrupt the 'natural' flow of his subject's actions.

After shooting the film, Bryan and Derin went together to the customs office of Sirkeci in Istanbul to pick up some of the reserve film which Bryan had left there upon entering Turkey. Derin writes that although they had already mentioned to the director of customs that Bryan's mission was to present Turkey abroad, it took the officials far too long to finish the bureaucratic procedure. Bryan, who noticed Derin's frustration with the procedure, consoled him by saying: 'These things are everywhere more or less the same. Also in Russia and Italy.'[42]

Leaving aside the impermeable bureaucracy around the president, Bryan had an exclusive journalistic experience in Turkey. After all, Atatürk had been a very generous host, opening the doors of spaces that had remained shut to most other journalists. When Atatürk returned to the Dolmabahçe Palace from the Florya summer residence two days later, he allowed Bryan to take some more pictures of the palace. It did not even matter to the president when Bryan blew out the palace fuses by using photo floodlights for the interior shots.⁴³ Bryan summarized his experience of visiting Atatürk as follows: 'The whole experience of photographing this amazing man, whom I regard as one of modern history's miracles, was exciting enough, but I think my biggest thrill came from knowing that not a soul in Istanbul had believed I would be allowed to set foot inside the palace.'⁴⁴

The many afterlives of Bryan's footage

After filming Atatürk, Bryan continued his journey within Turkey. He shot some 20,000 feet of black and white 35-mm negative film of almost all aspects of life in the country.⁴⁵ In a report on Turkey written retrospectively in 1961, he states that the material was used for his illustrated lecture *Turkey Reborn* and was still available and in good condition.⁴⁶ According to the website of the International Film Foundation of which Bryan was executive director, the motion picture *Turkey Reborn* exists.⁴⁷ Their records state that it is a 35-mm, silent film, ninety minutes long, produced in the 1930s. The film is described as a 'Theater Lecture' and Bryan is identified as its cinematographer. However, in my interview with Sam Bryan, his son and current executive director of the IFF, he indicated that to his knowledge the motion picture has not survived. Nevertheless, some parts of the film were used in other documentaries, as will be discussed later on.

Although the film in its complete form most probably no longer exists,⁴⁸ its contents can partly be reconstructed on the basis of film catalogues, newspaper reports and memoirs. According to the American Film Institute's catalogue, for instance, *Turkey Reborn* showed scenes from Turkey and highlighted the changes after Atatürk's rise to power.⁴⁹ The summary of the film suggests it contained scenes shot on Istanbul's historical peninsula, depicting mosques, bazaars, stores, restaurants and cafés. It also presented scenes shot along the waterfront as well as new factories and buildings as specimens of modern architecture. Displaying the use of the new Latin alphabet, the film emphasized the cultural reforms introduced by Atatürk. It also showed the traditional Turkish shadow play, and scenes from Turkish and Balkan folk dances performed at a festival as well as Turkish actors on stage performing William Shakespeare's *Macbeth*. Significantly, *Turkey Reborn* also contained the intimate shots of President Atatürk at work and play in his summer residence in Florya, including the scenes of Atatürk playing with his little adopted daughter Ülkü and teaching her the new Turkish alphabet on a blackboard, and the footage of Atatürk chairing the conference of the Turkish Language Association, the shooting of which has earlier been described.

What Bryan's screening and lecture looked like may be learned from a report in a local newspaper published on 9 December 1937. It describes Bryan's screening of *Turkey Reborn* at the Nineteenth Century Woman's Club in Oak Park, Illinois as follows: 'Tracing the story of Turkey briefly through the period of the degenerate Sultan to the revolution of 1923 out of which a new country was forged, he [Bryan] remarked that in no country in the world that he has visited have there been such drastic changes as Turkey has known in the last few years'.[50] According to the newspaper:

> The pictures opened with Istanbul, showing early Hittite carvings, the minareted mosque of St. Sofia, many other examples of architecture and in the streets men without fezes and women minus the former face veils. The old Arabic is gone and signs bloom with words very similar to English. By the ruins of the ancient walls of Justinian and Constantine run smooth modern roads and new architecture vies with the old even as does the new education with that under the Sultan. Moslem theological seminaries have all been closed and people are turning away from the Moslem religion. Oddly he [Bryan] finds that his Christian American audiences find that a fine thing while deploring the same turning away from the established church of Russia, even though in both instances there is an exciting new religion, in Turkey based on a strong social philosophy. The second reel showed the new education with boys and girls, looking very much like those of our own schools, learning side by side, a thing that would not have been possible a few years ago. Formerly 95 per cent illiterate, about 50 per cent of the Turkish people can now read and write. The next reel showed Smyrna, now Izmir according to the edict of the little group headed by Ataturk, which is responsible for drastic changes. This picture showed the fig industry from picking in the orchards through processing, 95 per cent of which is done by hand, to packaging and shipping all over the world. Continuing with industry, reels were shown of sugar production from beets washed, shredded, cooked, turned into syrup, crystallized and cut, boxed or bagged which now furnishes 100 per cent of their sugar all of which had to be important 14 years ago. An eight-million textile plant, with machinery from Russia on liberal credit terms to be paid for out of

the government taxes which have a 25 per cent minimum income tax, was shown from the raw cotton, which Turkey hopes to grow soon, through winding and weaving to the labeled bolts of goods with women unveiled working everywhere. Other reels showed Ankara with its water supply, old buildings backing the new, young women learning to make flowers, millinery and clothes or to cook or talking commercial subjects alongside of the boys in this new Turkey that has a greater per cent of its budget set aside for social welfare, public health and education, and so on, than we have. Here young people are given four years of higher education with free room and board, but there is a string tied to it. At its conclusion they must give four years' service teaching in smaller towns. A hospital equipped with all sorts of mechanical gadgets for manipulation and exercise was shown, but Turkey's crying need is for fifty times as many trained nurses and doctors. The final reel showed the only intimate pictures Mr. Bryan knows of taken of Kemal Ataturk whom practically everyone he talked to said had made Turkey what it is today, doing a significant job in fourteen years and Mr. Bryan thinks, a fairly patriotic job with the money they have going for the country rather than in graft. Pictures of Ataturk showed a large stern-visaged, bay-widowed man of scanty hair that might have been taken from any industrial board meeting in this country. Walking in his garden with his little four-year-old adopted daughter, teaching her at the blackboard, swimming with her, moving about his house, sitting with his cabinet the man showed no signs of pomp and power, but everybody 'jumps at his decree', and the little daughter disobeyed him more in the two days Mr. Bryan was his guest than others have dared in years.[51]

According to the available records, the film was shown at several locations in the United States, including clubs, institutes and museums as well as embassies and the White House. On 3 December 1937, for instance, another local US newspaper, *The Oakparker*, describes Bryan's illustrated lecture in Oak Park, Illinois as follows: '"Turkey Reborn" is the only great pictorial record of the New Turkey. Mr. Bryan will give you intimate glimpses of Kemal Ataturk at work and at play.'[52]

Although local newspapers do not report much on how American audiences received the film, a letter written by the Turkish Ambassador Mehmet Münir Ertegün, in Washington, DC, on 14 May 1937 to the prime minister's office in Turkey, gives some insight on this issue. Ertegün writes that, after having received permission from the Ministry for Foreign Affairs to display Bryan's film at the Turkish embassy in Washington, DC, on 29 March 1937, the embassy organized a soiree for 200 people, Americans and foreigners, including American state dignitaries and members of the opposition party in parliament.⁵³ Ertegün states that the film, which was screened with a short description by Bryan, was received with great interest.⁵⁴

Ertegün also mentions Bryan's film screening at the White House. He writes that Mr. Roosevelt invited Bryan and his female companion to spend the weekend at the White House. On the evening of 27 March, Bryan screened films on Turkey for around one and a half hours for the president, his family and other invited guests.⁵⁵ According to Ertegün, the president watched the pictures with great interest and, after the film, requested some additional information from Bryan and told him he wanted to write to Atatürk about these pictures. Ertegün's letter further details the positive impression Mrs. Roosevelt had of the film. In fact, on 29 March, she wrote a laudatory article on it in her column 'My Day',⁵⁶ which appeared daily in various US newspapers. In the column, she writes:

> Mr. and Mrs. Julian Bryan brought down their pictures of Turkey and the latest 'March of Time' which includes in brief some of the pictures which they showed us at great length. These Turkish pictures are extraordinarily interesting in that they show what has been done in a very few years to change a country which had remained apparently untouched by modern ways or machinery, into a mechanized nation. Let us hope that it will mean greater happiness for the people. They certainly seem to have taken to modern clothes and modern buildings with extreme rapidity.⁵⁷

Ertegün notes in his letter that Bryan talked about Turkey in a laudatory way. According to Ertegün, after the talk, Bryan asked the audience rhetorically whether they had known anything about the things he showed of Turkey before his talk, and stated that he too would never have thought he would see such things and that his travels had been a 'révélation' for him.⁵⁸

Ertegün also shares his own opinion about the general impact of the film in the United States. According to him, America was a wide continent generally lacking in knowledge of countries overseas.⁵⁹ Addressing the misconceptions about the Turks in the American imagination, he mentions that in some places, Americans think of the 'Turkish people as black, like people from Africa, and Americans who watched the films on Turkey were astonished that the Turkish statesman and the Turks looked very similar to the American statesman and businessman'.⁶⁰ He goes on to write: 'Considering these misconceptions, this kind of enterprise is highly useful in order to introduce Turkey to the American public opinion and counter the propaganda that has been spread before about our country and nation in the past and which will be repeated in the future by our enemies'.[61] But these misconceptions concerning Turks in the American imagination at the time warrant articulation. Who were the enemies of Turkey that Ertegün mentions in his letter and what were they propagating? And why did Ertegün find Bryan's enterprise so valuable to counter the propaganda that had been spread about Turkey and the Turkish nation?

Despite Atatürk's and his Kemalist followers' efforts to create a modern, civilized and progressive image of the Turkish nation on the international stage, the image of Turks in the American public opinion was quite negative during the interwar era. If an American citizen had an image of a Turk in his or her mind at all, this was mostly the image of the 'terrible Turk',[62] a stereotype that the young Turkish Republic inherited from the old Ottoman Empire. The prejudices against the Turks in the American public opinion were also reflected in an academic survey on cultural stereotypes conducted at Princeton University in 1932. When students were asked to choose character traits of various nationalities from a list of eighty-four adjectives, they generally chose negative ones to describe Turks. The students' top twelve adjective selections for Turks were: cruel, very religious, treacherous, sensual, ignorant, physically dirty, deceitful, sly, quarrelsome, revengeful, conservative and superstitious.[63]

Underlying this negative image of the Turks in the US public opinion was the widespread Western Orientalist discourse. Another, more recent, factor was the Ottoman Empire's treatment of the Armenians during the deportations and massacres of 1915, and their coverage in the US media.[64] Even after the Ottoman Empire collapsed and the Turkish Republic was established in 1923, most of the Armenian diaspora as well as anti-Turkish groups living in the United States continued to demand, in various media, formal recognition of the Ottoman massacres and forced deportations by the Turkish Republic. This contributed to the negative image of Turks in US public opinion.

The Turkish authorities were very sensitive about the image of the Turkish nation abroad, and they sought to prevent the propaganda activities of the Armenian diaspora and anti-Turkish groups in the United States. When Ertegün, for instance, heard of the Metro-Goldwyn-Mayer motion picture studio's plan to film the Austrian author Franz Werfel's historical novel *Die vierzig Tage des Musa Dagh* (The Forty Days of Musa Dagh, 1933) in 1934, he immediately contacted the US Department of State to prevent the film's production.⁶⁵ According to Ertegün, the film 'risked triggering hostility toward Turkey by presenting a distorted picture of Turkish treatment of Armenians'.⁶⁶ Consequently, MGM, under pressure from the US State Department as well as the Turkish government, agreed to withdraw the film project in 1935.⁶⁷

One might think that the tragic events related to the Ottoman past should not be a problem for the Kemalists; after all, they were the new government of the young Turkish Republic, who wanted to break with the Ottoman past and start a new relationship with the Western world. Moreover, they criticized Ottoman history as much as Westerners did. However, the Kemalists' relationship with Ottoman history was much more complex than it first appeared. First, the Kemalists knew that, outside Turkey, Ottoman history was seen as Turkish history. Although they liked to criticize the Ottoman past within the country, they were not happy when foreigners criticized it or made negative remarks at the expense of Turkish state and nation, as the case of the MGM film project shows.

To prevent anti-Turkish propaganda and promote a positive image of the Turkish nation in the United States and elsewhere, Atatürk and his Kemalist followers engaged in many public relations activities during the interwar era. The filming of Atatürk on his Forest Farm by Fox film, discussed in the last chapter, was one of those activities aimed at altering the negative image of Turkey in the United States. Atatürk's generosity towards Bryan can also be seen as part of the effort to improve the image of Turkey in US public opinion.

To underscore 'the impact and possible future impact of the films on American public opinion', Ertegün attached a letter sent to him by Representative Sol Bloom.⁶⁸ In the letter, which is dated 1 April 1937, Bloom states how much he, his wife and daughter enjoyed watching the films of Turkey screened at the Turkish embassy on Monday night. Bloom further writes:

> They were a vivid revelation to everyone there, I am sure, of the almost miraculous achievements of your country in the last few years, under the guidance of your very great President – in every field – in education, agriculture and industry. It was such a pleasure to see the eager interest on the children's faces in different schools, and the enthusiasm shown by all of the people in so many walks of life.⁶⁹

Bloom was not the only guest who had been fascinated by what he saw on the screen that evening. After Bryan presented his lecture at the Turkish embassy in Washington, DC, the German ambassador approached him and complained about the negative press treatment given by Americans to German affairs.[70] Reportedly, he said: 'That was such a fine presentation and an honest view of Turkey, why do not you do that in Germany, why do not you do that for us?'[71] This was the perfect opportunity for Bryan to ask the German ambassador for permission to enter Nazi Germany.

Highly impressed by Bryan's coverage of Kemalist Turkey, the German ambassador quickly made a special arrangement for Bryan not only to enter Germany but also to make films there.[72] Thus, in 1937, Bryan went to Germany for seven weeks, during which he produced 20,000 feet of sensational film footage, which included scenes of Adolf Hitler, other Nazi leaders and the Hitler Youth, as well as of party rallies, anti-Semitic propaganda activities and everyday life.[73] The footage was used in several lectures Bryan delivered throughout the United States upon his return, and was incorporated into a 1938 episode of the famous newsreel series *The March of Time* called 'Inside Nazi Germany' directed by Jack Glenn.[74]

Similarly, Bryan's film footage of Atatürk was used by The *March of Time* newsreel series to produce an episode called 'Father of All Turks' in 1937, which I will discuss in the next chapter.[75] However, Bryan's footage not only inspired Atatürk's contemporaries when he was alive but also continued to be among the most well-known images of him long after his death, appearing on Turkish television channels every Atatürk commemoration day. The footage also formed the inspiration for a popular advertisement for a bank, Türkiye İş Bankası, released during prime time on several national television channels on 10 November 2007, the sixty-ninth anniversary of Atatürk's death.[76] The advertisement's story is clearly modelled after Bryan's footage. Atatürk is played by the famous Turkish actor Haluk Bilginer, made up to look like Atatürk as featured in Bryan's footage wearing the exact same outfit, a short-sleeved white shirt with a sweater vest. However, the advertisement replaces Ülkü with a young boy, and Atatürk's garden at the summerhouse with a rose garden. The beautiful rose garden functions as an allegory for Turkey, with the thorn that at one point pricks Atatürk's finger standing for the challenges he had to face while creating it. Thus, it could be said that by allowing himself to be filmed by Bryan in his summerhouse in the fall of 1936, Atatürk not only influenced how his contemporaries saw him when he was alive but also how future generations would remember him.

Conclusion

At a critical time in Europe, with the young republic facing the threat of a new war, Atatürk understood the power of the motion picture. He knew he had to sell the image of Turkey as a strategically important country for the balance of power in the world to both its friends and enemies. He had to persuade people abroad, especially in the West, that Turkey was a strong and modern country, and that he, as its modern, democratic president, would stand up for universal peace and the wellbeing of mankind. The American film-maker Julien Bryan's visit to Turkey in the fall of 1936 coincided with a time when Atatürk was already constructing an image of himself and his country as a peacemaker on the international stage. To convey this image to the broader public, film was the most powerful tool, not only because it was a medium that the Western audience was familiar with but also because it was regarded as the most objective medium of the time. Through film, Atatürk wanted to allow Western audiences, which might not imagine Turkey as conforming to modern Western standards, to witness the changes happening right in front of their eyes; he knew that seeing was believing.

During Bryan's stay in Turkey, Atatürk was a generous host who allowed him to shoot in exclusive spaces and to take intimate pictures of his daily life. Atatürk's generosity to the American film-maker shows his investment in public relations and, by extension, his belief in the power of film to influence public opinion. To project a modern, civilian and democratic presidential image, Atatürk hosted Bryan at the Florya Summer Residence and Dolmabahçe Palace, and allowed him to film him while working in his office, playing with his adopted daughter Ülkü and attending an academic meeting on language policy. Consequently, Atatürk appeared in the film in diverse roles: as a bureaucrat working in the service of his people, as a statesman modernizing Turkey, as a father taking care of his child and as a democratic leader taking part in everyday activities associated with Western civilization, such as swimming and sunbathing in public spaces. Bryan's report suggests that Atatürk's natural appearance in the film was part of a performance. Unexpected incidents such as the security officers' intervention between Atatürk and the people were seen to disrupt the performance of his role as a democratic president. This incident was therefore considered a 'disgraceful scene'.

Since the *Turkey Reborn* film has not survived, it cannot be fully known how Bryan presented Atatürk in it. However, based on Bryan's later comments, newspaper articles and audience responses, it is likely that Atatürk was featured in a positive light to the American audience. Through his charisma, generosity and cooperation, Atatürk managed to impress Bryan, who would retrospectively call him 'one of modern history's miracles'. The diplomatic correspondence as well as the journal articles concerning Bryan's film screenings also make clear that in his presentations Bryan praised Atatürk's accomplishments, spoke about him enthusiastically and welcomed the great changes he had accomplished in Turkey.

Bryan's positive coverage of Atatürk and Kemalist Turkey not only attracted thousands of people in the United States but also provided him with an exclusive entrance visa to Nazi Germany for filming. When asked to compare Hitler and Atatürk in an interview in 1940, Bryan remembered Atatürk as 'a sensible guy who did not have "Mein Kampf" lying around and was not concerned with all the "lebensraum" stuff'.[77] He further stated that Atatürk 'was a high type of military leader from the very beginning, while Hitler was only a corporal through the whole World War'.[78] According to Bryan, 'nationalistic principles guided both men but Atatürk stopped at his own borders'[79] and, instead of waging war, 'decided to build his country into a strong nation'.[80]

One local newspaper, reporting on Bryan's screening of *Turkey Reborn*, welcomed the social, cultural and economic changes Atatürk had realized in Turkey and compared the country favourably to its own past and to other countries. It noted how the Christian American audience saw Turkey's secularization in a positive light, while criticizing Russia's more extreme rejection of religion. The article also drew attention to Turkey's expenditure on social welfare, which was higher than that of the United States. Thus, the newspaper portrayed Atatürk not as a leader of 'pomp and power', but still authoritarian in his own distinctive way.

The official and personal letters examined in this chapter show how Atatürk managed to impress not only Bryan, who met him in person, but also many people thousands of miles away, who could only see him on a screen. According to the Turkish Ambassador Ertegün, Bryan's film was a great success in the United States, helping the American audience to abandon their misconceptions about Turkey and enabling them to sympathize with the Turkish people. Representative Sol Bloom, who participated in the film screening at the Turkish embassy in Washington, DC, praised Atatürk for his achievements. The German ambassador wanted to have a similar film made about his own country and government. After watching the film, First Lady Eleanor Roosevelt in her column wished the Turkish people, who had adopted a modern way of life with extreme rapidity, great happiness. Finally, the pictures impressed President Franklin Roosevelt so much that he wrote a personal letter to congratulate Atatürk on the marvellous things he had done, expressing his hopes of one day meeting him in person. At a moment of increasing aggression in Europe, the pictures of Atatürk playing with his little daughter conveyed his vision of a peaceful world more forcefully than any political action could. In fact, what Bryan captured is still known as one of the greatest films of Atatürk, one that has defined his memory and continues to express a desire for peace at home and peace in the world.

In the next chapter, I will continue to follow the journey of Bryan's footage onto US screens in the episode of *The March of Time* newsreel series called 'Father of All Turks', and to explore how Atatürk's public image was constructed and communicated in film.

Notes

1 'Roosevelt Lauds Ataturk's Regime', *New York Times,* 1 August 1937. The translated Turkish version below is taken from Yurdagül Yüksel, 'Atatürk ve Roosvelt', *Atatürk Araştırma Merkezi Dergisi* 44 (1999): 782–3.

Beyaz Saray, Washington, 6 Nisan 1937

Azizim Bay Cumhurbaşkanı,

Ahiren Türkiye'de Bay Julien Bryan tarafından alınmış olan filmi, birkaç akşam evvel, Beyaz Ev'de seyrettim. Nispeten kısa bir zamanda meydana getirdiğiniz pekçok şayan-ı hayret hususatı görünce hissettiğim şevk ve heyecanı size arz etmek istedim.

Kıymetli şahsiyetinizin, evinde ve plajda küçük kızınız ile oynarken çekilmiş olan resimlerinizi seyretmekle bilhassa bahtiyar oldum. Bu, sizin ve benim bir gün birbirimize mülâkı olmak fırsatı bulacağımız ümidini bende bir kat daha takviye etti.

Nadir olan istirahat zamanlarımda, bana göndermek lütfunda bulunduğunuz Türk posta pulları koleksiyonunu seyretmekteyim. Bunlar üzerinde resmedilmiş olan manzaraları, bir gün kendi gözlerimle görmeyi ümit ediyorum.

Samimi saygılar ve halisâne temennilerimle.

Vefakârınız
Franklin D. Roosevelt [sic]

2 'Roosevelt Lauds Ataturk's Regime', *New York Times*, 1 August 1937. The untranslated Turkish version below is taken from Yurdagül Yüksel, 'Atatürk ve Roosvelt', *Atatürk Araştırma Merkezi Dergisi* 44 (1999): 783–4.

Ankara, 25 Mayıs 1937

Azizim Bay Cumhurbaşkanı,

Ahiren Türkiye'de Bay Julian Bryan tarafından alınmış olan filmi seyretmekten duyduğunuz memnuniyeti bildiren 6 Nisan 1937 tarihli lütufkâr mektubunuzu hakiki sevinç ile aldım. Mektubunuzda, ahvalü şerait müsaade eder etmez, birbirimize bir gün mülâki olacağımız ümidini de izhar buyuruyorsunuz.

Samimi duygularınız ve modern Türkiye'de elde edilen terakki hakkındaki takdirkâr telakkinizden dolayı size fevkalâde müteşekkir olduğuma inanmanızı rica ederim, Bay Cumhurbaşkanı.

Bu fırsattan istifade ederek Amerika Birleşik Devletleri hakkındaki hayranlığımı tekrar bildirmek isterim, bilhassa ki, bizim iki memleketimiz, umumi sulh ve insanlığın saadetini'istihdaf eden ayrı ideali gütmektedir.

Size bir an evvel mülâki olmak benim de samimi arzum olduğundan harikulade işler yapmış sevimli ve kuvvetli şahsiyetinizi Türkiye'de selâmlayacağım güne sabırsızlıkla intizar ediyorum.

Samimi duygular ve hâlisane temennilerimle,

Vefakârınız
K. Atatürk

3 Bryan's first name is sometimes spelled with an 'a' as Julian and sometimes with an 'e' as Julien. In a personal interview with Bryan's son Sam, he told me that his father's first name was actually Julien. Bryan's mother was a French protestant and she named her son Julien after an uncle, who was also French. Nevertheless, Sam Bryan said that even his father gave up on correcting the spelling of his first name after a while. To do justice to his memory, I will call him Julien Bryan throughout this study. Sam Bryan (The son of Julien Bryan and current executive director of the International Film Foundation), interview by the author, New York, 30 July 2015.

4 Raymond Fielding, *The March of Time: 1935–1951* (New York: Oxford University Press, 1978), 119.
5 The format of the travel lectures is reminiscent of today's PowerPoint presentations, but whereas you can show such presentations slide by slide, in Bryan's lectures the film would run continuously behind him while he delivered his presentation.
6 Jane M. Loy, 'The Present as Past: Assessing the Value of Julien Bryan's Films as Historical Evidence', *Latin American Research Review* 12, no. 3 (1977): 106, accessed 5 August 2015, http://www.jstor.org/stable/2502471.
7 Ibid. See also 'Films', International Film Foundation, accessed 10 August 2015, http://www.internationalfilmfoundation.org/films/?Sort=yd&start=10.
8 In my interview with Sam Bryan, he stated that his father's lectures commonly started right away without an introductory talk, with the motion picture projector running as Bryan talked along with it. Then he would show some photo slides and, finally, there was a question and answer session, particularly at universities. Sam Bryan, interview by the author, New York, 30 July 2015.
9 Ibid.
10 'Mustafa Kamâl Builds Nationalist State From Ruins of War-Torn Turkish Empire', *Photo Reporter*, January/February 1937, 7.
11 Ibid.
12 Ibid.
13 Ibid.
14 Ibid.
15 Ibid.
16 Ibid. The editors of Photo Reporter did not seem to know the filming of Atatürk in his Forest Farm that was produced by Fox Film, which I found and discussed in the previous chapter.
17 Ibid.
18 Ibid.
19 Julien Bryan, 'Turkey' (Report, Sam Bryan Private Collection, New York, 1961), 4.
20 Ibid.
21 Ibid.
22 Ibid.
23 Ibid. See also 'Mustafa Kamâl Builds Nationalist State', 7.
24 'Mustafa Kamâl Builds Nationalist State', 7–8.
25 Roger R. Trask, *The United States Response to Turkish Nationalism and Reform, 1914–1939* (Minneapolis: The University of Minnesota Press, 1971), 217.
26 Mango, *Atatürk*, 486.

27 On page 1 of his report, Bryan suggests that he shot 1,000 or 1,200 feet of film of Atatürk himself, while on page 4 of the same report, he states that he shot about 1,000 feet of 35-mm film. See Bryan, 'Turkey', 1, 4.
28 He also filmed the president swimming in the sea, drying himself and taking a rest on the beach. Furthermore, he filmed Atatürk with a young female secretary working in his office, and sitting at the table in the dining hall with his personal dentist, Sami Günzberg. Ibid., 4.
29 Bryan, 'Turkey', 5.
30 Haldun Derin, *Çankaya Özel Kalemini Anımsarken (1933–1951)*, ed. Cemil Koçak (Istanbul: Tarih Vakfı Yurt Yayınları, 1995), 111–12.
31 Ibid., 112.
32 Ibid.
33 Ibid.
34 Atatürk's words in Turkish: 'Rezilane bir sahne yaptınız'. See ibid.
35 Peter Burke, *Eyewitnessing: The Uses of Images as Historical Evidence* (Ithaca: Cornell University Press, 2008), 71.
36 Ibid. The word 'demotic' comes from the Greek *dēmos* and refers to 'the people', 'populace' and 'the common people of an Ancient Greek state'. Demotic, then, means relating to or favouring the 'common people'.
37 Ibid., 71.
38 Adam Cohen, 'The First 100 Days', Time, accessed 6 January 2016, http://content.time.com/time/specials/packages/article/0,28804,1906802_1906838_1906979,00.html.
39 Burke, *Eyewitnessing*, 71.
40 Derin, *Çankaya Özel Kalemini Anımsarken*, 112.
41 'Mustafa Kamâl Builds Nationalist State', 8.
42 Derin, *Çankaya Özel Kalemini Anımsarken*, 112.
43 'Mustafa Kamâl Builds Nationalist State', 8.
44 Ibid.
45 Bryan, 'Turkey', 1.
46 Ibid. Julien Bryan's son, Sam Bryan told me in a personal conversation that he gave a part of this film material to the Library of Congress.
47 'Turkey Reborn', International Film Foundation, accessed 15 August 2015, http://www.internationalfilmfoundation.org/films/show/825.
48 Bryan, interview by the author.
49 'Turkey Reborn', American Film Institute, accessed 18 August 2015. http://www.afi.com/members/catalog/DetailView.aspx?s=1&Movie=8646.

50 "'March of Time' Reporter Is Century Club's Speaker", *Oak Leaves*, 9 December 1937.
51 Ibid.
52 'Julien Bryan to Give Illustrated Lecture on "Turkey Reborn" on Monday', *The Oakparker*, 3 December 1937.
53 Mehmet Münir Ertegün'ün Baş Bakanlığa Türkiye Filmleri Hakkında Mektubu, 14 Mayıs 1937, Fon No: 30 10 0 0, Kutu No: 268, Dosya No: 804, Sıra No: 4. Başbakanlık Devlet Arşivleri Genel Müdürlüğü, Ankara.
54 Ibid.
55 Ibid.
56 In her column, Mrs. Roosevelt mentions some of the guests who came to spend Easter at the White House with them. These guests were Miss Helen Reynolds from Poughkeepsie, Mr. and Mrs. William Dana, and Mr. and Mrs. Raymond Adolphe. It is probable that they attended Bryan's film screening. See Eleanor Roosevelt, 'My Day, March 29, 1937', *The Eleanor Roosevelt Papers Digital Edition* (2008), accessed 31 July 2015, http://www.gwu.edu/~erpapers/myday/displaydoc.cfm?_y=1937&_f=md054603.
57 Ibid.
58 Mehmet Münir Ertegün'ün Baş Bakanlığa Türkiye Filmleri Hakkında Mektubu.
59 Ibid.
60 Ibid.
61 Ibid.
62 Şuhnaz Yılmaz, 'Challenging the stereotypes: Turkish–American relations in the inter-war era', *Middle Eastern Studies*, 42, no. 2 (2006): 223–37, accessed 8 April 2017, doi: 10.1080/00263200500417520.
63 Ibid., 86.
64 Ibid. 85–6.
65 George S. Harris, 'Cementing Turkish-American Relations: The Ambassadorship of (Mehmet) Münir Ertegün (1934–1944)', in *Studies in Atatürk's Turkey: The American Dimension*, ed. George S. Harris and Nur Bilge Criss (Leiden, Boston: Brill, 2009), 184–5.
66 Ibid., 184.
67 Ibid., 185.
68 Sol Bloom was also the director general of the United States Constitution Sesquicentennial Commission. Ertegün also attached to this letter a copy of Mrs. Roosevelt's column 'My Day', published in *The Washington News*. See Mehmet Münir Ertegün'ün Baş Bakanlığa Türkiye Filmleri Hakkında Mektubu.
69 Ibid.

70 Sam Bryan, interview by the author. Raymond Fielding tells a different story about Bryan's entry into Germany. According to him, Bryan got the permission to enter Germany from a high-ranking Gestapo officer, whom Bryan met at an embassy party in Turkey in 1937. He supposedly said, 'Why can't you Americans report our programs a little more objectively?' See Fielding, *The March of Time*, 188.
71 Bryan, interview.
72 Fielding, *The March of Time*, 188–9.
73 Ibid., 187–201.
74 Not caring much about Bryan's commitment to objective journalism, The *March of Time* staff turned his footage into an explicitly anti-Nazi film. Bryan was angry about this and considered suing them. *Inside Nazi Germany*, which included additional and staged scenes as well as narration, was released on 21 January 1938 in the United States. Up to today, Bryan's footage continues to be used in documentary films on the Nazi regime. Ibid.
75 Bryan's footage of Atatürk also appeared in other newsreel series, including the Pathé Gazette under the title 'Turkey Mourns Kemal Ataturk' (1938), as well as in another film entitled 'Turkey: A Nation In Transition' (1962), produced by Julien Bryan and Seymour Hymowitz. In my correspondence with the Turkish army's General Staff Photo and Film Center, I was informed that they hold two minutes of footage of Atatürk and Ülkü as part of a film called 'Atamtürk'ten Atatürk'e' (From my ancestor/father Turk to Atatürk [Father Turk]), but that they had no information on who shot the footage. The centre provided me with one minute of this footage on CD, on the basis of which I can confirm that it is indeed Bryan's.
76 Significantly, Atatürk was one of the bank's founders.
77 Earle Marckies, 'Ataturk Fuehrer Compared', *Berkeley Daily Gazette*, 7 March 1940.
78 Ibid.
79 Ibid.
80 Ibid.

5

Father of all Turks:
How *The March of Time* newsreel series represented Atatürk

Mustafa Kemal Atatürk wanted to create Turkey in his own image as 'modern', 'civilized' and 'democratic'. To achieve this aim, he introduced abundant reforms and presented himself as a democratic leader who had modernized his country and raised the standard of living. Despite all his efforts, however, some Western media were still prejudiced against the new Turkey and its creator. They represented Atatürk and his revolution differently than he intended, partly by reframing the carefully controlled film footage he had sent out into the world.

In this chapter, I focus on an episode of the famous American newsreel series *The March of Time* (MOT) from 1937 featuring Atatürk. By analysing this episode, which is titled 'Father of All Turks', I explore not only how Atatürk constructed and communicated his image to the Western world but also how this image was partially reframed by a Western newsreel series in light of how the Turkish president was viewed in the United States. The chapter offers insights into the making of Atatürk's image and his contemporary representation in Western media. It also outlines how the Kemalist modernization programme was seen in the Western world.

The chapter is divided into two parts. In the first part, I explain the format of the newsreel and The *March of Time* series. In the second part, I analyse the 'Father of All Turks' episode, concentrating on the scenes showing Atatürk and his reforms, and on how they are reframed in the American context for American audiences, showing that Atatürk's original intentions for particular footage did not necessarily survive as the footage travelled internationally.

Newsreel and *The March of Time*

The newsreel was a mixture of motion picture news footage, mostly lasting five to ten minutes, shown regularly in movie theatres throughout the world.¹ It was an important source of information in the first half of the twentieth century, long before television as a mass medium was born and at a time when literacy was not as high as today. Moreover, travelling was an expensive and difficult undertaking in those days, so the newsreel travelled on behalf of those who could not afford to do so. From their beginning, newsreels were produced partly for journalism and partly for entertainment purposes; therefore, they were informative and entertaining in content. Some of the newsreels showed actual events, others staged them,² but all newsreels tended to represent events so 'realistically' that they managed to fascinate audiences.

By the end of the 1920s, a weekly visit to the cinema had become a popular leisure activity for millions of people in the United States and Western Europe. Movie theatres showed newsreels as a standard part of their programme, mostly before a feature film in order to entertain and inform the audience about current affairs. Sound newsreels were introduced in 1927, which increased the popularity of newsreels among the public. The sound newsreel brought audiences the voices of prominent world leaders such as Churchill, Stalin, Hitler and Mussolini, as well as important news events such as the Olympic Games, the explosion of the Hindenburg Zeppelin and the Second World War. After the introduction of sound films and alongside the growth of international tensions in the 1930s, new cinemas were introduced to exclusively show newsreels and documentaries: a genre that came to flourish in these years. While members of the public could read about the events of the day in the newspaper or listen to the radio news, newsreels provided them with vivid imagery of events, making it seem as if they could see the entire world with their own eyes.

According to the American film scholar Raymond Fielding, 'at their height, newsreels produced by various companies throughout the world were viewed by more than 215 million people each week'.³ Several companies produced newsreel series under different titles. Pathé Film, for instance, produced the *Pathé News* newsreel series; Fox Film Inc. the *Fox Movietone News*; Universal Studios the *Universal Newsreel*; the Hearst Corporation the *Hearst Metrotone News*; Paramount Pictures the *Paramount News*; and Time-Life Inc. *The March of Time*. During his political career, Mustafa Kemal Atatürk appeared in at least three of these: *Pathé News*, *Fox Movietone News* and *The March of Time*, the last one being the most popular and influential newsreel series of its time (1935–51).[4]

Made by Time-Life Incorporated, *The March of Time* was designed to explore contemporary national and international affairs. It appeared on American movie screens for the first time in 1935 and introduced a new kind of pictorial journalism called 'interpretative journalism'. While most of the competitor newsreel series on the market carefully avoided any kind of controversy by trying to remain 'objective', *The March of Time* provoked controversy by offering highly interpretative and partial narratives.[5] Due to its provocative and sensational journalistic style, *The March of Time* became enormously popular among the public. Its makers were not afraid to touch sensitive issues or to criticize political figures, including Stalin, Mussolini and Hitler, on motion picture screens.[6]

At a time when an overt political analysis of National Socialism and its *Führer* was still taboo in American movie theatres, for instance, *The March of Time* was the first American newsreel to report comprehensively on Nazi Germany with the 1938 anti-Nazi film 'Inside Nazi Germany'.[7] Some of the scenes in this film were shot by Julien Bryan in Germany, but others were staged in Hoboken, New Jersey, by the crew of The *March of Time*.[8] It is still known as one of the most controversial films ever shown in America.

Father of all Turks

The March of Time episode titled 'Father of All Turks' is a black and white sound film, approximately eight minutes long. Much of the footage used in this episode was provided by Julien Bryan and Louis de Rochemont, the filmmaker and producer of *The March of Time* newsreel series.[9] The episode, which was narrated by Cornelius Westbrook Van Voorhis, was released in the United States on 19 February 1937,[10] and then in the rest of the world. It is a fact that at the height of their popularity, at least forty million people in the United States and more than two hundred million people throughout the world watched weekly American newsreels,[11] with each individual episode having an audience of more than twenty million.[12] It is thus likely that the

'Father of All Turks' episode had considerable influence shaping American and international public opinion about Turkey and Atatürk.

The newsreel starts with the Turkish national anthem playing in the background while a voice-over notes:

> On an arid plateau in Asia Minor, where stood, not long ago, a herdsman's village, there rises today a modern city. Its streets are broad to allow for future traffic. Its buildings imposing, to house the activities of a growing government, for this is Ankara, new capital of the new Republic of Turkey. Here, alone in a guarded mansion lives the man who out of blood and steel and ambition created both city and republic, Mustafa Kemal, now called Atatürk or Father of the Turks.

As the narrator utters these words, the newsreel shows scenes of Ankara and its modern urban architecture. The narrative links the emergence of this capital city of the new republic from what used to be a village to the single-handed achievement of one man, Mustafa Kemal Atatürk, by showing him at work in his office seated behind his desk. Although the presidential palace Çankaya Köşkü (Çankaya Mansion) in Ankara appears before the shot of Atatürk, the office scene seems to have been shot not in Ankara, but in the Florya summer residence in Istanbul by Julien Bryan, as the interior design of the room shows. The first image of Atatürk is that of a modern statesman wearing a casual, Western-style suit with an open-collared shirt and a handkerchief in his pocket working in his office. The newsreel could just as easily have started with Atatürk's impressive military career, introducing him as a victorious general in military uniform, but it rather chose to introduce Atatürk to US audiences in this way for reasons that will now be discussed.

The image of a president working at his desk in his office may look familiar to our modern eyes, but this has not always been the case. To comprehend the cultural significance of it, we need to go back to eighteenth-century Europe and try to understand how the public image of political leaders changed in the Western tradition, particularly after the French Revolution in 1789. According to the British historian Peter Burke, before the revolution, European rulers were commonly represented in an idealistic fashion in various visual media.[13] This was a time when absolute monarchies prevailed in Europe and it was believed that monarchs had a 'divine right' to rule over the people. Thus, in visual media, rulers tended to be depicted as dignified and distant from the common people.[14]

Burke argues that after the French Revolution changed the political system, the images of rulers had to change as well. The old conventions of royal portraiture had to be adapted to the ascending ideology of 'progress, modernity, liberty, equality and fraternity'.[15] Over time, new conventions developed. For instance, unlike the old kings, the French king Louis Philippe I (1830–48) was portrayed not in grandiose coronation robes, but in an unpretentious military uniform.[16] Moreover, the king's portrait was painted closer to the eye level of the onlooker than had previously been done.[17] All these changes were made to associate the king with the new values of the revolution in the eyes of the citizens.

Another important image signifying the shift in the conventions of ruler portraits is Jacques-Louise David's portrait *The Emperor Napoleon in His Study at the Tuileries* (1812). In this portrait, David depicted Napoleon as a bureaucrat standing next to his desk, spending the night in his study in order to create the Napoleonic code.[18] With this portrait, David emphasized a new feature of the ruler's power, namely, his administrative role. According to Burke, this portrait served as a model for the images of various rulers of later generations, such as François Gérard's *Louis XVIII in His Cabinet* (1824) and F. Reshetnikov's *Stalin in His Office* (1948).[19]

New media such as photography and film also contributed to the emerging image of the modern ruler. A number of Atatürk's contemporaries, including Vladimir Lenin and Franklin D. Roosevelt, were photographed or filmed working at their desks in their offices. Thus, by introducing Atatürk in this way at the very beginning of its narrative, The *March of Time* episode used a familiar convention, signifying his modernity as well as his administrative achievements. Similarly, by allowing Bryan to film him in his office in Western clothes, Atatürk wanted to show the American audience that he was a modern, civilian and democratic leader, who shared the vision of Western democracies and worked tirelessly in the service of his people.

Intertitle 1

After the scene of Atatürk at his desk, the national anthem stops and dramatic music starts to play. An intertitle appears: 'Predecessors of Kamâl Atatürk were the Sultans, world-powerful rulers in the days when Turkey was the Ottoman

Empire.' Images from the late Ottoman and early republican period appear as the narrator tells the audience the following:

> Four centuries ago, Constantinople was the capital of an empire that ruled half the Mediterranean, thundered at the gates of Vienna, threatened the Christian world, but gradually the empire shrank to a demoralized little sultanate. Almost driven from Europe, it nevertheless turned to the mastery of the Dardanelles, strategic passageway to Russia's Black Sea. Deep into squalor, Turkey sank. Ninety two per cent of its people could neither read nor write the complex Arabic script. And foreign enterprise was elbowing the Turks out of their own land. Turkey became to outsiders just the land of the harem and the fez. After the World War came final catastrophe. As with Allied warships of the Dardanelles, the frightened sultan, by the Treaty of Sèvres, signed over his country for dismemberment. Allied troops patrolled Constantinople, while the Greeks, traditional Turkish enemies, occupied Asiatic Turkey.

Significantly, the images accompanying this narration contain a number of Western Orientalist clichés and stereotypes. The sequence begins by showing mosques in Istanbul, followed by a still image of a map of the Ottoman Empire at its zenith, demonstrating its vast territorial spread over three continents, reaching all the way up to Vienna. Appearing at the beginning of the newsreel, the image of the map provides important insights into how its producers viewed Turkey. The newsreel was produced at a time when Axis aggression was hovering over Europe and, if a war were to break out, the geographical location of Turkey between Europe, the Middle East and Asia would make Turkey strategically important to the European balance of power. According to the narrator, although the Ottoman Empire lost almost all of its territory when it turned into a 'demoralized little sultanate'; it still held the 'Dardanelles, strategic passageway to Russia's Black Sea'. By verbally blurring the geographical differences between the Ottoman Empire and the new Turkey, he underlines the continuing strategic importance of Turkey.

After the map, the newsreel shows some traditional-looking scenes of the streets of Turkey and its architecture as the narrator describes the squalor of the late Ottoman Empire. The scenes with shops and others from the streets feature men and women in traditional costumes (fezzes, kalpaks and turbans for the men, and veils or headscarves for the women). The appearance of these scenes in the newsreel in this particular sequence is far from random, but designed to indicate the presumed 'backwardness' of the Ottoman Empire before Atatürk's Westernizing reforms. They serve as rhetorical tools to mark a sharp contrast between the old, traditional Ottoman Empire and the young, modern Turkish Republic. The newsreel continues with images of the Allied occupation of Turkey followed by the scenes of the last Ottoman sultan, Mehmed VI, which were probably shot at a ceremonial event. The sultan is shown walking down some stairs, getting into a horse carriage and being driven away.

Intertitle 2

A dramatic musical score starts to play in the background and a new intertitle appears: 'But as the victors prepared to partition the prostrate country, a new movement was taking shape in the mountains of Asia Minor.' The narrator continues as follows:

> Hiding away with his army, with a price on his head, was a former World War General, Mustafa Kemal, ruthless, unscrupulous, brilliant. He was the one character in Turkey strong enough to rise above defeat. Rallying a few generals around him, he defied his sultan, repudiated the Treaty of Sèvres, aroused Turkey to frenzied nationalism. In a campaign that startled the world, he drove the Greeks out of Asia Minor in utter rout. And out of blazing Smyrna began streaming the first refugees in a tragic migration that was to sweep Turkey clean of unwanted foreigners. [The Turkish national anthem starts to play in the background.] Negotiating a new treaty, Kemal kept intact all of Turkey in Europe and Asia Minor. But he agreed that Dardanelles should remain unfortified and open to all nations. The Ottoman Empire was dead, but for the first time in a century, Turkey belonged to the Turks. And the only sovereign flag in the land was the star and crescent.

This part of the newsreel begins by showing an image of an Anatolian town, followed by a close-up of Mustafa Kemal. He has his kalpak on and looks very briefly at the camera. As mentioned in the second chapter, the kalpak indicates that this scene must have been shot before the proclamation of the republic. In the next scene, Mustafa Kemal and the commanders of the National Movement are walking down the stairs of a building. Mustafa Kemal wears a long, dark, buttoned coat with a fur collar and carries a walking stick in his right hand. He descends on the right side of the stairs, ahead of the commanders, talking to Fevzi (Çakmak) Pasha, who is one step behind him on his left. Kazım (Karabekir) Pasha, the commander of the eastern front, walks behind them in his military uniform, followed by İsmet (İnönü) Pasha, the commander of the Western Front, also in uniform. At the end of this scene, Fevzi Pasha and Mustafa Kemal get into a car. In many of the films and still photographs that exist of him, Mustafa Kemal is shown one step ahead of the group. This was partly due to his role as the leader of the movement, but also to his average stature; standing in front allowed him to appear taller.[20]

The newsreel continues with a scene of the Turkish National Assembly's troops entering Istanbul, followed by images of Turkish troops in İzmir and elsewhere. The newsreel also shows Greek refugees, as well as the great fire of İzmir shot from the vantage point of the seashore. This scene, in all likelihood, was shot by Louis de Rochemont while he was on duty with the US Navy around the time of the War of Independence. Significantly, the newsreel represents the refugees, most of whom were probably from Anatolia, in a reductionist way, referring to them as 'unwanted foreigners'. The newsreel continues by showing the raising of the Turkish flag on a building, probably the Vali Konağı (Governor's Mansion) of İzmir, accompanied by applause from a Turkish crowd. The section ends by showing two imams performing *namaz* (a canonical prayer) on board of a ship, while the Turkish flag waves behind them at the stern.

This image serves as a partial ending for the newsreel. It does not bring the story to a full narrative closure, nor does it connect the dots to explain how Atatürk has modernized Turkey, as the newsreel had suggested at the beginning of its narrative. Rather, it marks the watershed between the old 'Oriental Turkey' and the new 'Modern Turkey' of Atatürk that cuts the narrative in half. In the first half, the newsreel set up the story by introducing the hero and presenting the conflict between him and his adversaries. In addition, it showed how the hero resolved an essential part of the conflict. But the hero has not yet reached his final goal; he has to continue his journey and deal with further challenges. How he does this is what the newsreel shows next.

Intertitle 3

A new piece of dramatic music starts to play and another intertitle appears: 'So far victorious, Kamâl Atatürk turns his ambitions towards his next goal – to make Turkey a modern nation, himself its absolute ruler'. To introduce this part, the narrator states the following:

> For resources, Kamâl Ataturk's new nation had to do with agriculture. A people seventy per cent peasants, living and working by Mohammedan laws fifteen hundred years old. And nowhere anyone to carry on industry. With his power as president and dictator he begins his reform, into European dress he forces both men and women, sweeping away the veil and the fez. In one of the great reform movements of modern time, he outlaws Arabic writing, keeps his cabinet sitting day after day, studying the Latin alphabet. He gives youngsters a new ABC to study, along with his name and story. He gives his people two years to learn reading and writing the simpler European way. He sends his soldiers out to give the oldsters surprise examining. Packing off to jail go old townsmen. Everywhere signs are changed to fit the worlds' first truly phonetic language. To make Turkish youth tough and healthy, he orders them out to the athletic field. He commands young Turks to go to business school. He brings in foreigners to show girls how to dress, how to manage their homes, the European way. He imports doctors and equipment to teach Turkey the wonders of medicine and therapy. On model farms, Turkey learns the methods of big scale agriculture. Hoping to make the nation self-sufficient through industrialization, he subsidizes new industry, builds cotton mill. Turkish sugar beets are ground refined at home. Today above all, all over the world come ships to trade in Turkish market.

Visually, this part begins by showing peasants, men and women, engaged in agricultural activity, in traditional clothes and without machinery. These images, like earlier ones, are presented to illustrate the situation before Atatürk's reforms. The newsreel then shows Atatürk at his desk in his office again, smoking a cigarette and reading some documents. This is a medium shot taken from his left by Julien Bryan at the summer residence in Florya. The newsreel then shows some more street scenes, this time featuring people in European clothing, coinciding with the narrator's description of Atatürk's dress reforms. To understand the new, modern image of Turkey presented here, we need to know how Atatürk and his followers crafted it.

'Clothes make the man', the proverb says, and Atatürk agreed. Although he prided himself on his distinguished military career, he put aside his uniform and did not wear it again when he became president. Leaving his traditional clothing style behind, he began to dress like a European bourgeois gentleman.[21] By adjusting his own image, Atatürk not only wanted to adopt a 'civilized' outlook but also aimed at becoming a model for his people, showing them how to dress in a 'civilized' fashion. He performed his role by always dressing appropriately for the occasion, as well as by paying meticulous attention to his clothing style. In his daily life, he was generally dressed in *tenue de ville*. For official celebrations and receptions, he frequently appeared in evening dress with a top hat. A close follower of contemporary European fashion, he even wore plus fours, after Edward, the Prince of Wales, made them fashionable in Europe and America in the 1920s.[22]

Dressing in a 'civilized' fashion was by no means a private matter for Atatürk; it was designed to signify a sense of belonging to a particular civilization, and that of the modern Western one.[23] Accordingly, he initiated a series of reforms to change the dress code of the Turkish nation. To convince the public of the necessity of these reforms, he visited the cities of Kastamonu and İnebolu in a Western suit and Panama hat between 23 and 31 August 1925.[24] There, he gave a number of speeches in which he harshly criticized and ridiculed the traditional clothes that were still being worn by some people. According to him, these clothes were 'wasteful', 'uncomfortable' and 'ridiculous'; above all, they were 'uncivilized' and therefore not appropriate for the new Turkish nation.[25]

On 24 August, in Kastamonu, he asked a local tailor: 'What is cheaper, local dress with baggy trousers or international clothes?'[26] The tailor, who could spot Atatürk's preference in fashion, did not wait long to give the right answer: 'international clothes'.[27] 'Quite so', confirmed Mustafa Kemal, 'and you will have enough cloth for two suits'.[28] Mustafa Kemal then turned to another man at the gathering, who wore a traditional hat called a *fez*,[29] and said to him: 'Take off your fez'.[30] The man followed this order immediately, but underneath his fez, he still had a skullcap.[31] Seeing this, Mustafa Kemal stated: 'Skullcaps, fezes, turbans – it all costs money which goes to foreigners'.[32] He finished his talk with the following words: 'We will become civilized. ... We will march forward. ... Civilization is a fearful fire which consumes those who ignore it'.[33] His next stop was İnebolu. There, he not only made a strong impression by walking through the market place in his chic Western suit and Panama hat[34] but also gave a speech that carried an intimidating message to his opponents. On 27 August,[35] he told the crowd:

> Gentleman, the Turkish people who founded the Turkish republic are civilized; they are civilized in history and reality. But I tell you as your own

brother, as your friend, as your father, that the people of the Turkish Republic, who claim to be civilized, must show and prove that they are civilized, by their ideas and mentality, by their family life and their way of living. In a word, the truly civilized people of Turkey … must prove in fact that they are civilized and advanced persons also in their outward aspect. [...] Is our dress national? (Cries of no!) Is it civilized and international? (Cries of no, no!) I agree with you. This grotesque mixture of styles is neither national nor international.… My friends, there is no need to seek and revive the costume of Turan. A civilized, international dress is worthy and appropriate for the Turkish nation, and we will wear it. Boots or shoes on our feet, trousers on our legs, shirt and tie, jacket and waistcoat – and of course, to complete these, a cover of brim on our heads. I want to make this clear. This head covering is called 'hat'.[36]

Mustafa Kemal's view on how to dress in a civilized fashion was not limited to male citizens, but also included female ones. He continued his speech by addressing women's attire, a highly sensitive subject that nobody had dared to touch before. After expressing his discontent regarding the covering of women's faces with veils that he had witnessed in villages and towns in Anatolia, which, according to him, must have been particularly uncomfortable in the hot summers, he concluded that this tradition was the outcome of 'male selfishness' and 'scruples about purity'.[37] He stated to the crowd: 'But, friends, women have minds, too. So teach them morals and then stop being selfish. Let them show their faces to the world, and see it with their eyes. … Do not be afraid. Change is essential, so much so that, if need be, we are prepared to sacrifice lives for its sake.'[38] Before returning to Ankara, Mustafa Kemal stopped in Kastamonu one more time, giving another speech. Pointing to a citizen in the crowd, he said: 'I see a man in the crowd in front of me.'[39] 'He has a fez on his head, a green turban wound round the fez, a traditional waistcoat [*mintan*] on his back, and on top of it a jacket like mine. I can't see what is below. Now, I ask you, would a civilized man wear such peculiar clothes and invite people's laughter?'[40]

Mustafa Kemal was a man of action. One day after he returned to Ankara, on 2 September 1925, the government passed a decree that permitted the wearing of religious dress such as turbans and robes only for Islamic officials recognized by the state and regulated the costume of civil servants. From then on, all civil servants had to wear what was 'common to the civilized nations of the world', namely, a 'Western suit' and 'hat'.[41] A month later, the government passed another decree that made the wearing of tails and top hats for civil servants on ceremonial occasions compulsory.⁴²

For Mustafa Kemal, there was to be no return to the past for the Turkish nation. On 1 November 1925, he stated in parliament: 'The nation has taken the final decision to adopt in essence and in form the life and resources which contemporary civilizations grant to all nations'.⁴³ Whether or not 'the nation' agreed with him, state interventions concerning the dress style of Turkish citizens continued with more drastic measures. In the beginning, the government decrees only applied to civil servants, but soon they would also concern ordinary citizens. On 25 November 1925,⁴⁴ the government passed a new law declaring: 'The hat [Western-style] is the common headgear of the Turkish people'.⁴⁵ The law also stipulated that 'the government forbids the contrary'.⁴⁶ This meant that if a Turkish citizen wanted to wear something on his head, it had to be a (Western-style) hat. Citizens could no longer wear a fez, a turban or any other traditional form of headdress.

Enforcing a type of headwear may sound ridiculous to a contemporary reader, but it was a deadly serious matter for the Kemalists. To survive in the modern world, they wanted to create a new society that would become a part of what was considered 'modern civilization' in both 'essence' and 'form'. For them, the hat was more than just a headdress; it signified a choice of a lifestyle as well as a move towards 'civilization'. Rejecting it meant rejecting the Turkish Revolution and keeping the nation from the path of progress. Consequently, whoever opposed the law in the assembly was deemed to be a 'reactionary', or an 'enemy of the popular will' by the Kemalist deputies.⁴⁷

Mustafa Kemal was not the first leader in Turkish history to initiate a dress reform that received a negative response from the public. As part of his modernization reforms, Sultan Mahmud II had introduced a law in 1829 that specified the clothing and headgear to be worn by religious officials and that introduced the fez for civil and military officials. The law was aimed at eliminating visible distinctions between the official and subject classes, as well as between Muslims and non-Muslims.⁴⁸ Although the fez had initially faced some resistance from some conservative Muslims who saw it as an 'infidel innovation', the Muslim middle classes and many non-Muslims quickly adopted it.⁴⁹ Over time, the fez became an increasingly common symbol of Muslim identification among the subjects of the empire, as well as for Muslims around the world.⁵⁰ The popularity of the fez among Muslims was partly due to its shape. Since the fez did not have a brim, like most Western-style hats, it was preferred by Muslims and helped them distinguish themselves from the Westerners. From the nineteenth century onwards, many Muslim Ottoman gentlemen in Istanbul and elsewhere in the empire dressed in the Western fashion, relying on their fez to indicate their Muslim and Ottoman identity.

This was precisely the problem for the Kemalist regime, which envisioned removing all distinctions between the 'civilized nations' and the Turkish nation. Consequently, the fez as the emblem of Oriental cultural identity had to disappear. By replacing it with the Western-style hat, Atatürk removed the last symbol of Muslim and Ottoman identification, as well as the visual distinction between the Turkish nation and the 'civilized nations of the world'.[51] Besides its 'civilizing' aim, it is also possible to read the new law in a Foucauldian manner as an exertion of disciplinary power through which the government sought to control the bodies of its citizens.[52]

Not everyone agreed with Mustafa Kemal's reforms. For many male Muslim citizens, wearing a Western-style hat was a hard decision to make, because in their eyes, Islam as a belief distinguished itself through common symbols of belonging such as dress and headdress. Moreover, clothing – particularly headgear – had signified identity, status and rank in Ottoman society. As a result, hat riots erupted in several cities throughout the country. Nevertheless, as he had announced, Mustafa Kemal and his followers were ready to sacrifice lives for the sake of change. According to Mango, to cope with violent local riots against the reforms, the Ankara Independence Tribunal was sent to the hotbeds of violence and implemented judicial terror, pronouncing 138 death sentences between 1925 and 1926, of which around twenty were related to the hat riots.[53] Invested by the Ankara government with extraordinary powers, the tribunal resembled in many aspects the *Tribunal révolutionnaire* (Revolutionary Tribunal) of the French Revolution, which executed the 'enemies' of revolution.

By applying disciplinary power to the bodies of Turkish citizens as well as by refashioning themselves as 'civilized' bureaucrats, the Kemalists managed to give Turkish society a somewhat Westernized appearance in public space, as can be seen in the newsreel. Unlike the earlier images of the streets of the old Ottoman Empire, which looked 'traditional' and 'Oriental', the images of the new Turkey with streets full of male and female citizens dressed in European fashion (wearing either a Western-style hat or nothing on their heads, as the law demanded) appear 'modern' and 'Occidental'. If the narrator had not announced that this was Turkey, it would have been impossible to tell whether the scenes were shot there or in a Western European country. Thus, Atatürk and his followers seem to have succeeded in convincing the newsreel producers that Turkey had indeed become a fully modern, Western country. The newsreel shows virtually no difference between the Turkish nation and other 'civilized nations', firmly incorporating Turkey in this category.

While the newsreel is showing the footage shot by Bryan of Atatürk at the meeting of the Turkish Language Association (TLA) at the Dolmabahçe Palace, the narrator explains Atatürk's *Harf Devrimi* (letter reform): 'In one of the great reform movements of modern time, he outlaws Arabic writing, keeps his cabinet sitting day after day, studying the Latin alphabet'. Yet the people shown in this scene are not the cabinet, but members of the TLA. Atatürk is seen sitting at a large table with some scholars, while Agop Dilaçar illustrates a language issue at the blackboard. Although it is hard to identify each person due to the camera's position, one can recognize İbrahim Necmi Dilmen, the secretary of the TLA, sitting on the right side of Atatürk.

As the newsreel suggests, the letter reform was one of Atatürk's most radical reforms. It had – and still has – many supporters as well as opponents. The Kemalists passed a law changing the alphabet from Arabo-Persian to a Latin-based alphabet on 1 November 1928.[54] To justify and validate the reform, they made several arguments. First of all, they believed that the Latin alphabet was phonetically more suited to the Turkish language. They also argued that the Arabo-Persian alphabet was not an appropriate medium for writing Turkish. Indeed, it was not easy to write a language like Turkish, containing eight vowels (a – e – ı – i – o – ö – u – ü) in an alphabet that has only four vowels (ا – ي – و – ه). According to the Kemalists, the Arabo-Persian alphabet also took more time to learn and was difficult to print, thus hindering educational and cultural development.[55]

An alphabet reform had already been discussed among Ottoman intellectuals in the second half of the nineteenth century. An important reason for the discussions was the issue of literacy. The emergence of print media (or print capitalism) in the Ottoman Empire, particularly in the form of newspapers and journals, depended on a literate public. Thus, a standard or simplified orthography would enable the Ottoman press to speak to a larger audience as well as increase public literacy. Nevertheless, the debates surrounding the Ottoman alphabet were generally about reforming it rather than about changing it completely. There were even some experiments with simplifying the Ottoman alphabet. From 1913 onwards, the Minister of War Enver Pasha, for instance, tried to implement the so-called *Enver Paşa Yazısı* (Enver Pasha Writing) or *Ordu Elifbası* (Army Alphabet) in order to make military communication as well as official correspondence easier.[56] However, due to the First World War and the impracticality of the Army Alphabet, the experiment failed. Discussions on reforms continued until Atatürk's initiative in 1928.

Atatürk supported Romanization for a number of reasons. First of all, he found the Latin alphabet a more convenient medium for writing Turkish. Since he and the other founders of the Turkish Republic had military backgrounds, it is not surprising that they were in favour of a letter system that made reading and writing both more precise and simpler. In military communication, after all, the incorrect writing of a place or name could lead to fatalities. Moreover, Atatürk believed that the adoption of the Latin alphabet could increase the literacy rate in Turkish society. In fact, it would increase the literacy rate from 9 per cent in 1924 to 65 per cent in 1975, 82 per cent in 1995[57] and 96 per cent in 2014.[58] Nevertheless, for Atatürk, the alphabet reform was by no means only a technical issue; it was a political one as well. As Benedict Anderson suggests, Atatürk implemented the reform to decrease Islamic identification and increase Turkish national consciousness.[59] By switching from Arabo-Persian to the Latin script, he was breaking Turkey's ties to both the Ottoman past and the global Islamic community, and creating a new national community that would be associated with Western civilization.

The introduction of Latin or the so-called *Gazi Elifbası* (Gazi Alphabet)[60] gave Mustafa Kemal yet another role, namely, that of head teacher of the nation. Having given his first class at the Dolmabahçe Palace on 11 August 1928,[61] Mustafa Kemal went on a tour of the country with a blackboard and easel to teach Turkish citizens the new alphabet, urging other members of the parliament to follow his example. National schools were also established throughout the country to teach citizens how to read and write.[62] Undoubtedly, Mustafa Kemal's project of bringing 'civilization' to the remote corners of Turkey bore fruit. According to Mango, the literacy rate doubled from 10 per cent to 20 per cent by 1936.[63]

The newsreel shows part of these efforts in a classroom scene featuring a boy and four girls writing on a blackboard using the new alphabet. Although it does not look striking to our modern eyes, there is an important detail in this scene that needs to be pointed out. Before Atatürk, a single-sex education system prevailed in schools in Turkey, but from 1924 onwards, this system was abandoned: a mixed-gender education system began in primary schools in the same year.[64] With this change, Atatürk also made the classrooms of Turkey look like the ones in greater parts of the 'civilized world'.

As 'Father of All Turks' shows Atatürk's attempts to make his people literate, the narrator notes: 'He gives youngsters a new ABC to study, along with his name and story.' In one of the images, a young girl can be seen learning how to read from a book on which Atatürk's name, story and image are printed. The significance of the name 'Atatürk' and its importance in school curricula at the time will now be deconstructed.

Atatürk is the assigned surname of Mustafa Kemal. On 21 June 1934, the Kemalists passed a law that made the adoption of a surname compulsory for every Turkish citizen. In the traditional Ottoman system, a Muslim man was known by his personal name, given at birth. This was usually complemented with a second name given during childhood, a nickname or a name based on occupation, area of residence, place of birth, and so on. Although some Muslim families used surnames, this was not common among the majority of Muslims. The Kemalists believed that the traditional way of naming was confusing and did not meet the needs and standards of a modern society. So like the citizens of modern Western countries, Turkish citizens had to adopt family names. This, of course, included Mustafa Kemal, but what surname should the first president of the Republic of Turkey adopt?

According to official sources, on 24 November 1934, the Grand National Assembly granted Mustafa Kemal the surname 'Atatürk', which literally means 'Father Turk' or 'Ancestor Turk', in gratitude for his service to the Turkish nation.[65] But this is only half of the story. The Turkish historian Mehmet Ö. Alkan suggests that Mustafa Kemal and his followers had thought long and hard before settling upon the name 'Atatürk'. They even established a special committee consisting of linguists and historians to find a suitable surname for Mustafa Kemal. The committee had to make sure that the name gave the president a positive image and would be of Turkish origin. Before the name Atatürk was adopted, thirteen other surnames had already been suggested to him. Mustafa Kemal was not satisfied with the names on the list, but he liked Safvet Arıkan addressing him as 'Ata Türk', a title that he had initially found ambitious, but finally adopted officially.[66] It quickly became the name by which he was best known.

The name 'Atatürk' has several implications. Most importantly, it implies the existence of a united Turkish people that has found a protective father in Mustafa Kemal. Bestowing upon him the honorific 'Atatürk' also implied both the original moment, and the person from which the nation of the Turks and its members (the modern Turks) emerged along with their progeny. In this sense, every Turkish citizen is a child of Atatürk. The foundational myth of the Turkish nation lies not only in a common ancestral past or genealogy but also in the common present of Mustafa Kemal's leadership, which establishes itself as the past of a future yet to come. The name Atatürk marked the foundation of the Turkish Republic as a new beginning and its leader as a new ancestor, a new father, who constituted a point of reference and an ideal-image of the Turk for generations to come. As the little girl featured in the newsreel shows, the national schools played a central role in the creation of a new 'imagined community' by teaching millions of children not only how to read and write in the new alphabet (and in a standard language) but also who 'Atatürk' was and what he meant to the 'Turkish nation'.

What this does not explain is why Atatürk's name keeps appearing as 'Kamâl' instead of 'Kemâl' Atatürk in the newsreel's intertitles. Was this a typographical mistake? I want to suggest it was not. On the contrary, by writing Atatürk's first name in this way, the newsreel was actually showing great sensitivity to the Turkish president's policies. To understand how a single letter can matter so much, we have to understand another aspect of Atatürk's world view at the time: his conception of the Turkish language and its history.

Mustafa Kemal's adoption of the family name Atatürk as well as the changed spelling of his given name was part of a larger movement related to the quest for an origin and identity for the 'Turkish nation'. With nationalism ascendant across the world in the 1930s, Mustafa Kemal and his followers were intensely searching for an origin story of the Turkish nation that would prove to the Western world that the Turks had always been a civilized, white race and a first class nation rather than a barbaric, 'yellow race' and second class, as was claimed by some Western historical discourses at the time.[67]

To undermine these racist discourses and to underscore the central role of 'Turks' in world history,[68] they developed a 'scientific' thesis called the Türk

Tarih Tezi (Turkish History Thesis) under the supervision of Mustafa Kemal. This thesis was published in 1930 as a book entitled *Türk Tarihinin Ana Hatları* (The Outline of Turkish History).[69] Furthermore, it was taught between 1931 and 1941 in high schools and its influence continued until the end of the twentieth century.

According to the Turkish History Thesis, in prehistoric times the homeland of the Turks was Central Asia, where there were plenty of water sources and immense inland seas.[70] In 9000 BC, Central Asia was a very fertile ground – a place like heaven, so to speak. While other peoples of the world were still living in stone and tree hollows, this fertile area was the cradle of civilization. People there had not only reached the level of the Iron Age but also domesticated animals and harvested agriculture for the first time in history.[71] Besides, they already knew mining, tool production and probably writing, making them culturally and technologically superior to all others.[72]

With the end of the Ice Age, however, the glaciers that fed the inland seas, rivers and creeks melted. As the majority of the water sources dried out, the green fertile plains turned into arid and barren deserts. Due to the droughts and the disappearance of inland seas, 'Turkish Migrations' began around 7000–5000 BC. According to the thesis, what was a great catastrophe for the Turks became a great benefit for the rest of the world as everywhere the Turks went, they spread civilization and taught peoples still living in more primitive stages their own skills in mining, farming and domesticating animals, as well as making tools, art works and probably writing.

The thesis solved many problems at once. It 'scientifically' proved that the Turks were not a second-class people or barbaric occupiers of other people's lands but were civilized and superior. There was a special emphasis on the whiteness of the Turks in the thesis, because in the racist discourses of many Western physical anthropologists at the time, Turks were classified as belonging to the 'yellow race' alongside Mongolians and other Asians, and deemed incapable of spreading civilization like white people. In other words, with the thesis, Mustafa Kemal and his followers wanted to say to the Europeans: we are one of you and we may even have made you what you are.

The thesis asserted that the Turks were 'the ancestors of world civilization', including the Western one. If this was true, adopting Western customs was not shameful but merely constituted a rediscovery of an ancient cultural heritage. Furthermore, the thesis aimed at bolstering national pride and the self-esteem of the citizens of a newly built country exhausted after many years of war with Europe. By establishing a link between the current people of Turkey and the 'Turks' of a mythical past, it aimed to tell contemporary Turkish society: be proud of your glorious history; your ancestors built a great Turkish civilization in the past and you can do the same today. Moreover, by promoting a unified national identity, the thesis suggested that all citizens of the Turkish Republic, despite their various ethnic backgrounds, were in fact already Turkish. Finally, by asserting a hereditary relationship between the prehistoric people of Anatolia and modern Turks, the thesis was designed to protect the new Turkish Republic from possible historical territorial claims by the Kurds, the Armenians, the Italians and the Greeks.

Still, the thesis also raised an important question for Mustafa Kemal and his followers. If the Turks not only constituted the origin of all human civilization but also were those who had developed and spread it throughout the world, their language must have influenced all other languages. To answer this question, Mustafa Kemal and his followers adopted, in 1935, the so-called Güneş Dil Teorisi (Sun Language Theory), based on the thesis of an obscure Viennese scholar called Dr. Herman Feodor Kvergić.[73] According to Kvergić's psycho-linguistic theory, language began with primitive people's realization of their own identity in relation to surrounding external objects, to which they first referred with gestures and then with sounds.[74] Kvergić suggested that Turkish pronouns reflect this most closely and he therefore proposed that Turkish must have been the prototypical human language.[75]

As doubtful as this theory was, it provided timely support for the Turkish History Thesis's argument that the Turks stood at the origin of world civilization. Not surprisingly, therefore, Kvergić's framework provided crucial inspiration for the language theory instrumentalized by Atatürk and the members of the TLA. According to this theory, it was specifically the sun through which primitive man became aware of his identity.[76] Language originated with primitive man looking towards the sun and shouting 'Aa!' Suitably, the vocal Aa or 'Ağ' in Turkish 'was the first-degree radical of the Turkish language'.[77] It originally meant 'sun', making it likely that other words such as 'yağmur (rain)' and 'çamur (mud)' were derived from this primitive root as primeval man's vocal expressions developed.[78] With great enthusiasm and energy, Mustafa Kemal and his followers began to 'prove' that, contrary to what Europeans had believed so far, the etymology of words in Western languages was actually Turkish.

In the scene from the newsreel showing Atatürk and the members of the TLA, they were probably working on these issues. İbrahim Necmi Dilmen, who was sitting on Atatürk's right side in the footage, had the theory, for instance, that the English word *god* and the German word *Gott* derived from the Turkish word *kut*, which means 'luck'.[79] He also asserted that the word *electric* derived from the Uyghur (a Turkic ethnic group) word *yaltrık*, meaning 'gleam, shining'.[80] Similarly, Agop Dilaçar, who stood at the blackboard, suggested that the word *philosophy* did not derive from the Greek words '*phil-*' (to love) and *sophia* (wisdom), but from the Turkish words *bil-* (to know) and *sav* (word-saying).[81] Although it is hard to see in the newsreel, Agop Dilaçar has written some words on the blackboard, including Tokar: Tsar, şar = El, most probably to show that the roots of another word are also 'Turkish'.

Before this theory was introduced, Mustafa Kemal had already initiated a *Dil İnkılabı* (language reform) by changing the alphabet from Arabo-Persian to Latin in 1928. Nevertheless, this was just the beginning of a long journey. The Kemalists also wanted to simplify the Turkish language and purify it from foreign influences. In 1930, Mustafa Kemal declared the following goal: 'The Turkish nation, which is well able to protect its territory and its sublime independence, must also liberate its language from the yoke of foreign languages.'[82] The purification drive was directed in the first place at Arabic and Persian grammar and vocabulary in Ottoman Turkish. Ottoman Turkish was not a vernacular language, but the administrative and literary language of the empire; it mainly consisted of Turkish-Arabic-Persian grammatical structures and vocabulary. By eliminating Arabic and Persian from the Turkish language and replacing them with 'pure Turkish' words and grammar structures, the Kemalists aimed at closing the gap between the official and popular language, and at creating a simplified standard language that would be accessible to ordinary citizens.[83]

As part of these efforts, in 1932, Mustafa Kemal established the Turkish Society for the Study of Language, which became the TLA in 1936.[84] In the same year, under the supervision of Mustafa Kemal, the First Turkish Language Congress took place.[85] The systematic study of the language began with the task of simplifying and purifying it. Old dictionaries and popular language books were scoured in order to find 'pure Turkish' words, methods were developed to derive new words from Old Turkic roots and popular words of foreign origin in daily use were replaced.[86] Moreover, researchers were sent to remote corners of the country in order to record the 'pure Turkish' words that were still used there.[87]

The whole country was mobilized to find replacements for 'foreign' words. Prepared by the Turkish Society for the Study of Language, booklets with slips were distributed throughout Turkey. State agents such as teachers, doctors and army officers, who had contact with common people, were supposed to collect 'pure Turkish' words from the local people, write them onto the slips and send them back to the association.[88] By examining, selecting and organizing these words, as well as by gathering other Turkish words from private individuals, old dictionaries and various texts, scholars compiled and published long lists of Turkish replacement words between 1932 and 1934.[89] Published by the Turkish Society for the Study of Language in 1934, *Tarama Dergisi* (The Search Journal) was the most prominent outcome of these efforts.[90] Newspapers and radio stations, too, were employed nationwide to collect 'pure Turkish' replacements from their audiences and to publicize them.[91] Ironically, however, as the heir of the multi-ethnic Ottoman Empire, Turkey had a mixed ethnic population so many non-Turkish words or even fake words collected from local populations or invented by the state agents and others entered the lists and *Tarama Dergisi* as 'pure Turkish' words. It was during the heyday of this movement, in 1934, that the surname 'Atatürk' was conferred upon Mustafa Kemal. He attributed great significance to the fact that his new name 'ata' was a word of Turkish origin.[92] However, the father/ancestor of Turks did face a problem concerning his given names, Mustafa Kemal, since both were of Arabic origin. Or were they?

Mustafa Kemal had never liked his birth name Mustafa, which was given to him by his family.[93] Mustafa was a name of Arabic origin meaning 'the chosen one'[94] and was a very popular male name in the Islamic world because it was also an epithet of the prophet Mohammed. According to Atatürk's sister Makbule Atadan, the name Mustafa was given to him by their father Ali Rıza Efendi. When Ali Rıza Efendi was a child, he accidentally caused his brother Mustafa's death while pushing him on a swing. To cherish his brother's memory, he named his son after him.[95]

As much as Mustafa detested his first name, he loved his second name Kemal, because this was a name he had earned in his youth. According to Atatürk's account, when he was in the military preparatory school in Salonica, his interest and success in mathematics attracted the attention of his mathematics teacher, whose name was also Mustafa. One day, his teacher suggested, 'My son, your name is Mustafa and so is mine. This won't work. There must be a distinction. From now on your name should be Mustafa Kemal.'[96] Kemal was another name of Arabic origin, meaning 'maturity' or 'perfection'.[97] The Arabic origin of the name, however, did not really seem to matter much at the time. After all, Kemal was also the name of one of Mustafa Kemal's favourite poets, Namık Kemal. In those days, many young Ottomans adored the famous patriotic poet or 'poet of liberty', particularly because of his opposition to the absolutist Ottoman regimes.[98]

According to Alkan, Atatürk seems to have embraced the name Kemal during his army years; accordingly, his name appeared as M. Kemal on the three books he authored on military subjects.[99] After receiving the surname Atatürk on his first identity card in 1934, his given name appeared as Kemal and his surname as Atatürk.[100] It seems that Mustafa had disappeared altogether. As mentioned before, these were the years of language reform, when Atatürk was trying to liberate the Turkish language from the hegemony of foreign languages. Consequently, the father of the Turks could not possibly have a name of Arabic origin.

But what about Kemal? Was that not also a name of Arabic origin? It was, but it did not matter, because in February 1935 Atatürk began to use his supposedly 'original' name Kamâl. According to *Tarama Dergisi* (1934), *kamal* meant 'fortification', 'castle', 'army' and 'shield'.[101] In 1935, a new identity card was prepared with this name, which was introduced to the public in the *Ulus* (Nation) newspaper on 22 January.[102] When the press noticed the presidential name change in the bulletins, they thought it must be a mistake and asked for a clarification from the government.[103] On 4 February 1935, the government's official news agency Anadolu Ajansı gave the following explanation:

> We have seen that the leader Atatürk's original name was written as Kamâl in today's bulletin. The ground reason for such writing is understood after our enquiry in this matter.[104] In the light of our information, the name 'Kamâl' that Atatürk bears is not an Arabic word, nor does it have the meaning indicated by the Arabic word kemal ['maturity', 'perfection']. Atatürk's [original] personal name, which is being retained, is 'Kamâl', the Turkish meaning of which is army and fortification. As the circumflex accent on the final a softens the k the pronunciation closely approximates that of the Arabic 'Kemal'. That is the full extent of the resemblance.[105]

Whether the public believed this explanation or not, it meant that all official 'Kemals' had to change as well. In 1935, the ideology of Kemalizm turned into Kamâlizm, the government's international propaganda journal *La Turquie kemaliste* became *La Turquie kamâlist*, and in all other official documents, the name would henceforth appear as Kamâl.[106] Many foreign publications also showed sensitivity to the change in a single letter of the Turkish president's name.[107] As the intertitles of the newsreel show, the producers of *The March of Time* chose to incorporate the change, writing Atatürk's name as Kamâl Atatürk.

Atatürk used his novel Turkish name Kamâl enthusiastically for a while, but one-and-a-half years later he realized that 'kamal' was neither a Turkish word nor meant what it was supposed to. However, since there had already been a huge effort to turn all official Kemals into Kamâls, it was difficult to retreat publicly. To make a soft transition, he avoided using the name as much as he could, either by not using it at all or by signing documents as K. Atatürk.[108] Following his example, all official Kamâls were changed back to the old spelling of Kemal. An official explanation was never given, so we have no way of knowing the full reasons behind it. Nevertheless, it is obvious that the issue with Atatürk's name was linked to the Turkish Language Reform.

Linguistic nationalism was not only a popular concern in Turkey but almost everywhere at the time. As Burke notes, language purification has always been an important issue in the history of nationalism.[109] There were strong movements during the nineteenth and twentieth centuries in European countries to eliminate foreign words.[110] As was the case in the Turkish Language Reform, peasants were often romanticized by these movements. Supposedly less exposed to foreign cultures, their language was considered 'pure' or 'unspoiled', and therefore taken as a model for the 'national language'.[111] In her book *Purity and Danger*, Mary Douglas shows that purity and impurity (or, in other words, clean and dirty) are symbolic concepts that serve to create and maintain a community's cultural boundaries.[112] Since shared language is one the most significant symbols of a community, 'foreign' words can be seen as a threat to the unity and integrity of the national community.[113] As Atatürk's struggle with his own name shows, however, attempts at purification did not always work.

What happened to the Turkish Language Reform? Atatürk gradually lost his interest in the Sun Language Theory, partly due to the lack of academic support for it in the international arena, and eventually abandoned the extreme purification of the Turkish language. Instead, he increasingly concentrated on developing a technical vocabulary, even publishing a book called *Geometri* (1937) introducing several new Turkish words of his own invention that are still in use today.[114]

And what of the two men who appeared with Atatürk at the recorded meeting of the TLA? With the introduction of the surname law, Hagop Martanyan, who was of Armenian origin, was endowed with the Turkish family name Dilaçar by Atatürk, in recognition of his contributions to the Turkish language. He became known as Agop Dilaçar, with 'dil' meaning 'language' in Turkish and 'açar' a neologism manufactured from the Turkish verb *açmak* 'to open', which replaced the Greek word *anahtar* for 'key'. Dilaçar means, then, a language key or someone who unlocks the language. Similarly, İbrahim Necmi received the surname 'dilmen' from Atatürk in recognition of his contributions, becoming İbrahim Necmi Dilmen. According to the TLA's dictionary, Dilmen signifies a person who knows the language and who articulates it beautifully.[115] Atatürk only devised surnames for people he liked and it was considered a great honour to obtain a surname from him at the time.[116]

Returning to the newsreel, after the scene of the school children learning to read and write, it continues by showing the Kemalist government's efforts to teach the new alphabet to every Turkish citizen. We see some men, dressed in European fashion, sitting and reading in a café. A Turkish military officer together with two soldiers enters the café and opens a roll on which is written 'Hayat Alfabesi' (Life Language). He undertakes a surprise examination of one of the men, asking him to read words written in the new alphabet. After the man shakes his head, indicating that he cannot read, the scene changes and two prisoners are shown behind iron bars. While these scenes are shown, the narrator tells us: 'He [Atatürk] gives his people two years to learn reading and writing the simpler European way. He sends his soldiers out to give the oldsters surprise examining. Packing off to jail go old townsmen.'

As mentioned before, *The March of Time* newsreels frequently used restaged scenes and re-enactments in studios in order to make their footage look real. In 'Inside Nazi Germany' (1938), for instance, there was a scene showing a Nazi storm trooper entering a house in order to collect funds from a housewife. This was a restaged scene shot in Hoboken, New Jersey, where there was a large German community.[117] The similar scenes at the café and the jail in 'Father of All Turks' also appear to be staged. Although the Kemalist regime did make the new Turkish alphabet compulsory, it banned the public use of Arabic script in 1928 and even examined the literacy of civil servants in the new script;[118] there were no prison sentences for those who could not read it.

With the prohibition of the public use of the Arabic alphabet, all signs in public spaces had to be replaced with signs in the Latin alphabet. The newsreel shows some examples of these new signs such as: 'Otomobil–Pasaport Vizalari', 'Tramvay Mecburi Durak', 'Max Baer – American Tiraş Biçaklari', 'Telgraf' and 'Sokoni Vakum Oyl Kompani'. As with the visible change in headdress, with this reform, the Kemalists managed to give public spaces, shops and companies a Westernized look, as the newsreel shows.

In the next scene of the newsreel, a group of male students are putting on their shoes in a tribune. They are not fully dressed and wear only white shorts. This scene must have been shot by Julien Bryan at the Gazi Education Institute in Ankara, because scholarly research conducted in his son Sam Bryan's private archives uncovered a still photo from it. On the back of the photo is a handwritten note by Julien Bryan stating 'Students Dressing for Track Meet at Gazi Atatürk, Ankara'. Opened in 1926, the Gazi Education Institute was one of the new educational institutes set up to train teachers. A true follower of Enlightenment ideals, Atatürk believed in the power of science and education to change and improve society. Therefore, during his time in power, he campaigned for widespread public education, and opened several schools and educational institutes in Turkey such as the Gazi Education Institute. The newsreel scene shows young men running around the track towards the camera, while the narrator says: 'To make Turkish youth tough and healthy, he orders them out to the athletic field.' Atatürk specifically supported physical education in schools, making it a compulsory part of the curriculum, to create fit and healthy youths or, in other words, a strong nation. However, this scene seems designed above all to counter the Western Orientalist image of the old Ottoman Empire as the 'sick man of Europe' by presenting the American audience with the young, masculine and strong bodies of Turkish citizens.

After the scene showing athletic activity, the newsreel shows young people in a business school class. In contrast to the images of the Ottoman Empire featured in Western Orientalist discourse, in which women were represented as secluded in domestic spaces such as the home and the harem, or wearing the veil in public spaces, the newsreel introduces the image of the new 'liberated' republican Turkish woman who is unveiled, dressed in a European fashion and shares public spaces such as the business school with men. Like many previous scenes, these images create the impression that there was virtually no difference between the new Turkey and the West. A business school classroom in New York, London or Paris in the 1930s would have looked much the same as the classroom presented here. When the American audience saw these pictures from Turkey in the 1930s, they would seem familiar, for in the United States, too, young women and men were learning the new, crucial skills of typing and stenography for business. This would help them to identify with the Turkish youth and maybe even to think: they are just like us.

After this scene, the narrator states, 'He [Atatürk] brings in foreigners to show girls how to dress, how to manage their homes, the European way' as the newsreel shows images of young women tailoring European clothes, followed by a scene of a group of young women looking at a fashion magazine and images of two women in uniform setting a dinner table in the European way. These scenes seem to have been shot by Julien Bryan at a girls' institute, most probably Ismet Pasha's Girls' Institute in Ankara.[119] Established in the 1920s, the girls' institutes were secondary-level vocational schools built by the Kemalist regime in order to educate girls with a special emphasis on their training as housewives.[120] The Girls' Institutes distinguished themselves as imparting a 'modern' education to young women, and thus emphasized new skills over traditional ones. The schools took Western, and particularly Parisian fashion as a model when teaching girls how to produce clothes.[121] This is indicated in the newsreel by the images of young girls looking at women's clothing in a magazine. Furthermore, as the newsreel shows, they instructed girls in laying tables the French way. Like many other educational institutes, the girls' institutes were considered agents of social change. They were established to create the ideal type of woman, befitting the modern, secular and Westernized vision of the Kemalist regime. The newsreel suggests that they were successful in this aim.

The next scenes show modern medical practices in Turkey, while the narrator says: 'He [Atatürk] imports doctors and equipment to teach Turkey the wonders of medicine and therapy.' From 1933 onwards, Atatürk modernized Turkey's health care system through a series of reforms.[122] As German-speaking scholars, most of whom were Jewish, were escaping the rise of National Socialism in Central Europe, Kemalist Turkey opened its doors to them. More than a hundred distinguished scholars and their families took refuge in Turkey. The Kemalist government's decision to welcome these scholars was humanitarian as much as it was pragmatic. Impoverished by the long wars and reduced in population, the young republic urgently needed experts in every imaginable field, but primarily in medicine, as there were acute problems in public health. The infant mortality was high and life expectancy was low. Issues such as local water standards and malnutrition had to be dealt with immediately.[123] In addition, there were epidemic diseases among the population, such as malaria, tuberculosis and syphilis. Bringing with them the latest knowledge and technology, the émigré scholars made major contributions to both medical education and practice in Turkey. Above all, they introduced modern concepts and methods of public health care, collecting data from the local population and compiling the first nationwide public health statistics.[124] They also played an important role in the prevention, diagnosis and treatment of public diseases.

By opening Turkey's doors to the refugee academics, Atatürk fulfilled a great humanitarian task. He offered them and their families a safe haven in Turkey where they could stay and continue their career. Yet Turkey's welcoming of the refugees cannot only be explained by their value to the young republic. In those days, many Western countries needed qualified personnel and had the power to take care of them better than financially straitened Turkey, but most of them turned their backs on the Jewish refugees, refusing to give employment or even visas. Some of them did not dare to make the Nazi regime their enemy, while others were subject to a prevalent anti-Semitic atmosphere. As Arnold Reisman points out, the United States had very restrictive immigration laws and anti-Semitic hiring policies at its universities at the time.[125] Even a distinguished scholar like Albert Einstein considered Turkey as an option while waiting for an answer from Princeton, because he had been told that they would not 'hire Jews'.[126]

The newsreel continues by showing scenes illustrating Atatürk's reforms in the economic sphere. First, a model farm is shown with a large amount of crops. The next scene features a tractor ploughing a field as the voice-over states: 'On model farms, Turkey learns the methods of big scale agriculture.' As already mentioned in the previous chapter, modern farms and tractors were important symbols of the industrialization of Turkish agriculture. The huge amount of crops gathered at the model farm shows the farm's productivity. Significantly, the farmer driving the tractor is dressed in Western-style clothing, dons a Western-style hat and wears dark glasses for protection from the sun and dust. This image contrasts with earlier images of Turkish peasants mostly dressed in the traditional way and undertaking manual agricultural activities. By showing images of the model farm, the newsreel suggests that Turkey is learning a new type of large-scale agriculture.

At the beginning of the twentieth century, small- and large-scale agriculture constituted two different types of farming.[127] Small-scale agriculture was mostly undertaken by individual farmers with help from their family members on a family-owned small piece of land. This type of farming relied on human and animal labour. It was mostly associated with inefficiency and low productivity, and was seen as a sign of economic underdevelopment from the perspective of industrialized countries such as the United States. Large-scale agriculture, on the other hand, was based on corporate (in the United States) or state (in the Soviet Union) ownership, managed and run by professional employees on large pieces of land. Unlike small-scale farming, it was characterized by the extensive use of modern techniques, farming machinery and chemical fertilizers. Associated with efficiency and high productivity, it was considered an important feature of a developed/industrialized country. By showing scenes of a productive, large-scale model farm with a tractor, the newsreel implies that, thanks to Atatürk's reforms, Turkey was rapidly catching up with the industrialized countries of the West.

The next scene shows the Sümerbank textile factory in Kayseri, which was opened in 1935. The camera first focuses on the modern architectural design of the factory buildings from the outside, and then shows images of textile and cotton mills at work from the inside. Over these images, the narrator states: 'Hoping to make the nation self-sufficient through industrialization, [Atatürk] subsidizes new industry, builds cotton mills.' As mentioned in the newsreel, 'self-sufficiency' is a key term in the rationale behind Atatürk's economic policies. As a result of the First World War and the Turkish War of Independence, Turkey's economy was largely devastated when Atatürk came to power. In the nineteenth century, the Ottoman state had been unable to keep up with industrial developments in capitalist Europe, and its economy had become increasingly peripheral in relation to Europe.[128] Although Turkey was still part of the European capitalist economic system, it rather served as a market for Europe or as a supplier of food and raw materials.[129] Thus, its economy gradually became dependent on Europe and accumulated huge foreign debts, which contributed to the failure of the Ottoman state.

The Turkish nationalists wanted to change this situation by gaining economic independence. Raw materials such as cotton, which were previously sold to Europe, were to be processed by Turkish industry and then sold on national and foreign markets. The plan looked good on paper, but Turkey lacked processing capacity. To build an adequate national industry, it needed capital and know-how. Thus, the Turkish government turned to an old comrade, the Soviet Union, to realize its industrialization programme. The Soviet Union not only provided loans to the Turkish government but also helped to build the Sümerbank textile factory (*kombinat*) in Kayseri, something the newsreel does not mention. With its 33,000 mechanical spindles, this factory was considered one of the greatest industrial achievements of the young republic.[130] Besides the main factory building, it comprised a small town with facilities for workers, including housing, a day-care centre and a social club, sports facilities, a swimming pool and a cinema. With all these features, the factory was an emblem of modern Turkish industry. By displaying the machines of the factory in action, the newsreel conveys the message that Atatürk was mechanizing Turkey and turning it rapidly into a modern, industrialized country.

Because Turkey was an agrarian society, the government prioritized industries based on agricultural products such as cotton and, above all, sugar, which was a staple need for the country.[131] The Ottoman state had not succeeded in building a national sugar industry, thus, the country had to import almost all of the sugar needed. During the First World War, for instance, crystalized sugar was imported from Russia, and sugar cubes from Austria and the Netherlands.[132] Due to the conditions of war, there were problems delivering the sugar, which caused an enormous hike in prices.[133] Therefore, as soon as the republic was established, building a national sugar industry capable of processing sugar beets at home became one of the primary economic aims for the new government. Sugar factories were opened in Uşak and Alpullu in 1926, in Eskişehir in 1933 and finally in Turhal in 1935.[134] The newsreel shows workers loading sugar beets onto freight trains and beets being taken to be processed by industrial machines. This signalled the industrial accomplishments of Atatürk's regime and, by extension, certified Turkey's economic development.

After this, the newsreel shows a long shot of a bustling Turkish port, followed by a close shot of the names of foreign cargo ships and their cities of origin: Mardinian-Liverpool, Predsjednik Kopajtić-Split, Hercules-Amsterdam and Angora-Bremen. The varied locations from which these ships have come illustrate Turkey's status as an expanding market and hub for international trade.

Intertitle 4

The Turkish national anthem begins to play as a new intertitle appears: 'As his country moves slowly towards internal security, Dictator Atatürk takes his steps to ensure its international security.' The voice-over states:

> Late in 1936, under cover of Europe's squabbles, Kemal Atatürk secretly fortifies the Dardanelles. Too late for refusal, he politely asks and gets permission of the League of Nations. Then in full possession of one of the Mediterranean's most vital strongholds, he relaxes, sends his envoys out to fish in the pond of international politics. Besides agreements with Russia, the Balkans and Great Britain, suave foreign minister Dr. Tevfik Rüştü Aras negotiates a new understanding with France and the League of Nations about Syria; he makes a new friend out of potent Italy. But all these things Turkish diplomats must do without committing Turkey to any of Europe's isms. For the father of the Turks is no political theorist, and what he has built up, he has built up not for Fascism, not for Communism, but for Turkey.

In order to make sense of these words, it is important to look at Europe's political situation and Atatürk's foreign policy during the interwar period. As mentioned in the previous chapter, in the late 1930s, the prospect of war was looming over Europe. The Nazi Germany and Fascist Italy wanted to redraw the map of Europe and the rest of the world. In 1936, Italy invaded Ethiopia, claiming it as their territory. The Civil War broke out in Spain in the same year. Mussolini's Italy and Hitler's Germany openly supported the nationalists led by General Franco against the Republicans. Renouncing the Locarno Treaties that guaranteed European borders, Germany occupied the Rhineland on 7 March 1936. Although Germany's action alarmed the former Allies of the Great War, they could not prevent the remilitarization of the Rhineland. Also, the League of Nations had proven impotent against fascist aggression in Europe. While

Germany was a rather distant concern for the Turkish government, Italy posed a serious threat to the country's security because it possessed the Dodecanese Islands near the Turkish coast, which it had already fortified.¹³⁵ Mussolini's territorial claims to Asia and Africa also reminded the Turkish government of the Italian occupation of southwest Turkey after the First World War.¹³⁶

Atatürk knew how to turn Europe's political crises into opportunities. At the Lausanne conference in 1923, Turkey had signed a strait convention stipulating demilitarization of the Straits area (Bosphorus and Dardanelles) and control of all civilian and military traffic by an international commission. At this point, Atatürk could have chosen to use brute force to overthrow the international commission and remilitarize the straits, but instead he used peaceful means.¹³⁷ These consisted of bringing the issue in front of the League on 10 April 1936 and pressing for a revision of the straits convention in view of the political situation in Europe and Turkey's apprehensions concerning its security and sovereignty.¹³⁸

Atatürk's peaceful move was more than welcome at a time when international law had been violated repeatedly and the European situation was becoming increasingly tense. In response to his request, Turkey received the support of almost all countries in the league, except for Italy. Negotiations led to the Montreux conference (22 June–20 July 1936), from which Turkey emerged with a new straits convention.¹³⁹ Signed on 20 July 1936, the Montreux Convention not only gave control of civilian and military transits in the straits to the Turkish government but also allowed remilitarization of the area.¹⁴⁰ This was a great diplomatic and moral victory for the Ankara government, which eventually achieved sovereign control over the straits.

The newsreel refers to these events by showing a French map of the straits marking the fortified area, followed by a shot of a huge cannon, symbolizing the strong defensive capability of Turkey. The cannon is watched over by a disciplined soldier, indicating with his alert body language the readiness of the Turkish army to respond to any aggressions. Over these images, the narrator states: 'Late in 1936, under cover of Europe's squabbles, Kemal Atatürk secretly fortifies the Dardanelles. Too late for refusal, he politely asks and gets permission of the League of Nations.'

This example clearly shows that news does not simply show what happened but rather tells a story about what happened. The newsreel suggests that Atatürk had already fortified the Dardanelles before getting permission from the league and that the league agreed only because it was too late to say no. Although this was not quite the case, the newsreel portrays Atatürk as a shrewd politician, essentially tricking the league. Although the newsreel generally depicts Atatürk in a positive light, this part betrays some scepticism about his foreign policy.

In the next scene, Atatürk is shown on the beach, coming out of the sea after a swim at his summerhouse in Florya. He is shown being offered a bathrobe by a man and drying himself. According to the newsreel, these are images of Atatürk relaxing after gaining 'full possession of one the Mediterranean's most vital strongholds'. After this, the newsreel shows scenes from a convention of the League of Nations, followed by images of some diplomats including the Turkish foreign minister Tevfik Rüştü Aras. While showing these images, the voice-over informs the audience about Turkey's diplomatic efforts: 'Besides agreements with Russia, the Balkans and Great Britain, suave foreign minister Dr. Tevfik Rüştü Aras negotiates a new understanding with France and the League of Nations about Syria; he makes a new friend out of potent Italy.'

In the late 1920s and early 1930s, Turkey made several agreements and built alliances in order to provide it with security. In 1928, the Turkish government signed a treaty of neutrality with Italy. In 1930, it signed a treaty of friendship with Greece, a country that had previously invaded Turkey. Ankara's policy of neutrality and its peaceful international relations, even with its former invaders, played an important role in Turkey's admission to the League of Nations in 1932. Later on, however, Mussolini's expansionist policy in the Mediterranean prompted the Turkish government to establish close relationships with the non-revisionist Balkan states. Thus, Turkey entered the Balkan Pact (Entente) with Greece, Romania and Yugoslavia on 9 February 1934. Because of his efforts to maintain peace, Atatürk was even nominated for the Nobel Peace Prize by the Greek Prime Minister Eleftherios Venizelos.[141]

As in the Balkans, in the Near East Turkey was seen as a peacemaker. After the Great War, Turkey had lost its Sanjak of Alexandretta (District of İskenderun and Antakya) to French-mandated Syria. When France made the first steps to relinquish their mandate in Syria in 1936, Atatürk sent his foreign minister Tevfik Rüştü Aras to the League of Nations to negotiate with France.[142] The Sanjak, which had become the Republic of Hatay in 1938, finally joined the Turkish Republic in 1939. Atatürk did not live to see this, yet he was the one who paved the way to a solution without violating international law.

So, the newsreel was actually reporting about the negotiations between Turkey and France while they were still taking place.

During the interwar era, then, the main purpose of Turkey's foreign policy was maintaining peaceful relations with other countries. Even with its potential enemy Italy, Turkey avoided direct confrontation and tried to solve issues by diplomatic means. The narrator's comment that Atatürk made a 'new friend' out of 'potent Italy' is an exaggeration; it only applies to the period before Italy's invasion of Ethiopia in 1936 and even then it was hard to speak of a friendship. The relationship between Turkey and Italy was rather neutral, consisting of short-lived collaborations in certain political, economic and military matters.[143] Nevertheless, from the perspective of the American newsreel, this relationship seems to have still been too close for comfort.

It is significant that the newsreel calls the foreign minister 'suave'. This can be a positive label, referring to someone who is sophisticated, but it can also have an undertone of negativity, implying that someone is a little too smooth. In the way it comments on Atatürk's foreign policy, the newsreel is clearly taking an American perspective that includes a certain suspicion. There is, therefore, a noticeable disparity between the image Atatürk seeks to project and the image that the newsreel conveys to the American public. Atatürk intended to appear to Bryan's camera as a democratic and transparent leader, but the newsreel used the same footage to portray him as a benevolent dictator or an enlightened despot. The voice-over is what enables the introduction of a discrepancy between what Atatürk wanted to project and what the newsreel suggests.

In the second-to-last scene, the newsreel shows Atatürk taking off his bathrobe, putting it on a table and lying down on the beach to sunbathe, with one leg crossed over the other. As these images are shown, the narrator states: 'For the father of the Turks is no political theorist, and what he has built up, he has built up not for Fascism, not for Communism, but for Turkey.' Finally, the newsreel returns to the image of the cannon on the straits with the soldier keeping watch over it, only now the soldier is no longer standing still but marching. This constitutes a perfect ending for *The March of Time* and the narrator finishes the episode by saying: 'Time marches on'. At this point, the Turkish national anthem stops playing and 'THE END' appears.

The ending of the newsreel brings the story to a neat narrative closure. Throughout, the newsreel showed the audience how Atatürk – as the hero of the narrative – resolved all conflicts successfully. Having saved, built and developed Turkey, the final scenes show the mythical hero resting on the beach after doing his job. This last part of the newsreel contains some interesting metaphors. Atatürk's emergence from the sea, for example, conveys a sense of the country's rebirth. The seaside, moreover, defines Turkey's borders both literally and metaphorically, so if Atatürk can relax on the beach at such a critical geopolitical time, the suggestion is that Turkey must be prepared to counter any military attack on its sovereignty. If the penultimate image of Atatürk in his swimsuit on the beach was not convincing enough to deliver this message, the final image of the cannon with the marching soldier would certainly do the job.

Conclusion

This chapter analysed an episode of *The March of Time* newsreel series titled 'Father of All Turks' in order to understand how Atatürk and his revolution was represented to Western audiences in the 1930s. The newsreel offered glimpses of the making of Atatürk's image and his representation in contemporary media and showed how the Kemalist modernization programme was perceived in the Western world. Throughout his time in power, Atatürk sought to achieve and project a vision of Turkey as modern, civilized and democratic. To realize this goal, he made constant reforms and carefully constructed his image across various media as a Western-style leader who had successfully modernized and secularized his country.

Despite his attempts to present himself as a democratic and Western-style leader, *The March of Time* newsreel's presentation of Atatürk shows that he could ultimately not fully control the message conveyed by his representation on film. By editing the footage and adding a voice-over, *The March of Time* created its own narrative for the carefully constructed images, portraying Atatürk very differently than he had intended. Atatürk would most certainly not have wanted to be referred to as a dictator or as someone who had deceived the League of Nations by asking for permission for reinforcements that were already in place. Although the newsreel offers a largely positive image of Atatürk and his reforms, there are a few moments where it is clear that it presents an American perspective of him that also includes some scepticism.

Furthermore, it establishes a binary opposition between the benevolent 'dictatorship' of Turkey and the liberal democracy of the United States.

Although it is not known how cinema audiences received the newsreel episode 'Father of All Turks' in the United States or Europe, it is clear that the president of Turkey managed to impress its producers. Although they referred to Atatürk as a dictator throughout the newsreel, the images and narrative characterized him as a benevolent one. In its narrative, the newsreel presented Atatürk as a heroic figure, almost single-handedly saving Turkey from its various enemies and building, through cultural, educational and economic reforms, a modern Turkish Republic on the ruins of the Ottoman Empire. Paying particular attention to Turkey's strategic importance at a time of heightened international tensions, the newsreel projected an image of Atatürk as a clever statesman taking shrewd steps to protect Turkey's security. It finished Atatürk's story with a happy ending in which the hero of the narrative resolved all conflicts and turned Turkey into a strong, modern and independent nation-state on whose shores he could peacefully rest.

Notes

1. Raymond Fielding, *The American Newsreel, 1911–1967* (Oklahoma: University of Oklahoma Press, 1980), 3–5.
2. Ibid., 37–45.
3. Raymond Fielding, *The American Newsreel: A Complete History, 1911–1967*, 2nd ed. (Jefferson, North Carolina: MacFarland: 2006), 1.
4. Raymond Fielding, *The March of Time: 1935–1951* (New York: Oxford University Press, 1978).
5. Ibid., 6–7.
6. Ibid.
7. Ibid., 187–201.
8. Ibid., 191.
9. According to Fielding, the combat footage in 'Father of All Turks' was shot by De Rochemont when he was in Turkey and later incorporated into the film by him. Louis de Rochemont, who used to be an officer in the US Navy, had filmed Mustafa Kemal's retaking of İzmir and the great fire of İzmir in 1922 when still on active duty. See ibid., 171.
10. Fielding, *The March of Time*, 337.

11 Ibid., 4.
12 Raymond Fielding, 'Time Flickers Out: Notes on the Passing of The "March of Time"', *The Quarterly of Film Radio and Television* 11, no. 4 (1957): 354–61. doi:10.2307/1209995.

   See also Stephen E. Bowles, 'And Time Marched On: The Creation of The March of Time'. *Journal of the University Film Association* 29, no. 1 (1977): 7. http://www.jstor.org/stable/20687350.
13 Peter Burke, *Eyewitnessing: The Uses of Images as Historical Evidence* (Ithaca: Cornell University Press, 2008), 65–9.
14 Ibid., 68.
15 Ibid., 69.
16 Ibid., 29.
17 Ibid.
18 Ibid., 69.
19 Ibid., 71.
20 Turkish sociologist Emre Kongar states that not everybody was allowed to take Atatürk's photo whenever they wished; photographers had to wait for Atatürk to strike a pose. According to Kongar, photos of Atatürk were also mostly taken from a low position to make him appear taller than he was. See Emre Kongar, 'Atatürk'le devam eden bir hayat ...' in *O Daima Şıktı: Gazi'nin Son Tanıkları Anlatıyor*, ed. Nebil Özgentürk (Istanbul: Bir Yudum Insan Yayınevi, 2010), 190.
21 Bernard Lewis, *The Emergence of Modern Turkey*, 3rd ed. (London: Oxford University Press, 2002), 292.
22 Erik-Jan Zürcher, 'In the name of the father, the teacher and the hero: Atatürk personality cult in Turkey', in *Political Leadership Leaders and Charisma*, ed. Vivian Ibrahim and Margit Wunsch (London: Routledge, 2012), 137.
23 Civilization meant the modern civilization of the West for Atatürk. See Lewis, *The Emergence of Modern Turkey*, 292.
24 Utkan Kocatürk, *Doğumundan Ölümüne Kadar Kaynakçalı Atatürk Günlüğü*, 2. Basım (Ankara: Atatürk Araştırma Merkezi, 2007), 376–8.
25 Andrew Mango, *Atatürk* (London: John Murray, 2004), 433–7. See also Lewis, *The Emergence of Modern Turkey*, 267–71.
26 Mango, *Atatürk*, 434.
27 Ibid.
28 Ibid.
29 A fez is a short cylindrical red felt cap, generally with a tassel attached to the top.
30 Mango, *Atatürk*, 434.

31 Ibid.
32 Ibid.
33 Ibid.
34 Kocatürk, *Doğumundan Ölümüne Kadar Kaynakçalı Atatürk Günlüğü*, 376–8.
35 Ibid.
36 Lewis, *The Emergence of Modern Turkey*, 268–9.
37 Mango, *Atatürk*, 434.
38 Ibid.
39 Lewis, *The Emergence of Modern Turkey*, 269. See also Mango, *Atatürk*, 435.
40 Mango, *Atatürk*, 435.
41 Lewis, *The Emergence of Modern Turkey*, 269. See also Mango, *Atatürk*, 435.
42 Mango, *Atatürk*, 435.
43 Ibid.
44 Ibid., 436.
45 Ibid.
46 Ibid.
47 Ibid.
48 Donald Quataert, 'Clothing Laws, State, and Society in the Ottoman Empire, 1720–1829', *International Journal of Middle East Studies* 29, no. 3 (1997): 403, 405, accessed 2 February 2015, http://www.jstor.org/stable/164587.
49 Ibid., 413–14. See also Lewis, *The Emergence of Modern Turkey*, 267.
50 Lewis, *The Emergence of Modern Turkey*, 267.
51 Ibid., 268–9.
52 Michel Foucault, *Discipline and Punish: The Birth of the Prison*, trans. Alan Sheridan (London: Penguin, 1991).
53 Mango, *Atatürk*, 436.
54 Lewis, *The Emergence of Modern Turkey*, 278.
55 Ibid. 279.
56 Geoffrey Lewis, *The Turkish Language Reform: A Catastrophic Success* (New York: Oxford University Press, 2010), 29.
57 Ibid., 37.
58 Turkish Statistical Institute, *Turkey in Statistics* (Ankara: Türkiye İstatistik Kurumu Matbaası, 2014), 25.
59 Benedict Anderson, *Imagined Communities: Reflections on the Origin and Spread of Nationalism* (London: Verso, 2006), 45.
60 Lewis, *The Turkish Language Reform*, 35.
61 Mango, *Atatürk*, 466.
62 Ibid., 467.

63 Ibid.
64 Yücel Özkaya, 'Cumhuriyetin İlanı ve Rejim Olarak Eğitime Katkıları', *Atatürk Araştırma Merkezi Dergisi* 56 (2003): 471–81.
65 Mehmet Ö. Alkan, '"Atatürk" Soyadı Nasıl Bulundu?' *Toplumsal Tarih* 205 (2011): 49–50.
66 The name was used for the first time by Safvet Arıkan when he addressed Mustafa Kemal as 'our great leader Ata Türk Mustafa Kemal' during a speech delivered at a meeting of the Türk Dili Tetkik Cemiyeti (Turkish Society for the Study of Language) in Ankara on 26 September 1934. See ibid., 50–2.
67 For Atatürk and the republican elits' interest in anthropology, see Zafer Toprak, *Darwin'den Dersim'e Cumhuriyet ve Antropoloji* (Istanbul: Doğan Kitap, 2012).
68 *Türk Tarihinin Ana Hatları: Kemalist Yönetimin Tarih Tezi* (İstanbul: Kaynak Yayınları, 1996), 25.
69 Ibid., 18.
70 Ibid., 57–9.
71 Ibid. 58.
72 Ibid., 325, 340.
73 M. Şükrü Hanioğlu, *Atatürk: An Intellectual Biography* (Princeton: Princeton University Press, 2011), 176.
74 Lewis, *The Turkish Language Reform*, 57.
75 Ibid.
76 Ibid.
77 Ibid.
78 Ibid., 58.
79 Ibid., 60.
80 Ibid.
81 Ibid.
82 Ibid., 42.
83 Ibid., 2.
84 Ibid., 45.
85 Ibid., 47.
86 Ibid., 49.
87 Mango, *Atatürk*, 495.
88 Lewis, *The Turkish Language Reform*, 49.
89 Ibid., 50.
90 The full title of the dictionary was as follows: Osmanlıcadan Türkçeye Söz Karşılıkları Tarama Dergisi (Search Journal of Equivalents in Turkish for Ottoman Words).

91 Lewis, *The Turkish Language Reform,* 50.
92 Alkan, '"Atatürk" soyadı nasıl bulundu?', 52.
93 Mehmet Ö. Alkan, 'Mustafa'dan Kamâl'a Atatürk'ün İsimleri', *Toplumsal Tarih* 204 (2010): 57.
94 Ibid.
95 Ibid.
96 Ibid.
97 Hanioğlu, *Atatürk,* 23.
98 Ibid.
99 Alkan, 'Mustafa'dan Kamâl'a Atatürk'ün İsimleri', 58–9.
100 Ibid., 59.
101 Lewis, *The Turkish Language Reform,* 55.
102 Alkan, 'Mustafa'dan Kamâl'a Atatürk'ün İsimleri', 59.
103 Ibid., 59–60.
104 Ibid., 60.
105 Ibid., 62. See also Lewis, *The Turkish Language Reform,* 55.
106 Alkan, 'Mustafa'dan Kamâl'a Atatürk'ün İsimleri', 60.
107 Ibid.
108 See, for instance, his correspondence with President Roosevelt in Chapter 4.
109 Peter Burke, *Languages and Communities in Early Modern Europe* (Cambridge: Cambridge University Press, 2004), 169–71.
110 Ibid.
111 Ibid.
112 Mary Douglas, *Purity and Danger* (Routledge: London, 2003).
113 Ibid. See also Burke *Languages and Communities,* 156.
114 Lewis, *The Turkish Language Reform,* 65.
115 *Türk Dil Kurumu: Büyük Türkçe Sözlük,* 'dilmen', accessed 10 February 2016, http://tdk.gov.tr/index.php?option=com_bts&arama=kelime&guid=TDK.GTS.57bfa38756a8f2.47488988.
116 Mango, *Atatürk,* 498.
117 Fielding, *The March of Time,* 191.
118 Lewis, *The Emergence of Modern Turkey,* 278.
119 Ismet Pasha's Girls' Institute was the first girls' institute, opened in 1928, after which they spread throughout Turkey.
120 Fatma Gök, 'The Girls' Institutes in the Early Period of the Turkish Republic', in *Education in 'Multicultural' Societies: Turkish and Swedish Perspectives,* ed. Maria Carlson et al. (Bromma: Swedish Reseach Institute in Istanbul, 2007), 94.

121 Ayten Sezer Arığ, 'Türkiye'de Kız Enstitüleri: Gelenekten Geleceğe', *Hacettepe Üniversitesi Türkiyat Araştırmaları Dergisi* 20 (2014): 198.
122 Arnold Reisman, *Turkey's Modernization: Refugees from Nazism and Atatürk's Vision* (Washington: New Academia Publishing, 2006), 135–90.
123 Ibid., 135–6.
124 Ibid.
125 Ibid., 2.
126 Ibid., xxiii, 320.
127 Philip M. Raup, 'Economies and Diseconomies of Large-Scale Agriculture', *American Journal of Agricultural Economics* 51, no. 5 (1969): 1274–83, accessed 5 March 2016, http://www.jstor.org/stable/1238003.
128 Şevket Pamuk, *The Ottoman Empire and European Capitalism, 1820–1913: Trade, Investment and Production* (Cambridge: Cambridge University Press, 1987).
129 Ibid.
130 Lewis, *The Emergence of Modern Turkey*, 286–7.
131 Mehmet Karayaman, 'Atatürk Döneminde Şeker Sanayi ve İzlenen Politikalar', *Atatürk Araştırma Merkezi Dergisi* 82 (2012): 54–8.
132 Ibid., 55.
133 Ibid.
134 Ibid., 61.
135 Mango, *Atatürk*, 504.
136 Ibid.
137 Roger R. Trask, *The United States Response to Turkish Nationalism and Reform, 1914–1939* (Minneapolis: The University of Minnesota Press, 1971), 228.
138 Ibid.
139 Ibid., 229.
140 Ibid.; see also Mango, *Atatürk*, 504–5.
141 One year later, in 1935, the Thessaloniki City Council donated Atatürk's birth house to the Turkish state, immortalizing him with an inscription describing him as 'the renovator of the Turkish Nation and champion of the Balkan Pact'. The house, which stands next to and on the same property as the Turkish consulate, today serves as the Atatürk Museum.
142 Trask, *The United States Response to Turkish Nationalism*, 234–6. See also Mango, *Atatürk*, 506–9.
143 Dilek Barlas, 'Friends or Foes? Diplomatic Relations between Italy and Turkey, 1923–36', *International Journal of Middle East Studies* 36 (2004): 231–52, accessed 18 April 2016, http://www.jstor.org/stable/3880033.

Epilogue:
Atatürk in retrospect

In this study, I have explored Atatürk's relationship to cinema by going beyond the well-known quotations and anecdotes attributed to him. This study had three major aims. First, it strove to analyse the image of Atatürk established in film in order to better understand the evolution of his public image over the course of his time in power and the contribution it made to the developing concept of the Turkish nation. Second, unlike much of Turkish historiography, which tends to present Atatürk as a man whose ideas, including those on cinema, were far ahead of his time, this study aimed to place Atatürk in his historical context in order to understand how he used cinema in order to answer the major problems of his time. Third, it sought to understand the social, cultural and political uses of cinema in the modernization process and the building of a nation-state in early twentieth-century Turkey. To sum up, this study has attempted to understand the relationship between media and power, and, more specifically, the role of cinema in the making of the image of Atatürk and the modern Turkish nation-state in the early twentieth century.

Film played a significant and somewhat paradoxical role in making Atatürk and Turkey's new 'modern' image visible to both the national and the international community. It not only recorded the construction of the Turkish nation-state but also helped Atatürk significantly in its making. Even today, his cinematic images shape how most people in Turkey continue to imagine Atatürk: as a military hero who saved the fatherland, a teacher who taught modern ways to his students, a father who took excellent care of his many children, and a reforming statesman who created a new and modern state on the ruins of the Ottoman Empire.

Atatürk, however, instead of being far ahead of his time, was highly influenced by the social and cultural milieu from which he came, and thought about cinema within the framework provided by that environment. Growing up as a Turkish-Muslim, middle-class male in the urban centres of Ottoman modernization, and being part of the Ottoman army – an elite institution in the empire – Mustafa Kemal belonged to the ranks of the Westernized elite, which made him aware of the cultural and political value of cinema. He was especially drawn to this new medium because cinema was perceived as one of the significant symbols of Western modernity.

Similarly, cultural influences and role models are likely to have influenced his attempts to construct and communicate his public image as a political leader. To conclude the study, I will place Atatürk's image in a historical perspective and make a few comparisons. First, I will compare Atatürk with political rulers of his time and of earlier periods in order to better understand how their public image, communicated through different forms of media, but particularly cinema, influenced his self-representation. Since Atatürk's public image has been a cornerstone in the creation and maintenance of the Turkish nation-state, transformations in how it has been presented and received mark important changes in Turkish political culture and society. Therefore, I will also compare his image in the media of his day and in today's media. Finally, I will make some concluding remarks on further research possibilities.

Atatürk compared to other leaders of his time and of earlier periods

Atatürk was certainly not the only political leader in Turkish history who was concerned with his public image and its communication through different forms of media. He was influenced by many leaders preceding him, and influenced many who would follow him. He constructed his public image in relation to others and learned from their image politics. He also defined himself in contrast to others and competed with them.

Growing up in the Hamidian era, Atatürk must have been aware of the strong personality cult of Sultan Abdul Hamid II. In much the same way as the sultan created his image as a devout caliph, father and saviour of all Muslims, Atatürk constructed his image as a secular president, father and liberator of the Turks.[1] Unlike many 'modern' European monarchs, the sultan was reluctant to display himself in visual media such as portraits, photography and film, but he still employed different media such as ceremonies, coats of arms, decorations, official musical compositions, public works, religiously symbolic items, motifs and other artefacts to propagate his power and omnipresence to the public. Despite his hesitance to show his image in public spaces, as mentioned in Chapter 1, he was filmed during the Friday prayer ceremony (Selamlık). This makes him the first Ottoman ruler who used cinema to communicate his image to the public.

Although Sultan Abdul Hamid II did not show much interest in visual media, Atatürk was greatly attracted by these media. Perhaps his inability to claim legitimacy by descent made him more dependent on the strategic use of visual media to create a favourable image of himself in the public eye. Unlike Sultan Abdul Hamid II, who focused on traditional modes of self-presentation, Atatürk paid particular attention to Western modes of self-representation in paintings, photographs and films in order to appear as a modern European type of political leader. As Turkish historian Selim Deringil suggests, the sultan's aim was to create 'vibrations of power' without being seen.[2] Contrary to the sultan, Atatürk formed part of his power by being seen and appearing accessible to his people. In this respect, he followed the demotic style of enlightened European rulers after the French Revolution.

The reforming Ottoman sultans, particularly Mahmud II (1785–1839), who initiated a Western-style dress reform in 1828 and commissioned many portraits of himself in the European ruler portraiture tradition with the aim of having them hung in state offices, were certainly a model for Atatürk. According to Atatürk's adoptive daughter Afet Inan, Atatürk was an admirer of Mehmed II (a.k.a. Mehmed the Conqueror, 1432–81),[3] who had a great interest in European art and culture. Although we do not know to what extent Mehmed II influenced his image politics, we do know that he was known as the first Ottoman ruler who employed a Western artist (Gentile Bellini from Venice) to portray him, and struck medals with this portrait in 1480. Sultan Mehmed II's openness to new ideas and cultural exchange was an example for many of his Turkish successors, including Atatürk.

Sultan Abdul Hamid II was rather sceptical about using modern visual media to project his image, but his successor Mehmed V. Reşâd (1844–1918) was not. His image was promoted through modern visual media such as photography and cinema at home and abroad. Sultan Reşâd had also a different style of rulership than his elder brother. Unlike Sultan Abdul Hamid II, who only rarely left Yildiz Palace and made little effort to get in touch with the population outside the capital, Sultan Reşâd made two symbolically significant journeys to the provinces to show his love and respect for the people. He visited the old Ottoman capitals of Bursa, Edirne and the province Izmit, and also made an extensive journey to the Ottoman Balkans, where he made a conscious effort to make himself visible and get in touch with his people.

In his approach to cinema, Sultan Reşâd was also much more open than his elder brother. When he was visiting Monastir (Bitola) in 1911, for instance, he was filmed by the Manaki brothers. According to a well-known anecdote, when the sultan was leaving the town hall, the Manaki brothers, who were waiting outside, began to shoot the film of the sultan. The bodyguards who saw this tried to prevent them. The sultan, who noticed the incident, supposedly said to one of his bodyguards: 'Let the boy play with it [the camera]'.[4] Whether this incident really happened or not, the anecdote is still frequently used to show the sultan's tolerant attitude towards the medium of cinema and the freedom of press in general.

The image-makers of Sultan Reşâd, particularly the CUP regime, promoted him as a popular monarch, visible and accessible to his subjects. He was presented as the 'father of the nation',[5] a role that was highly suitable for the old sultan both physically and mentally. Significantly, descriptions of Turkish rulers as 'fathers of the nation' seem to have been common in the Turkish-Ottoman tradition. Sultan Abdul Hamid II, for example, was known to Muslim Turks as Baba Hamit (Father or Daddy Hamid). Following this tradition, as mentioned in Chapter 5, Mustafa Kemal chose for himself the family name Atatürk, which means father of the Turks.

Likewise, country trips had been a tradition since Sultan Mahmud II, who was exposed to Western ruler practices after the French Revolution. At this time, the Ottoman sultans began to become more visible and leave their palaces more frequently – with the exception of Abdul Hamid II – in order to make personal contact with their people outside of the capital. Sultan Abdulmecit's (1839–61), Abdulaziz's (1861–76) and Mehmed V. Reşâd's country trips are just a few examples of this new practice.

Atatürk certainly appeared in public much more often than his Ottoman predecessors. During his country trips, he was often filmed by the Republican People's Party's cameraman Kenan Reşit Erginsoy, shaking the hands of ordinary citizens, listening carefully to their needs, receiving their petitions, visiting schools, teaching students Turkish history and talking to the public. The newsreels of Atatürk's country trips were carefully designed to present him as a popular leader, who was adored by the people.⁶ In contrast to the Ottoman sultans, he was shown as an egalitarian leader, close to his people and in fact not very different from them. In line with his republican ideals, he chatted with citizens at every opportunity, read his newspaper like any other responsible citizen would and even played games with other state dignitaries on board a ship. Whether his egalitarianism was genuine or not, such scenes would be difficult to imagine for the Ottoman sultans.

Among all Atatürk's predecessors, however, it was Enver Pasha who had the greatest influence on his image politics. Although most Turkish historians present Enver Pasha and Atatürk as rivals and complete opposites in terms of their character, in fact, there were many similarities, close connections and continuities between the two. When Atatürk was not yet a well-known officer, his peer Enver Pasha was, for instance, already known, also internationally, as the charismatic leader of the Young Turk Revolution of 1908, and subsequently the Ottoman Empire until 1918. Like Atatürk, Enver Pasha made much more extensive use of media than the Ottoman sultans had. This is perhaps not surprising as both were competing for political legitimacy with an Ottoman dynasty that had ruled since the thirteenth century. To assert their leadership, they needed much more propaganda than Sultan Abdul Hamid II, Mehmed V. Reşâd or Mehmed VI Vahideddin.

It might be even argued that a personality cult had already begun to develop around Enver Pasha. This can be observed in many of the propaganda materials of the period. The CUP government, in particular, made a deliberate effort to create a heroic image of Enver Pasha through the press. After the Young Turk Revolution of 1908, he was promoted as the 'hero of freedom', and after his recapture of Edirne from the Bulgars in 1913 he was presented as the 'conqueror of Edirne'. Besides devoting considerable space to Enver Pasha's actions in the press, marches were composed, theatre plays featuring him were staged and poems in praise of him were written. As a result, the name 'Enver' became lastingly popular among Muslims of the empire and beyond – the first names of political leaders such as Enver Hoxha of Albania and Anwar Sadat of Egypt are just a few prominent examples of this. The CUP government also used modern visual media such as postcards, photographs and films to propagate Enver Pasha's image to the public. As a member of the CUP, Atatürk must have observed his contemporary's meteoric rise to power and the role that propaganda played in his political success.

The Ottoman Empire's entrance into World War I on the side of the Central Powers was, however, a turning point in Enver Pasha's image-making, as it made his image part of a worldwide propaganda campaign. The experienced allies of the Ottoman Empire, Germany and the Austria-Hungarian Empire, began promoting his image beyond the national borders by using modern propaganda techniques. A war painter called Wilhelm Viktor Krausz, for instance, was sent to Istanbul and Çanakkale Fronts in 1915 by the Austria-Hungarian War Ministry Social Welfare Bureau (Kriegsfürsorgeamt des. k.u.k. Kriegsministeriums) for documentary and propaganda purposes.[7] Krausz made portraits of Ottoman state dignitaries such as Sultan Mehmed V. Reşâd, Grand Vizier Said Halim Pasha, the Minister of War and Deputy Commander-in-Chief of the Army Enver Pasha, as well as German and Turkish military commanders such as Generalfeldmarschall Liman von Sanders, Generalfeldmarschall Von der Goltz and General Major Esat Pasha. He also made the first known portrait of Colonel Mustafa Kemal, who was the commander of the Anafartalar Group at the time, at the battlefront. The album called *Paintings and Drawings from Turkey during World War* (Bildnisse und Skizzen aus der Turkei im Weltkrieg) was printed in Vienna and distributed in Europe and Turkey.

The main sponsor behind Enver Pasha's image campaign, however, was the German Empire, which reproduced his image on numerous medals, postcards and stamps. His pictures and photographs were also published in books, journals and newspapers, and distributed throughout Europe and the Muslim world. In propagating Enver Pasha's image, the Germans particularly emphasized his youth, dynamism and vitality, in contrast to the stereotypical image of the Ottoman sultans as old, lethargic and indolent. As mentioned in Chapter 1, the Germans also presented Enver Pasha in the famous newsreel series *Messter-Woche* a number of times. To honour the Turkish national hero, moreover, in 1915, his name was given to a bridge ('Enwer-Pascha-Brücke') in Potsdam, where he had stayed when he was serving as military attaché in Berlin between 1909 and 1912.

There were also attempts to make Enver Pasha a favourable figure in popular culture. A tobacco company from Dresden, for instance, named one its best-selling cigarette brands 'Enver Bey', printing his picture on the package. Buses on the streets of Berlin carried advertisements for Enver Bey cigarettes, while 'Enverland' was written instead of Turkey on trains going from Berlin to

Istanbul. In fact, in those days, not only the Germans but also most of the other Europeans referred to the Ottoman Empire as 'Enverland'. As an army member, it is highly unlikely that Atatürk was unaware of Enver Pasha's visual propaganda. He must have observed closely the political and military uses of media in creating a heroic public image. Moreover, he must have noticed how the Europeans were using new means of communication and modern propaganda techniques to persuade the public.

Besides these domestic influences, it would also be interesting to look at the foreign political rulers who may have influenced Atatürk's image construction. In fact, Atatürk was a keen follower of European fashion trends. Already as a young army captain, he wore Kaiser Wilhelm II's moustache style (called the imperial moustache), which was very popular among members of the Ottoman army and the Turkish intelligentsia of the period. In line with contemporary fashions, his moustache style changed over time until he shaved it off entirely after becoming the president of Turkish Republic in order to leave behind the traditional image of the Turks in the European imagination. It is clear that European bourgeoisie sensibilities had a strong impact on Atatürk's image construction. His taste for European fashion was most emphatically reflected in his extensive wardrobe, which consisted of clothes tailored in France, Italy, England, Germany and Switzerland. He also employed some Greek tailors in Istanbul, who made clothes for him in the European style. In fact, non-Muslim bourgeois dressing styles already had a strong influence on many modern Muslim Turks, including Atatürk, at the time of the Ottoman Empire. When he became president, he not only wanted to dress in contemporary European clothes himself, but wanted the Turkish army to do so as well. To give the Turkish army a modern look, he had their uniforms designed by Coco Chanel, who was a young but promising talent in the fashion industry at the time.[8]

In developing his own personal style, Atatürk was also influenced by Europe's fashion icons. He wore cuffed trousers (trouser turn-ups), which had been worn by the British King Edward VII, and plus fours after Edward, the Prince of Wales, made them trendy during his visit to the United States in 1924. Like many elites of the time, Atatürk must have followed the contemporary European fashion trends through visual media such as films and photographs in newspapers or magazines, and adapted some of them to create his own public image.

Western rulers from earlier periods also influenced his image politics. As a keen reader of history, he was well aware of the public image of famous political leaders such as Napoléon Bonaparte and George Washington, who, like him, had had successful military careers. Significantly, the foreign press frequently compared him with Napoléon and his wife Latife with Napoléon's first wife Joséphine.[9] The national press also often compared him with Western leaders. Journalist Ahmet Refik from Cumhuriyet, for instance, compared Atatürk in 1933 with three 'great men' of the Western world: Alexander the Great, Caesar and Napoléon. He concluded that Atatürk was more successful and yet more modest.[10] Such comparisons with rulers of the past were made to praise and justify Atatürk's leadership in the present.

Atatürk's image in the official media of his day and in today's media

As transformations in Atatürk's image signify changes in political culture and society, it is vital to place his image in the official media of his day in a comparative perspective, not only in relation to other leaders of his time or of earlier periods but also in relation to today's media. In the official media of his day, which were under the strict control of the Kemalist regime, Atatürk was presented as a flawless political leader and a heroic figure, who was virtually omnipotent and omnipresent. He was always portrayed as the hero of the story, who was larger than life, with his opponents cast as villains or stereotyped evil characters. Not surprisingly, these stories always ended with the triumph of good over evil, symbolized by Atatürk's victory over his opponents. Contemporary representations of Atatürk in official media served to legitimize his rule and justify his actions in the present through the creation of the myth of Atatürk.

As mentioned throughout this study, the myth of Atatürk was constructed and protected by the Kemalist regime and by Atatürk himself, particularly in cinema. To understand his relation to cinema more comprehensively, however, it is important to look at his image not only in documentary films but also in fictional films produced during his lifetime. Significantly, just as one man, namely, Atatürk, dominated the realm of politics in the early years of the republic, one director, namely, Muhsin Ertuğrul, monopolized the Turkish fiction film industry. Trained in Germany and the Soviet Union, Ertuğrul reproduced the cultural ideology of Atatürk and the republican elite in his films.

Significantly, although Ertuğrul made three fictional films about the Turkish War of Independence – *Ateşten Gömlek* (The Turkish Ordeal, 1923), *Ankara Postası* (Ankara Post, 1928) and *Bir Millet Uyanıyor* (The Awakening of a Nation, 1932) – he did not make Atatürk the central character in his films, show him[11] or allow him to be played by an actor. When Atatürk was alive, his image seems to have had an almost sacred status that could not be played with on the cinema screen in fictional films. I believe that this was partly due to Ertuğrul's personal respect for Atatürk's public image, but also to the political risks he would run if he misrepresented Atatürk. Although Atatürk was much more open than his Ottoman predecessors to propagating his image through various forms of media, he and his followers were still cautious when it came to do this on film, especially when they did not control the production process.

The myth of Atatürk has continued to survive after his death in 1938. The Turkish state, moreover, continued to act as a gatekeeper to ensure state control over Atatürk's portrayal in the official media. It authorized only particular narratives about him, those in which he was presented as a flawless political leader, a military hero, a caring father figure and a secular, modern statesman. The visual cultural memory of the leader was conserved either by using actual representations of Atatürk (in photographs or on film) or by creating fictional films about the War of Independence that reiterated the official narratives.

Significantly, until the 1980s, a biographical film about Atatürk could not be made. The main reasons for this were the strength of the myth of Atatürk and the way Kemalist discourse continued to propagate a godlike image of Atatürk in history, literature and the visual arts after his death. Due to the Kemalist discourse, it was – and still is – difficult to imagine or represent Atatürk in a free and creative way. Any alternative depictions of Atatürk that historicized or humanized him were rejected or marginalized by the Turkish state. In addition, Law 5816, titled 'The Law Concerning Crimes Committed Against Atatürk', which was passed thirteen years after Atatürk's death on 25 July 1951, made insulting his memory an offense punishable by up to three years in prison and constituted a great hindrance to representing him in an imaginative way for writers, visual artists and film-makers alike. No film producer or director would take the risk of making an Atatürk film diverting from the official discourse and ending up in court accused of defiling Atatürk's memory.¹²

It is, therefore, no surprise that the first fictional film in which Atatürk was played by an actor was produced not by the Turkish film industry, but by Hollywood. In 1970, the Northern Irish actor Patrick Magee played the role of Atatürk for the first time in an adventure film called *You Can't Win 'Em All*. It is also no surprise that the film was banned from being screened in Turkey by the state censorship commission, which considered it disrespectful to Atatürk and the Turkish people.

The Turkish state took the initiative to produce an Atatürk film for the first time in 1981. For the centenary of Atatürk's death, it ordered the production of three films: *I Stand for Your Dreams* (unknown director, budget 1.8 million US dollars), *Atatürk* (directed by Marc Mopty, budget 2 million US dollars)¹³ and *Atatürk ve Sanat* (Atatürk and Art, directed by Halit Refiğ, budget 40,000 US dollars). Nevertheless, the authorities did not find the films satisfactory.

The story of the television series *Yorgun Savaşçı* (Tired Soldier, 1978–83), which was about the Turkish War of Independence, is even more telling.¹⁴ Although the series, which was directed by Halit Refiğ, was a TRT production and was also supported by the Turkish army, after the coup d'état of 1980, the state censorship committee decided to burn it. This happened in 1983, preventing it from reaching an audience. The series' scenario was adapted from the famous Turkish writer Kemal Tahir's novel *Yorgun Savaşçı* (1965), which focused on the role of officers on the Committee of Union and Progress in the Turkish War of Independence. By offering an alternative narrative to the official historiography and by not representing Atatürk as the sole hero, the series probably disturbed the state censorship committee.

However, in the 1980s, more precisely after Turgut Özal became prime minister in 1983, Turkey found itself on the threshold of a shift from a state-controlled to a liberalized political economy. This shift had great implications for the country's cultural industries in the following decades. In parallel with the political and economic reforms, Atatürk's representation in cinema began to change. On 3 November 1988, for instance, the Ministry of Culture and Tourism organized a panel titled 'Atatürk Film' in Ankara in order to discuss the possibility of an Atatürk film with several Turkish film directors. The most notable speaker, the famous Turkish film director Metin Erksan, argued that an Atatürk Film would limit the audience's imagination of Atatürk and would therefore reduce their capacity to love, think, learn more and create myths about him. However, during the conference, he changed his mind and argued that if an Atatürk film had to be made, it should be made by a great American film director such as Martin Scorsese, Steven Spielberg or George Lucas.[15]

The Ministry of Culture and Tourism did not accept Erksan's thesis and ordered scenarios for an Atatürk Film from Turkish film-makers such as Halit Refiğ, Refik Erduran, Orhan Asena, Necati Cumalı, Güngör Dilmen, Recep Bilginer, Turan Oflazoğlu, Nezihe Araz, Ziya Öztan and Tarık Buğra. Finally, they chose two films projects: Halit Refiğ's *Gazi and Latife* and Refik Erduran's TV series *Metamorfoz*. The first film, which tells the story of Atatürk and Latife's relationship in the context of the political developments between 1922 and 1925, was never made,[16] and the audience showed little interest in *Metamorfoz*, which was about an English PhD student visiting Turkey in order to do research on Atatürk's revolution and the social changes it brought to Turkish society between 1922 and 1936. The disappointment with *Metamorfoz* led to other TRT productions such as the TV series *Kurtuluş* (Liberation, 1994) and *Cumhuriyet* (The Republic, 1998), which were directed by Ziya Öztan. Although both series reiterated the official history in general, they also revealed some untold stories about Atatürk's private life, such as his relationship with Fikriye Hanım.

In the 1990s, the broadcasting system, which had functioned under the strict monopoly of the Turkish Radio and Television Corporation (TRT), was transformed by an explosion of commercial television channels, paving the way for a multi-vocal cultural environment. As a result of this, the metanarrative of official historiography constructed around the heroic image of Atatürk started to be challenged by films and documentaries representing him in alternative ways and, at the same time, proposing other heroes. By using fictional characters and alternative historiography, the new independent films and documentaries began to tell stories that had never been told by the official historiography, questioning the metanarrative of old documentaries and films as well as their claims to historical accuracy. With Turkey's shift to a liberal economy and politics, Atatürk also began to be played by actors in bank and insurance advertisements, which served to justify the new economic system and led to the commercialization of his image.

The changes in Atatürk's representation in audiovisual media became particularly apparent when Turkey's European Union accession negotiations gained momentum in the early 2000s. In Ali Akyüz's documentary film *Latife Hanım* (2006), for instance, Latife wears Atatürk's clothes in order save her husband's life when he is besieged by Lame Osman. In Can Dündar's film *Mustafa* (2008), Atatürk is demythologized and shown to be as fallible as any human being. He appears as a tippler, a heavy smoker and a lonely figure dealing with disappointments and failed marriages. And in Mehmet Tanrısever's film *Hür Adam* (Free Man, 2011), Muslim Kurdish scholar Saîd Nursî is seen to challenge Atatürk, undermining his authority. These changes in Atatürk's representation show that the myth of Atatürk as an omniscient and omnipotent heroic figure, as presented by the official or state-sponsored media, will not be able to survive intact in a global era. In the future, we will probably see many different, contradictory representations of Atatürk and alternative heroes that, together, will challenge the official narrative of the Turkish nation-state.

Moreover, this narrative has also itself changed since the Justice and Development Party (Adalet ve Kalkınma Partisi, AKP) took power in 2002. The AKP government has tried to transform Atatürk's Westernization project inspired by Europe and secular nationalism into one inspired by the Ottoman and Islamic pasts. Thus, they have offered alternative narratives to the Kemalist one and have presented other heroes from the Turkish-Islamic past rather than Atatürk.

Concluding remarks

Before ending this study, it is necessary to make some remarks on further research possibilities. This study has focused on films featuring Atatürk aimed at audiences in Turkey and the Western world (mainly the United States), but more research is needed in order to fully understand Atatürk's relation to film as well as the image politics developed during his lifetime, not only from a Western but also from a global perspective. Significantly, Atatürk revised his public image several times and performed diverse roles for different audiences, depending on his political and cultural agenda.[17] During the War of Independence, for instance, his speeches resembled in many aspects those of the Muslim Bolshevik Mirsaid Sultan-Galiev, who propagated the unification of the Muslim proletariat in the East against Western imperialism.[18] The analysis of archival films such as, among others, *Afgan Kralı Amanullah Han'ın Türkiye Ziyareti* (The Visit of the Afghan King Amanullah Khan to Turkey, 1928), *İran Şahı Rıza Pehlevi'nin Türkiye Ziyareti* (The Visit of the Iranian Shah Rıza Pehlevi to Turkey, 1934) and *Ürdün Kralı Abdullah'ın Türkiye Ziyareti* (The Visit of the Jordanian King Abdullah to Turkey, 1937) would be illuminating to understand Atatürk's image-building for non-Western audiences.[19] The analysis of these films would also be useful to understand the impact of Atatürk's image politics in the Middle and Far East as its leaders such as the Iranian Shah Rıza Pehlevi, the Afghan King Amanullah Khan, the President of Egypt Gamal Abdel Nasser and the Prime Minister of India Jawaharlal Nehru were all highly impressed by his reforms and took the new Turkey as a model in modernizing their own countries.

Foreign non-Western film productions are equally important to understanding Atatürk's image politics and its effects outside of Turkey. The Soviet director Sergei Iosifovich Yutkevich and Lev Oskarovich Arnshtam's documentary film *Ankara-Serdtse Turtsii* (*Türkiye'nin Kalbi Ankara* or *Ankara: Heart of Turkey*, 1934, in English),[20] which is about Soviet–Turkish friendship and Turkey's post-war transformation, is perhaps the most remarkable of these productions. The film, which shows Atatürk's famous speech delivered during the 10-year anniversary celebrations of the Turkish Republic[21] and of Soviet support for the construction of the new Turkey, was screened not only in Turkey and Western states (e.g., the United States and Europe) but also in the Soviet Union and Eastern states (e.g., Iran and Afghanistan) in order to propagate the value of Soviet–Turkish friendship. A detailed analysis of this film could lead to a more comprehensively understanding of how Atatürk and his revolution were seen and reframed outside of Turkey.

The fate of *Heart of Turkey*, as well as of other film projects concerning Kemalist Turkey, is another topic that is worthy of further study. Although *Heart of Turkey* was intensely screened in Turkey in the mid-1930s, the Turkish-language copy of the film disappeared in the following years. The Russian-language copy of the film could only be aired on Turkish television in 1969, but it was cut by the censors midway through the broadcast as being communist propaganda. The censors probably saw Turkish–Soviet friendship in the past as a problem as Turkey was now a NATO member.[22] Soviet film-maker Esfer Schub's (a.k.a. Esther Schub) *Türk İnkılabı'nda Terakki Hamleleri* (Strides of Progress in Turkish Revolution, 1937) was another documentary film project on the Turkish reforms that was in the planning stages when Atatürk was still alive. At the moment, not much is known about how she depicted or planned to depict Atatürk or the new Turkey in this film, which has not been found, but archival materials may shed more light on its (envisioned) contents.

There are also rumoured to be other film projects in whose production Atatürk was personally involved. If more were known about these projects, this could enhance our understanding of his relation to cinema. According to Nizameddin Nazif Tepedelenlioğlu, who wrote the scenario of Muhsin Ertuğrul's fiction film *Bir Millet Uyanıyor* (The Awakening of a Nation, 1932), Atatürk wanted to see the scenario of the film before it was produced and had accepted the invitation to give a speech in front of the camera for a scene in the film. Turkish film critic Attila Dorsay also states that, having examined the scenario, Atatürk posed for the camera in front of a black curtain and gave his speech on the domestic and foreign affairs.[23]

The founder of the Mimar Sinan Film Archive, Sami Şekeroğlu, mentions a similar occasion, but assigns a different date. According to him, Cezmi Ar wanted to shoot *Atatürk's 4th Quarter Speech* (1934) in the Turkish parliament. Because the quality of the shots was not satisfactory due to the poor lighting, Atatürk decided to give the same speech again in front of a black curtain.[24] Both versions of Atatürk's speech, the version shot in the parliament and the version shot in front of a black curtain, would be interesting to compare and contrast in order to assess Atatürk's stage performance once they are made available to researchers.[25]

Atatürk was also supposedly involved in the process of writing a film scenario concerning the Turkish Revolution with Münir Hayri Egeli. Egeli states in his memoir *Bilinmeyen Yönleriyle Atatürk* (Atatürk and His Unknown Aspects)[26] that Atatürk told him that the film should show his own life in parallel with the life of a teacher, and that he dictated what the film should look like. After Egeli had delivered the first draft, Atatürk revised it page by page and made some additions. To realize this film project, he sent Egeli to Germany in order to learn the craft of film-making.[27] When Egeli returned from abroad with certificates stating his proficiency in film-making, Atatürk revised the scenario one last time and approved the making of the film.[28] According to Egeli, while they were shooting some film of Atatürk, Atatürk got sick and the film project could not be realized.[29] The analysis of this film scenario could also offer significant insights into how Atatürk wanted to project himself and

Turkey through the medium of film. What is clear, even without looking at the details of the various film productions Atatürk was involved in, is that he tended to support film projects about his leadership and the new Turkey as long as they remained under his control.

Atatürk's interest in cinema cannot be fully understood without comparing the Turkish state's cinema policy in his period with that of other countries. Lenin, for instance, supported the cinema industry in Soviet Union with the enduring slogan 'Cinema for us is the most important of the arts'.[30] In fact, in the Soviet Union, from the state's perspective, cinema was a medium for propaganda and not one for entertainment. It was primarily used to educate the masses by transmitting socialist ideas and images, including Lenin's own. In Italy, Mussolini founded Europe's largest film and movie studio, Cinecittà, in Rome in 1937 under the slogan 'Cinema is the most powerful weapon'. In doing so, he aimed at creating a strong national film industry and at promoting fascism through propaganda films and newsreels. In Germany, too, Hitler and his propaganda minister Joseph Goebbels were highly interested in cinema and saw it as a valuable propaganda instrument with great power. They subordinated the entire German film industry under the Ministry of Propaganda, and nationalized film production and distribution. Moreover, they supported big budget propaganda film productions such as *Der Sieg des Glaubens* and *Triumph des Willens*, as well as newsreels of vast Nazi rallies in which Hitler took on the role of a cinema star.

Atatürk achieved remarkable success as both a political and military leader, and he could perhaps have also become a cult figure through cinema if he had had a comparable cinema industry. However, although he and his Kemalist followers considered cinema an emblem of modernity and an important means of propaganda, they did not develop a systematic state policy for cinema or try to take the entire film industry under the state control.[31] In line with their mixed-economy view, they left the cinema sector largely to private enterprise, while keeping a watchful eye on the sector and its agents. Thus, for Atatürk and his Kemalist followers, cinema may not have been the most important of the arts, but it was still important enough not to leave it entirely to artists and entrepreneurs. Of course, cinema was only one medium among many; the role of other media such as photography, painting, sculpture and literature in constructing and communicating Atatürk's public image as well as in building the modern Turkish nation-state needs to be further studied in order to better understand the connection between media and power.

This research has focused on the construction of a positive public image for Atatürk. Significantly, an opposing image (equally mythical) portraying him as an evil figure also existed and circulated in Turkey and abroad. This antithetical myth of Atatürk could be another subject for further research. Moreover, the films featuring Atatürk are important not only for what they show but also for what they do not show. Although they underline Atatürk's importance in the War of Independence and the subsequent establishment of the Turkish nation-state, they downplay or elide the vital role of others in this process. They also do not show the negative aspects of the Kemalist modernization project, such as its authoritarian tendencies, its homogenizing nature and its denial of different ethnic/religious identities and social classes. In light of this, an analysis of the negative or non-representation of 'others' would be useful to form a better understanding of the strengths and weaknesses of the Kemalist modernization project and its representation on film.

Finally, although this study has concentrated on the construction of Atatürk's image in film rather than on the reception of this image, it has tried to offer some glimpses of responses by statesmen and journalists. The full effects of Atatürk's appearances on film on ordinary people as well as public opinion in Turkey and abroad during his lifetime are still unknown and deserve further study, even though data on audience numbers and responses may be difficult to find. Nonetheless, the analysis of Atatürk's filmic representations during his lifetime in this book has shown how the making of a leader's image illuminates the close relationship between media and power. In the end, I believe the true power of these pictures lies in the way they influenced the perception of not only his contemporaries when he was still alive but also that of later generations long after his death, who continue to imagine Atatürk as a hero, teacher, father and modern statesman.

Notes

1. M. Şükrü Hanioğlu, *Atatürk: An Intellectual Biography* (Princeton: Princeton University Press, 2011), 185.
2. Selim Deringil, *The Well Protected Domains: Ideology and the Legitimation of Power in the Ottoman Empire 1876–1909* (London and New York: I. B. Tauris, 2011), 18.

3 Afet İnan, *Atatürk Hakkında Hatıralar ve Belgeler* (İstanbul: İş Bankası Kültür Yayınları, 2009), 430-1.
4 In Turkish: 'Bırakın çocuk oynasın'. This means that 'let the boy play with the camera' or 'allow him to do the filming activity'. For some still photos of the film, see Savaş Arslan, *Cinema in Turkey: A New Critical History* (New York: Oxford University Press, 2011), 33-5.
5 Erik-Jan Zürcher, *The Young Turk Legacy and Nation Building: From the Ottoman Empire to Atatürk's Turkey* (New York: I.B. Tauris, 2010), 84-94.
6 The intertitles of the newsreels, which are both in Turkish and French, are a strong indication that these newsreels were not only directed to a national audience but also to an international one.
7 Bahattin Öztuncay, 'Wilhelm Viktor Krausz (1878-1959) The War Painter in the Ottoman Empire', in *Propaganda and War: The Allied Front during the First World War*, ed. Edhem Eldem et al. (Istanbul: Mas Matbaacılık, 2014), 8-39.
8 Vural Gökçaylı, 'Bir ulusun tasarımcısı: Atatürk', in *O Daima Şıktı: Gazi'nin Son Tanıkları Anlatıyor*, ed. Nebil Özgentürk (İstanbul: Bir Yudum Insan Yayınevi, 2010), 45.
9 İpek Çalışlar, *Latife Hanım* (İstanbul: Everest Yayınları, 2011), 331.
10 Bengül Salman Bolat, Milli *Bayram Olgusu ve Türkiye'de Yapılan Cumhuriyet Bayramı Kutlamaları (1923-1960)* (Ankara: Atatürk Araştırma Merkezi, 2011).
11 The archival version of *Bir Millet Uyanıyor* (The Awakening of a Nation, 1932), which I had the opportunity to see in the Turkish Film Archives, contains some scenes taken from documentary films of the period, which briefly show Atatürk dressed in a white tie and holding a top hat in his hand during a ceremony. While the Turkish army parades, the voice-over states: 'Be ready for the war, if you want peace and order' (Hazır ol cenge eğer ister isen sulh-ü salâh). The film ends with an image of Atatürk's head surrounded by an aura-like light painted on a Turkish flag. If this film was screened in this version in 1932, it was probably because the Turkish government was using cinema, including fiction films, to prepare the public for a war that could begin at any time.
12 The Turkish academic Semih S. Tezcan describes in his book *Atatürk Dizi Filmi Teşebbüsü Nasıl Baltalandı?* (How the Attempt to Make an Atatürk Film Series Was Sabotaged?) the desperate attempts made to produce an Atatürk film. According to Tezcan, when İsmet İnönü was still president, Adil Özkaptan wanted to produce a dramatic documentary film about Atatürk, but two CHP party deputies aggressively dissuaded him. This shows the deep distrust the authorities felt concerning any civilian's capacity to produce a worthy Atatürk film. With the support of president Celal Bayar, Adil Özkaptan tried again in 1951 and 1957, even bringing famous Hollywood actors of the period such as

Douglas Fairbanks Jr. and Yul Brynner to Turkey to play Atatürk, but again did not succeed due to the reluctance of the state bureaucracy. See Semih S. Tezcan, *Atatürk Dizi Filmi Teşebbüsü Nasıl Baltalandı? 1984–1987* (İstanbul: Yüksek Öğrenim Eğitim ve Araştırma Vakfı, 2005).

13 In his book *Sinema and Çağımız*, the Turkish film critic Atilla Dorsay writes about his experience of watching the *Atatürk* film directed by Marc Mopty in 1983, two years after its production. Dorsay states that the film's screening was delayed for an unknown reason, but that it was finally shown on TRT (Turkish State Television), not at primetime but at ten in the evening. Dorsay wrongly claims that this (and not *You Can't Win 'Em All*) was the first film in which Atatürk was played by an actor. Thus, according to him, it broke a taboo. Dorsay judges the film successful in general and, most importantly, argues that it opened the way to new dramatic films on Atatürk. See Atilla Dorsay, *Sinema ve Çağımız* (Istanbul: Remzi Kitapevi, 1998), 22–3.

14 Ömer Serim, *Devlet Yapar Devlet Yıkar (Yorgun Savaşçı Olayı)* (Istanbul: An Yayıncılık, 2003).

15 Metin Erksan, *Atatürk Filmi* (Istanbul: Hil Yayın, 1989), 76.

16 The Ministry of Culture and Tourism published the scenario of *Gazi and Latife* twice, first in 1993 and again in 1998. Alfa Yayınları republished the book in 2008 for the third time, which made the filming of the scenario an urgent issue. However, since no producer wanted to finance the film, it could not be realized. For the film's scenario, see Halit Refiğ, *Gazi ile Latife*: *Mustafa Kemal'in Yaşamından Bir Kesit* (Istanbul: Alfa Yayınları, 2008).

17 When Atatürk, for instance, heard that Edward, Prince of Wales, would come to visit him on a yacht, he ordered a navy blazer to fit the occasion. See Füreya Koral, 'Siyah pelerinli Atatürk', in *O Daima Şıktı: Gazi'nin Son Tanıkları Anlatıyor*, ed. Nebil Özgentürk (Istanbul: Bir Yudum Insan Yayınevi, 2010), 107.

18 Hanioğlu, *Atatürk,* 105.

19 The films 'İran Şahı Rıza Pehlevi'nin Türkiye Ziyareti' (The Visit of the Iranian Shah Rıza Pehlevi to Turkey, 1934), 'Afgan Kralı Amanullah Han'ın Türkiye Ziyareti' (The Visit of the Afghan King Amanullah Khan to Turkey, 1928) and 'Ürdün Kralı Abdullah'ın Türkiye Ziyareti' (The Visit of the Jordanian King Abdullah to Turkey, 1937) can be found in the Turkish Film Archives. This archive also holds other films that might be useful to gain a comprehensive understanding of Atatürk's relation to film, such as 'The Visit of the British King Edward VIII's to Turkey' (1936), 'Mustafa Kemal Atatürk's 5th Term, 2nd Opening Speech in the Grand National Assembly of Turkey' (1936) and 'Atatürk's Journey to Eastern Turkey' (1937).

20 The original Russian title of this film is *Ankara–Serdtse Turtsii*.
21 Based on a personal interview with Sergei Yutkevich the historian Abdul Anbievich Guseinov states in his book that the Western cinema companies Fox and Pathé were also there to film Atatürk's speech. The Western companies had much fancier sound equipment, and Yutkevich mentions that the Western cinematographers looked somewhat 'ironically' at the inferior Soviet gear. The Soviets attached a bulky, crude microphone to the stage and had to run a huge cable to their cameras in order to sync the audio. When Atatürk's convoy drove by, the heavy car severed the thinner Fox and Pathé cables, while the sturdier Soviet cable survived. As a result, the Soviets were the only ones to capture any audio of the speech. See Abdul Anbievich Guseinov, *Turetskoe kino: istoriia i sovremennye problemy* (Moscow: Nauka, 1978), 37.
22 Taylor Craig Zajicek, 'Modern Friendship: The "New Turkey" and Soviet Cultural Diplomacy, 1933–1934' (Master's thesis, University of Washington, 2014), 69.
23 Atilla Dorsay, *Sinema ve Çağımız*, 16.
24 In Sekeroglu's interview, Cezmi Ar states that Atatürk took the filming process very seriously. When his adoptive daughter Afet Inan and his aide-de-camp Salih bey entered the room, Atatürk became nervous and said angrily: 'We are shooting a film here, as you see. Go to the Parliament.' See Sami Sekeroglu, 'I am opening the 2nd gathering year of the 4th Quarter of the Parliament!...': A Nitrate Memory' in *This Film is Dangerous: A Celebration of Nitrate Film*, ed. Roger Smither and Catherine A. Surowiec (London: FIAF, 2002), 545.
25 Sekeroglu states that he found the original shots of Cezmi Ar among some films from the Army Photo Film Centre and united the two pieces (or versions) of the film, leaving the opening words of both versions, 'I am opening the 2nd gathering year of the 4th Quarter of the Parliament', so that the change in setting could be noticed. See ibid., 576.
26 Münir Hayri Egeli, *Bilinmeyen Yönleriyle Atatürk* (Ankara: Berikan, 2004), 89–92. The original title of the book that was published in 1954 for the first time was *Atatürk'ün Bilinmeyen Hatıraları* (Unknown Memories of Atatürk).
27 Another Turkish film-maker Faruk Kenç states in an interview that when Atatürk heard that he was going to Germany to learn the craft of film-making, he wanted a report from him on what needs to done to bring the craft of film-making in Turkey to level of European film-making. Nevertheless, Kenç could not present the report to Atatürk when he returned home, yet he still managed to shot his funeral ceremony in 1938. See Fuat Kenç, 'Sayın bayana da selam söyle', in *O Daima Şıktı: Gazi'nin Son Tanıkları Anlatıyor*, ed. Nebil Özgentürk (Istanbul: Bir Yudum Insan Yayınevi, 2010), 88–92.

28 The film, which was planned to be produced in 1936, was called *Ben Bir İnkılap Çocuğuyum* (I am a Child of the Revolution).
29 Egeli, *Bilinmeyen Yönleriyle Atatürk*, 90–2.
30 For a detailed analysis of the Soviet cinema see Zajicek, 'Modern Friendship', 62.
31 In 1929, a Turkish entrepreneur called Naci Bey submitted the first cinema report to the Turkish parliament. A detailed analysis of this report might offer interesting insights into how the cinema industry was perceived in this period.

Bibliography

Filmography

British Pathé (London)

Mustapha Kemal. Pathé Gazette, Audiovisual file, 1923, 29 sec. Accessed 3 May 2014. http://www.britishpathe.com/video/mustapha-kemal/query/Mustapha+Kemal.

Mustapha Kemel. Pathé News, Audiovisual file, 1920–1929, 20 sec. Accessed 3 May 2014. http://www.britishpathe.com/video/mustapha-kemel.

Turkey Mourns Kemal Ataturk. Pathé, Audiovisual file, 1938, 1 min. 21 sec. Accessed 20 July 2015. http://www.britishpathe.com/video/turkey-mourns-kemal-ataturk/query/ataturk.

Das Bundesarchiv (Koblenz)

Der Kaiser bei unseren türkischen Verbündeten. BUFA, Audiovisual file, 1917, 30 min. 17 sec. Accessed 22 September 2017. https://www.filmothek.bundesarchiv.de/video/565699?q=Enver+Pascha&xm=AND&xf%5B0%5D=_fulltext&xo%5B0%5D=CONTAINS&xv%5B0%5D=.

Türkische Militäraufnahmen aus dem Weltkrieg. Messter-Woche, Audiovisual file, 1915. 7 min. 18 sec. Accessed 22 September 2017. https://www.filmothek.bundesarchiv.de/video/574631?q=Enver+Pascha&xm=AND&xf%5B0%5D=_fullte xt&xo%5B0%5D=CONTAINS&xv%5B0%5D=.

Moving Image Research Collections (MIRC), University of South Carolina (Columbia)

Fox Movietone News Story 8-795-8796: *Miss Afet*. Crew Info: Squire 14 Young. Fox Movietone News Collections, Moving Image Research Collections, University of South Carolina. B&W Sound, 11 November 1930, Ankara, Turkey, 3.54 min.

Fox Movietone News Story 8–848: *Ataturk Entertains Grew on His Private Estate*. Crew Info: Squire 14 Young. Fox Movietone News Collections, Moving Image Research Collections, University of South Carolina. B&W Sound, 1 November 1930, Ankara, Turkey, 13.53 min.

Fox Movietone News Story 8–849: *Turkish Market Day*. Crew Info: Squire 14 Young. Fox Movietone News Collections, Moving Image Research Collections, University of South Carolina. B&W Sound, 3 November 1930, Ankara, Turkey, 9.09 min.

Fox Movietone News Story 8–854: *Turks Still Smoke the Old Way*. Crew Info: Squire 14 Young. Fox Movietone News Collections, Moving Image Research Collections, University of South Carolina. B&W Sound, 13 December 1930, Constantinople, Turkey, 9.64 min.

National Archives (Washington, DC)

Video Recording No: 200. MT.38; 'Father of All Turks'. Release Date: 19 February 1937; Records of The March of Time Collection, Vol. 3, No. 07, Record Group 200; National Archives at College Park, College Park, MD, 6 min.

Incredible Turk. National Archives and Records Administration, ARC: 651784, 263.2028., DVD, 1958, 26 min.

Turkish Film & TV Institute, Mimar Sinan Fine Arts University (Istanbul)

Atatürk'ün Amerikan Büyükelçisi Joseph C. Grew'u Orman Çiftliğinde Kabulü. Turkish Film & TV Institute, Mimar Sinan Fine Arts University, 35 mm. Nitrate Film, 1930, 9 min. 40 sec.

Lozan Sulh Heyetinin Karşılanması. Turkish Film & TV Institute, Mimar Sinan Fine Arts University, 35 mm. Nitrate Film, 1923, 4 min. 30 sec.

Archival sources

Austrian State Archives (Vienna)

KA, AOK, KPQ, Ktn. 60, Filmstelle 1917, 'Aktion Goldschmid', No. 3419, Mai 1917.

Başbakanlık Devlet Arşivleri Genel Müdürlüğü (Ankara)

Mehmet Münir Ertegün'ün Baş Bakanlığa Türkiye Filmleri Hakkında Mektubu, 14 Mayıs 1937, Fon No: 30 10 0 0, Kutu No.: 268, Dosya No: 804, Sıra No: 4.

Private sources (unpublished)

Bryan, Julien. 'Turkey'. Report, Sam Bryan Private Collection, New York, 1961.
Çeliktemel-Thomen, Özde. Email message to author. 12 July 2016.
Genelkurmay Başkanlığı. Letter to author. 16 July 2012.
Greg Wilsbacher. Email message to author. 21 July 2015.
Sam Bryan. Interview by Enis Dinç. New York, 30 July 2015.

Newspapers and journals

'Cumhuriyet Bayramı'. *Akşam*, 24 October 1930.
'Foks Film Ankara'da ne gibi resimler çekti'. *Akşam*, 1 November 1930.
'Gazi Hz'. *Akşam*, 18 August 1929.
'Gazi Hz. Dün Elhamra sinemasına giderek bazı filmleri temaşa ettiler'. *Akşam*, 5 December 1930.
'Günün Haberleri'. *Akşam*, 20 July 1929.
'Julien Bryan Tells of Country's Power in Turkey Reborn'. *Dunkirk Evening Observer*, 3 July 1939.
'Julien Bryan to Give Illustrated Lecture on "Turkey Reborn" on Monday'. *The Oakparker*, 3 December 1937.
'"March of Time" Reporter Is Century Club's Speaker'. *Oak Leaves*, 9 December 1937.
Marckies, Earle. 'Ataturk Fuehrer Compared'. *Berkeley Daily Gazette*, 7 March 1940.
'Mustafa Kamâl Builds Nationalist State From Ruins of War-Torn Turkish Empire'. *Photo Reporter*, January/February, 1937.
Roosevelt, Eleanor. 'My Day, March 29, 1937'. *The Eleanor Roosevelt Papers Digital Edition* (2008). Accessed 31 July 2015. http://www.gwu.edu/~erpapers/myday/displaydoc.cfm?_y=1937&_f=md054603.
'Roosevelt Lauds Ataturk's Regime'. *New York Times*, 1 August 1937.
Tasvir-i Efkar, 12 Teşrinisani 1338 (Kasım 1922).
'Ziyafet ve Balo'. *Akşam*, 31 October 1930.

Online sources

American Film Institute. 'Turkey Reborn'. Accessed 18 August 2015. http://www.afi.com/members/catalog/DetailView.aspx?s=1&Movie=8646.

Bardakçı, Murat. 'Beyaz enerji krizimiz bir yangınla başladı'. *Hürriyet*. Last modified 12 May 2001. Accessed 3 May 2014. http://arama.hurriyet.com.tr/arsivnewsmobile.aspx?id=-242952.

Bottomore, Stephen. 'Don Ramirez: Spanish showman active in Turkey'. *Who's Who of Victorian Cinema*. Accessed 2 February 2016. http://www.victorian-cinema.net/ramirez.

Çetin, Mustafa. 'Fuat Uzkınay Ailesi Tarafından Hazırlanan Özgeçmiş 2'. mustafacetin.org. Accessed 22 September 2017. http://www.mustafacetin.org/tr/fuat-uzkinay-ailesi-tarafindan-hazirlanan-ozgecmis-2.

Cohen, Adam. 'The First 100 Days'. *Time*, Accessed 6 January 2016. http://content.time.com/time/specials/packages/article/0,28804,1906802_1906838_1906979,00.html.

Encyclopedia Britannica Online. 'Crescent'. Accessed 3 May 2014. http://www.britannica.com/EBchecked/topic/142628/crescent.

Encyclopedia Britannica Online. 'Ortaoyunu'. Accessed 3 May 2014. http://www.britannica.com/EBchecked/topic/295642/Islamic-arts/13827/Ortaoyunu.

filmportal.de. 'Einzelsujets'. Messter-Woche, Audiovisual file, 1916, 2 min. 38 sec. Accessed 22 September 2017. http://www.filmportal.de/video/messter-woche-einzelsujets.

Genelkurmay Personel Başkanlığı Askerî Tarih ve Stratejik Etüt (ATASE) Daire Başkanlığı Yayınları. *Fotoğraflarla Atatürk*. Ankara: Genelkurmay Basımevi, 2015. Accessed 23 October 2015. http://www.ata.tsk.tr/content/media/07/ataturk_albumu_1.pdf.

International Film Foundation. 'Films'. Accessed 10 August 2015. http://www.internationalfilmfoundation.org/films/?Sort=yd&start=10.

International Film Foundation. 'Turkey: A Nation in Transition'. Accessed 20 July 2015. http://www.internationalfilmfoundation.org/films/show/752.

International Film Foundation. 'Turkey Reborn'. Accessed 15 August 2015. http://www.internationalfilmfoundation.org/films/show/825.

Kekül, Ufuk. 'Topal Osman'ın heykeli dikildi'. *Kentselhaber.com*. Last modified 08 August 2004. Accessed 3 May 2014. http://www.kentselhaber.com/V2/News/90518/Topal-Osman-in-heykeli-dikildi.

National Archives. '19th Amendment to the U.S. Constitution: Women's Right to Vote'. Accessed 30 June 2015. http://www.archives.gov/historical-docs/document.html?doc=13.

Radikal com.tr. 'İpek Çalışlar'a 'Latife' davası'. Last modified 19 August 2006. Accessed 3 May 2014. http://www.radikal.com.tr/haber.php?haberno=196265.

Toker, Metin. 'Atatürk ve Barış'. Atam.gov.tr. Accessed 3 May 2014. http://www.atam.gov.tr/dergi/sayi-09/ataturk-ve-baris-2.

Türk Dil Kurumu: Büyük Türkçe Sözlük. 'dilmen'. Accessed 10 February 2016. http://tdk.gov.tr/index.php?option=com_bts&arama=kelime&guid=TDK.GTS.576260 7ee66cc7.14198817.

Türkei (Konstantinopel): Kriegskundgebung der Bevölkerung bei der Fatih Moschee, Der Erste Weltkrieg und das Ende der Habsburgermonarchie, Audiovisual file, 1914, 45 sec. Accessed 21 March 2017. http://ww1.habsburger.net/de/medien/tuerkei-konstantinopel-kriegskundgebung-der-bevoelkerung-bei-der-fatih-moschee-film-d-1914.

Türkiye Cumhuriyeti Cumhurbaşkanlığı Kurumsal Internet Sitesi. 'Video Galerisi'. Accessed 15 May 2016. https://www.tccb.gov.tr/ata_ozel/video/.

Books and journal articles

Alkan, Mehmet Ö. 'Mustafa'dan Kamâl'a Atatürk'ün İsimleri'. *Toplumsal Tarih* 204 (2010): 56–64.

Alkan, Mehmet Ö. ''Atatürk' Soyadı Nasıl Bulundu?' *Toplumsal Tarih* 205 (2011): 48–53.

Allan, Kenneth. *A Primer in Social and Sociological Theory: Toward a Sociology of Citizenship.* California: Sage Publications, 2011.

Anderson, Benedict. *Imagined Communities: Reflections on the Origin and Spread of Nationalism.* London: Verso, 2006.

Andriopoulos, Stefan. 'The Terror of Reproduction: Early Cinema's Ghostly Doubles and the Right to One's Own Image'. *New German Critique*, no. 99 (2006): 151–70. Accessed 12 April 2015. http://www.jstor.org/stable/27669180.

Arığ, Ayten Sezen. *Atatürk Türkiye'sinde Kılık Kıyafette Çağdaşlaşma.* Ankara: Siyasal Kitabevi, 2007.

Arığ, Ayten Sezen. 'Türkiye'de Kız Enstitüleri: Gelenekten Geleceğe'. *Hacettepe Üniversitesi Türkiyat Araştırmaları Dergisi* 20 (2014): 193–215.

Arslan, Savaş. *Cinema in Turkey: A New Critical History.* New York: Oxford University Press, 2011.

Atay, Falih Rıfkı. *Çankaya: Atatürk'ün Doğumundan Ölümüne Kadar.* İstanbul: Sena Matbaası, 1960.

Ateş, Toktamış. *Türk Devrim Tarihi.* İstanbul: İstanbul Bilgi Üniversitesi Yayınları, 2010.

Avcı, Cemal. 'İsmet İnönü'nün Lozan Dönüşü ve Demeçleri (10 Ağustos 1923—23 Ağustos 1923)'. *Ankara Üniversitesi Türk İnkılâp Tarihi Enstitüsü Atatürk Yolu Dergisi*, 3, no. 12 (1993): 341–54.

Aydemir, Şevket Süreyya. *Tek Adam: Mustafa Kemal*, vol. 1. İstanbul: Remzi Kitabevi, 2011.

Bali, Rıfat N. *US Diplomatic Documents on Turkey II: The Turkish Cinema in the Early Republican Years*. Istanbul: The Isis Press, 2007.

Banoğlu, Niyazi Ahmet. *Atatürk'ün İstanbul'daki Günleri (1899-1919 /1927-1938)*. İstanbul: Alfa Yayınları, 2012.

Barlas, Dilek. 'Friends or Foes? Diplomatic Relations between Italy and Turkey, 1923-36'. *International Journal of Middle East Studies* 36 (2004): 231-52. Accessed 18 April 2016. http://www.jstor.org/stable/3880033.

Barnouw, Erik. *Documentary: A History of the Non-Fiction Film*. New York: Oxford University Press 1993.

Benjamin, Walter. 'The Work of Art in the Age of Its Technological Reproducibility: Second Version'. In *The Work of Art in the Age of Its Technological Reproducibility and Other Writings on Media*, edited by Michael W. Jennings, Brigid Doherty and Thomas Y. Levin, 19-55. Cambridge: Harvard University Press, 2008.

Betsy A. McLane. *A New History of Documentary Film*. London: Continuum, 2012.

Bolat, Bengül Salman. *Milli Bayram Olgusu ve Türkiye'de Yapılan Cumhuriyet Bayramı Kutlamaları (1923-1960)*. Ankara: Atatürk Araştırma Merkezi, 2011.

Börekçi, Günhan. 'The Ottomans and the French Revolution: Popular images of 'Liberty-Equality-Fraternity' in the late Ottoman Iconography, 1908-1912'. Master's thesis, Boğaziçi University, 1999.

Bowles, Stephen E. 'And Time Marched On: The Creation of The March of Time'. *Journal of the University Film Association* 29, no. 1 (1977): 7-13. http://www.jstor.org/stable/20687350.

Boyar, Ebru and Kate Fleet. 'Making Turkey and The Turkish Revolution Known to Foreign Nations without any Expense: Propaganda Films in the Early Turkish Republic'. *Oriente Moderno* 24 (85), no. 1 (2005): 117-32. Accessed 24 April 2015, http://www.jstor.org/stable/25817998.

Boyd-Barrett, Oliver and Terhi Rantanen, eds. *The Globalization of News*. London: Sage Publications, 1998.

Bozdoğan, Sibel. *Modernism and Nation Building: Turkish Architectural Culture in the Early Republic*. Seattle: University of Washington Press, 2001.

Bozis Yorgo and Sula Bozis. *Paris'ten Pera'ya Sinema ve Rum Sinemacılar*. Istanbul: Yapı Kredi Yayınları, 2013.

Briggs, Asa and Peter Burke. *A Social History of the Media: From Gutenberg to the Internet*. Cambridge: Polity Press, 2009.

Burke, Peter, ed. *New Perspectives on Historical Writing*. Pennsylvania: The Pennsylvania State University Press, 2001.

Burke, Peter, ed. *Languages and Communities in Early Modern Europe*. Cambridge: Cambridge University Press, 2004.

Burke, Peter, ed. *Eyewitnessing: The Uses of Images as Historical Evidence*. Ithaca: Cornell University Press, 2008a.

Burke, Peter, ed. *What Is Cultural History?* 2nd Edition. Cambridge: Polity Press, 2008b.

Burke, Peter, ed. *Cultural Hybridity*. Cambridge: Polity Press, 2009a.

Burke, Peter, ed. *The Fabrication of Louis XIV*. London: Yale University Press, 2009b.

Çalışlar, İpek. *Latife Hanım*. İstanbul: Everest Yayınları, 2011.

Carlyle, Thomas. *On Heroes, Hero-Worship, and the Heroic in History*. Edited by David R. Sorensen and Brent E. Kinser. New Haven and London: Yale University Press, 2013.

Casetti, Francesco. *Eye of the Century*: Film, *Experience, Modernity*. New York: Columbia University Press, 2008.

Çeliktemel-Thomen, Özde. 'The Curtain of Dreams: Early Cinema in Istanbul (1896–1923)'. Master's thesis, Central European University, 2009.

Çeliktemel-Thomen, Özde. 'Osmanlı İmparatorluğunda Sinema ve Propaganda (1908–1922)', Online International Journal of Communication Studies, Vol. 2, June 2010.

Çeliktemel-Thomen, Özde. '1903 Sinematograf İmtiyazı'. *Toplumsal Tarih* 229 (2013): 26–32.

Çeliktemel-Thomen, Özde. 'Denetimden Sansüre Osmanlı'da Sinema'. *Toplumsal Tarih*, 255 (2015): 72–9.

Chapman, James. *Film and History*. Basingstoke: Palgrave Macmillan, 2013.

Charney, Leo and Vanessa R. Schwartz, eds. *Cinema and the Invention of Modern Life*. Berkeley: University of California Press, 1995.

Christodoulou, Christos K. *The Manakis Brothers: The Greek Pioneers of the Balkanic Cinema*. Thessaloniki: Organization for the Cultural Capital of Europe Thessaloniki, 1997.

Çırakman, Aslı. 'From Tyranny to Despotism: The Enlightenment's Unenlightened Image of the Turks'. *International Journal of Middle East Studies* 33, no. 1 (2001): 53. Accessed 1 April 2015. http://www.jstor.org/stable/259479.

Çırakman, Aslı. *From the Terror of the World to the 'Sick Man of Europe': European Images of Ottoman Empire and Society from the Sixteenth Century to the Nineteenth*. New York: Peter Lang Publishing, 2002.

Clarke, Sally H. *Regulation and the Revolution in United States Farm Productivity*. New York: Cambridge University Press, 1994.

Daniel, Robert L. *American Philanthrophy in the Near East, 1820–1960*. Athens: Ohio University Press, 1970.

Darnton, Robert. *The Great Cat Massacre and Other Episodes in French Cultural History*. New York: Basic Books, 1984.
Demirci, Sevtap. *Belgelerle Lozan Taktik - Stratejik - Diplomatik Mücadele 1922-1923*. Çeviren Mehmet Moralı. İstanbul: Alfa Yayınları, 2011.
DeNovo, John A. *American Interest and Policies in the Middle East, 1900-1939*. Minneapolis: The University of Minnesota Press, 1963.
Derin, Haldun. *Çankaya Özel Kalemini Anımsarken (1933-1951)*. Edited by Cemil Koçak. Istanbul: Tarih Vakfı Yurt Yayınları, 1995.
Deringil, Selim. *The Well Protected Domains: Ideology and the Legitimation of Power in the Ottoman Empire 1876-1909*. London and New York: I.B. Tauris, 2011.
Derrida, Jacques. 'Archive Fever: A Freudian Impression'. Translated by Eric Prenowitz. *Diacritics*, 25, no. 2 (1995): 9-63. Accessed 28 September 2014. doi: 10.2307/465144.
Doane, Mary Ann. *The Emergence of Cinematic Time: Modernity, Contingency, the Archive*. Cambridge: Harvard University Press, 2002.
Dorsay, Atilla. *Sinema ve Çağımız*. Istanbul: Remzi Kitapevi, 1998.
Douglas, Mary. *Purity and Danger*. Routledge: London, 2003.
Egeli, Münir Hayri. *Bilinmeyen Yönleriyle Atatürk*. Ankara: Berikan, 2004.
Eisenstadt, Shmuel N. 'Multiple Modernities'. In *The Multiple Modernities*, edited by Shmuel N. Eisenstadt, 1-30. New York: Routledge, 2017.
Erdoğan, Nezih. 'The Spectator in the Making of Modernity and Cinema in Istanbul, 1896-1928'. In *Orienting Istanbul: Cultural Capital of Europe?*, edited by Deniz Göktürk, Levent Soysal and İpek Türeli, 129-43. New York: Routledge, 2010.
Erksan, Metin. *Atatürk Filmi*. Istanbul: Hil Yayın, 1989.
Fielding, Raymond. 'Time Flickers Out: Notes on the Passing of The "March of Time"'. *The Quarterly of Film Radio and Television* 11, no. 4 (1957): 354-61. doi: 10.2307/1209995.146.
Fielding, Raymond. *The March of Time: 1935-1951*. New York: Oxford University Press, 1978.
Fielding, Raymond. *The American Newsreel, 1911-1967*. Oklahoma: University of Oklahoma Press, 1980.
Fielding, Raymond. *The American Newsreel: A Complete History*, 1911-1967. 2nd ed. Jefferson, North Carolina: MacFarland, 2006.
Filmer, Cemil. *Hatıralar: Türk Sinemasında 65 Yıl*. İstanbul: Emek Matbaacılık ve İlâncılık, 1984.
Fortna, Benjamin C. *Learning to Read in the Late Ottoman Empire and the Early Turkish Republic*. Basingstoke: Palgrave Macmillan, 2012.
Foucault, Michel. *Discipline and Punish: The Birth of the Prison*. Translated by Alan Sheridan. London: Penguin, 1991a.

Foucault, Michel. 'The Great Confinement'. In *The Foucault Reader: An Introduction to Foucault's Thought*, edited by Paul Rabinow, 124–40. London: Penguin, 1991b.
Foucault, Michel. *Archeology of Knowledge*. Translated by A. M. Sheridan Smith. New York: Routledge, 2002.
Fumaroli, Marc. *When the World Spoke French*. Translated by Richard Howard. New York: The New York Review of Books, 2011.
Geertz, Clifford. *The Interpretation of Cultures*. New York: Basic Books, 1973.
Goethe, Johann Wolfgang von. *Faust: Der Tragödie erster und zweiter Teil, Urfaust*. Edited by Erich Trunz. München: C.H. Beck, 1986.
Gök, Fatma. 'The Girls' Institutes in the Early Period of the Turkish Republic'. In *Education in 'Multicultural' Societies: Turkish and Swedish Perspectives*, edited by Maria Carlson, Annika Rabo and Fatma Gök, 93–105. Bromma: Swedish Research Institute in Istanbul, 2007.
Gökçaylı, Vural. 'Bir ulusun tasarımcısı: Atatürk'. In *O Daima Şıktı: Gazi'nin Son Tanıkları Anlatıyor*, edited by Nebil Özgentürk, 44–5. Istanbul: Bir Yudum Insan Yayınevi, 2010.
Grew, Joseph C. *Turbulent Era: A Diplomatic Record of Forty Years, 1904-1945*, Vol. 2. Edited by Walter Johnson. Cambridge: The Riberside Press, 1952.
Gürkan, Emrah Safa. 'Mutual Cultural Influences'. In *Encyclopedia of the Ottoman Empire*, edited by Gábor Ágoston and Bruce Masters, 224–5. New York: Facts on File, 2009.
Guseinov, Abdul Anbievich. *Turetskoe kino: istoriia i sovremennye problemy*. Moscow: Nauka, 1978.
Hall, James A. *Hall's Dictionary of Subjects and Symbols in Art*. London: John Murray, 1991.
Hanioğlu, M. Şükrü. *Atatürk: An Intellectual Biography*. Princeton: Princeton University Press, 2011.
Harris, George S. 'Cementing Turkish-American Relations: The Ambassadorship of (Mehmet) Münir Ertegün (1934–1944)'. In *Studies in Atatürk's Turkey: The American Dimension*, edited by George S. Harris and Nur Bilge Criss. Leiden, Boston: Brill, 2009.
Hubertus, Jahn. *Patriotic Culture in Russia during World War I*. Ithaca, New York and London: Cornell University Press, 1998.
İnan, Afet. *Atatürk Hakkında Hatıralar ve Belgeler*. İstanbul: İş Bankası Kültür Yayınları, 2009.
Kaçar, Ayşe Duygu. *Kültür / Mekân, Gazi Orman Çiftliği*. Ankara: Koç Üniversitesi Vekam Yayınları, 2015.
Karaosmanoğlu, Yakup Kadri. *Atatürk*. İstanbul: İletişim Yayınları, 2014.
Karayaman, Mehmet. 'Atatürk Döneminde Şeker Sanayi ve İzlenen Politikalar'. *Atatürk Araştırma Merkezi Dergisi* 82 (2012): 54–96.

Kemal, Gazi Mustafa. *Nutuk*. Istanbul: Yapı Kredi Yayınları, 2015.

Kenç, Faruk. 'Sayın bayana da selam söyle'. In *O Daima Şıktı: Gazi'nin Son Tanıkları Anlatıyor*, edited by Nebil Özgentürk, 88–92. Istanbul: Bir Yudum Insan Yayınevi, 2010.

Keskinok, Çağatay. 'Bir Özgürleşme Tasarısı Olarak Atatürk Orman Çiftliği'. In *Bir Çağdaşlaşma Öyküsü: Cumhuriyet Devriminin Büyük Eseri Atatürk Orman Çiftliği*, edited by Yalçın Memluk et al., 70–90. Ankara: Koleksiyoncular Derneği Yayını, 2007.

Kinross, Patrick. *Atatürk: The Rebirth of a Nation*. London: Phoenix, 2005.

Kocatürk, Utkan. *Atatürk ve Türkiye Cumhuriyeti Tarihi Kronolojisi, 1918–1938*. 3. Baskı. Ankara: Türk Tarih Kurumu Basımevi, 2000.

Kocatürk, Utkan. *Doğumundan Ölümüne Kadar Kaynakçalı Atatürk Günlüğü*. 2. Basım. Ankara: Atatürk Araştırma Merkezi, 2007.

Kongar, Emre. *Devrim Tarihi ve Toplum Bilinci Açısından Atatürk*. İstanbul: Remzi Kitabevi, 1999.

Kongar, Emre. 'Atatürk'le devam eden bir hayat…'. In *O Daima Şıktı: Gazi'nin Son Tanıkları Anlatıyor*, edited by Nebil Özgentürk, 189–91. Istanbul: Bir Yudum Insan Yayınevi, 2010.

Koral, Füreya. 'Siyah pelerinli Atatürk'. In *O Daima Şıktı: Gazi'nin Son Tanıkları Anlatıyor*, edited by Nebil Özgentürk, 106–7. Istanbul: Bir Yudum Insan Yayınevi, 2010.

Kreiser, Klaus. *Atatürk: Eine Biographie*. München: Verlag C. H. Beck, 2008.

Kuhn, Annette and Guy Westwell. *A Dictionary of Film Studies*. Oxford: Oxford University Press, 2012.

Lasswell, Herold D. 'The Structure and Function of Communication in Society'. In *The Communication of Ideas: A Series of Addresses*, edited by Lyman Bryson, 37–51. New York: Institute for Religious and Social Studies, 1948.

Le Bon, Gustave. *Psychologie des foules*. Paris: Félix Alcan, 1895.

Lewis, Bernard. *The Emergence of Modern Turkey*. 3rd ed. New York: Oxford University Press, 2002.

Lewis, Geoffrey. *The Turkish Language Reform: A Catastrophic Success*. New York: Oxford University Press, 2010.

Loy, Jane M. 'The Present as Past: Assessing the Value of Julien Bryan's Films as Historical Evidence'. *Latin American Research Review* 12, no. 3 (1977): 103–28. Accessed 5 August 2015. http://www.jstor.org/stable/2502471.

Mango, Andrew. *A Speech on Atatürk's Universality*. İstanbul: Aybay Yayınları, 1996.

Mango, Andrew. *Atatürk*. London: John Murray, 1999.

Mauss, Marcel. *The Gift: The Form and Reason for Exchange in Archaic Societies*. Translated by W.D. Halls. New York: W. W. Norton & Company, 2000.

Memluk, Yalçın. 'Cephelerden Orman Çiftliğine'. In *Bir Çağdaşlaşma Öyküsü: Cumhuriyet Devriminin Büyük Eseri Atatürk Orman Çiftliği*, edited by Yalçın Memluk et al., 91-9. Ankara: Koleksiyoncular Derneği Yayını, 2007.

Meyer, Arline. 'Re-dressing Classical Statuary: The Eighteenth-Century 'Hand-in-Waistcoat' Portrait'. *The Art Bulletin*, 77, no. 1 (1995): 45-63. Accessed 20 January 2016. doi 10.2307/3046079.

Osmanoğlu, Ayşe. *Babam Sultan Abdülhamid*. İstanbul: Timaş Yayınları, 2013.

Özdemir, Nuray. 'Türk Kadınına Milletvekili Seçme ve Seçilme Hakkı Tanınması Üzerine Yapılan Kutlamalar'. *History Studies* 6, no. 5 (2014): 177-91. Accessed 21 April 2015, http://www.historystudies.net/Makaleler/2054201183_9-Nuray%20Özdemir.pdf.

Özen, Mustafa. 'De opkomst van het moderne medium cinema in de Ottomaanse hoofdstad Istanbul, 1896-1914'. PhD diss., Universiteit Utrecht, 2007.

Özen, Mustafa. 'Travelling Cinema in Istanbul'. In *Travelling Cinema in Europe*, edited by Martin Loiperdinger, 47-53. Frankfurt am Main: Stroemfeld Verlag, 2008.

Özen, Mustafa. 'Visual Representation and Propaganda: Early Films and Postcards in the Ottoman Empire, 1895-1914'. *Early Popular Visual Culture*, 6, no. 2 (2009): 145-57. doi: 10.1080/17460650802150408.

Özen, Saadet. 'Rethinking the Young Turk Revolution: Manaki Brothers' Still and Moving Images'. Master's thesis, Bogaziçi University, 2010.

Özkaya, Yücel. 'Cumhuriyetin İlanı ve Rejim Olarak Eğitime Katkıları'. *Atatürk Araştırma Merkezi Dergisi* 56 (2003): 471-81.

Özön, Nijat. *İlk Türk Sinemacısı Fuat Uzkınay*. İstanbul: Türk Sinematek Derneği Yayınları, 1970.

Özön, Nijat. *Türk Sineması Tarihi 1896-1960*. İstanbul: Doruk Yayımcılık, 2010.

Öztaner, Emine. 'Technology as a Multidirectional Construction: Electrification of Istanbul in the Late Nineteenth and Early Twentieth Centuries'. Master's thesis, İstanbul Şehir University, 2014.

Öztoprak, Izzet. *Atatürk Orman Çiftliği'nin Tarihi*. Ankara: Atatürk Araştırma Merkezi, 2006.

Öztuncay, Bahattin. 'Wilhelm Viktor Krausz (1878-1959) The War Painter in the Ottoman Empire'. In *Propaganda and War: The Allied Front during the First World War*, edited by Edhem Eldem et al. Istanbul: Mas Matbaacılık, 2014.

Öztürk, Serdar. *Erken Cumhuriyet Döneminde Sinema, Seyir, Siyaset*. Ankara: Elips Kitap, 2005.

Özuyar, Ali. *Babıâli'de Sinema*. İstanbul: İzdüşüm Yayınları, 2004.

Özuyar, Ali. 'II. Meşrutiyet'in Modernleşmede Önemli Bir Araç Olan Sinema Üzerindeki Etkileri'. In *100. Yılında II. Meşrutiyet Gelenek ve Değişim Ekseninde Türk Modernleşmesi Uluslararası Sempozyumu: Bildiriler*, edited by Zekeriya

Kurşun, Cemil Öztürk, Yasemin Tümer Erdem and Arzu M. Nurdoğan, 447–55. İstanbul: Ebru Matbaacılık, 2009.
Özuyar, Ali. *Sessiz Dönem Türk Sineması Antolojisi (1895–1928)*. Istanbul: Küre Yayınları, 2015.
Özuyar, Ali. *Sessiz Dönem Türk Sineması Tarihi (1895–1922)*. Istanbul: Yapı Kredi Yayınları, 2016.
Pamuk, Şevket. *The Ottoman Empire and European Capitalism, 1820–1913: Trade, Investment and Production*. Cambridge: Cambridge University Press, 1987.
Pronay, Nicholas and Peter Wenham. *The News and the Newsreel*. London: Macmillan Education Ltd, 1976.
Quataert, Donald. 'Clothing Laws, State, and Society in the Ottoman Empire, 1720–1829'. *International Journal of Middle East Studies* 29, no. 3 (1997): 403–25. Accessed 2 February 2015. http://www.jstor.org/stable/164587.
Quataert, Donald. *The Ottoman Empire*, 1700–1922. Cambridge: Cambridge University Press, 2000.
Raup, Philip M. 'Economies and Diseconomies of Large-Scale Agriculture'. *American Journal of Agricultural Economics* 51, no. 5 (1969): 1274–83. Accessed 5 March 2016. http://www.jstor.org/stable/1238003.
Refiğ, Halit. *Gazi ile Latife: Mustafa Kemal'in Yaşamından Bir Kesit*. Istanbul: Alfa Yayınları, 2008.
Reisman, Arnold. *Turkey's Modernization: Refugees from Nazism and Atatürk's Vision*. Washington: New Academia Publishing, 2006.
Ricoeur, Paul. *Time and Narrative*, Vol. 1. Translated by K. McLaughlin and D. Dellauer. Chicago: University of Chicago Press, 1990.
Rollberg, Peter. *Historical Dictionary of Russian and Soviet Cinema*. Lanham: Scarecrow Press, 2009.
Şahin, Feyza Kurnaz. 'Cumhuriyetin Kuruluşuna Kadar Türkiye'de Yardım Cemiyetlerinin Sinema Faaliyetleri ve Kamuoyunda Sinema Algısı (1910–1923)'. *Atatürk Araştırma Merkezi Dergisi* 88 (2014): 1–35.
Said, Edward W. *Orientalism*. London: Penguin Books, 2003.
Sakaoğlu, Necdet, 'Yangınlar: Osmanlı Dönemi'. In *Dünden Bugüne İstanbul Ansiklopedisi*. Vol 7. İstanbul: Kültür Bakanlığı ve Tarih Vakfı, 1994.
Scognamillo, Giovanni. *Türk Sinema Tarihi*. İstanbul: Kabalcı Yayınevi, 2010.
Sekeroglu, Sami. "I am opening the 2nd gathering year of the 4th Quarter of the Parliament!...': A Nitrate Memory'. In *This Film is Dangerous: A Celebration of Nitrate Film*, edited by Roger Smither and Catherine A. Surowiec. London: FIAF, 2002.
Şener, Erman. *Kurtuluş Savaşı ve Sinemamız*. Dizi Yayınları, 1970.
Şener, Erman. *Sinema Seyircisinin El Kitabı*. İstanbul: Koza Yayınları, 1976.

Serim, Ömer. *Devlet Yapar Devlet Yıkar (Yorgun Savaşçı* Olayı). İstanbul: An Yayıncılık, 2003.

Shakespeare, William. *As You Like It*. Edited by George Rice Carpenter. New York: Longmans, Green and Co., 1896.

Smith, Emily. *The Charlie Chaplin Handbook: Everything You Need to Know About Charlie Chaplin*. Emereo Pty Limited, 2011.

Sorlin, Pierre. 'War and cinema: Interpreting the Relationship'. *Historical Journal of Film, Radio & Television* 14 (1994): 357-66.

Tezcan, Semih S. *Atatürk Dizi Filmi Teşebbüsü Nasıl Baltalandı? 1984-1987*. İstanbul: Yüksek Öğrenim Eğitim ve Araştırma Vakfı, 2005.

Toprak, Zafer. *Darwin'den Dersim'e Cumhuriyet ve Antropoloji*. Istanbul: Doğan Kitap, 2012.

Trask, Roger R. *The United States Response to Turkish Nationalism and Reform, 1914-1939*. Minneapolis: The University of Minnesota Press, 1971.

Tunalı, Uğurlu. 'Atatürk Orman Çiftliği'. In *Bir Çağdaşlaşma Öyküsü: Cumhuriyet Devriminin Büyük Eseri Atatürk Orman Çiftliği*, edited by Yalçın Memluk et al. Ankara: Koleksiyoncular Derneği Yayını, 2007.

Türk Tarihinin Ana Hatları: Kemalist Yönetimin Tarih Tezi. İstanbul: Kaynak Yayınları, 1996.

Turkish Statistical Institute. *Turkey in Statistics*. Ankara: Türkiye İstatistik Kurumu Matbaası, 2014.

Véray, Laurent. 'Cinema'. In *The Cambridge History of the First World War Volume 3. Civil Society*, edited by Jay Winter, 475-503. Cambridge: Cambridge University Press, 2014.

Virilio, Paul. *War and Cinema: The Logistics of Perception*. London and New York: Verso, 1989.

Vree, Frank van. 'Media Morality and Popular Culture. The Case of the Netherlands 1870-1965'. In *Twentieth-Century Mass Society Britain and Netherlands*, edited by Bob Moore and Henk van Nierop, 79-92. New York: Berg, 2006.

Vree, Frank van. 'The Imagery of War: Screening the Battlefield in the Twentieth Century'. Paper presented at the International Conference and Summer School: Cultures of War and Peace, Peace Palace, The Hague, 15 June 2013.

Waley, Muhammed Isa. 'Images of the Ottoman Empire: The Photograph Albums presented by Sultan Abdulhamid II'. *The British Library Journal*, 17, No. 2 (1991): 111-27. Accessed 23 June 2015. http://www.jstor.org/stable/42554325.

White, Hayden. *Metahistory: The Historical Imagination in Nineteenth-Century Europe*. Baltimore: The Johns Hopkins University Press, 1975.

Yalçın, Memluk. 'Atatürk Orman Çiftliği'. In *Bir Çağdaşlaşma Öyküsü: Cumhuriyet Devriminin Büyük Eseri Atatürk Orman Çiftliği*, edited by Yalçın Memluk et al. 91-9. Ankara: Koleksiyoncular Derneği Yayını, 2007.

Yıldıran, İbrahim. 'Selim Sırrı Tarcan ve Türk Sinemasının Erken Dönem Tartışmalarına Katkı'. *Kebikeç* 27 (2009): 221–30.

Yılmaz, Şuhnaz. "Korkunç Türk' imajı ile mücadele', *Toplumsal Tarih* 120 (2003): 86–91.

Yılmaz, Şuhnaz. 'Challenging the stereotypes: Turkish–American relations in the inter-war era'. *Middle Eastern Studies*, 42, no. 2 (2006): 223–37. Accessed 8 April 2017. doi: 10.1080/00263200500417520.

Yüksel, Yurdagül. 'Atatürk ve Roosvelt', *Atatürk Araştırma Merkezi Dergisi* 44 (1999): 778–84.

Zajicek, Taylor Craig. 'Modern Friendship: The "New Turkey" and Soviet Cultural Diplomacy, 1933–1934'. Master's thesis, University of Washington, 2014.

Zürcher, Erik Jan. *The Unionist Factor: The Role of the Committee of Union and Progress in the Turkish National Movement 1905–1926*. Leiden: Brill, 1984.

Zürcher, Erik Jan. *Turkey: A Modern History*. London and New York: I.B. Tauris, 1998.

Zürcher, Erik Jan. *The Young Turk Legacy and Nation Building: From the Ottoman Empire to Atatürk's Turkey*. New York: I.B. Tauris, 2010.

Zürcher, Erik Jan. 'In the Name of the Father, the Teacher and the Hero: The Atatürk Personality Cult in Turkey'. In *Political Leadership Leaders and Charisma*, edited by Vivian Ibrahim and Margit Wunsch, 129–42. London: Routledge, 2012.

Index

advertisement 150
Afgan Kralı Amanullah Han'ın Türkiye Ziyareti (*The Visit of the Afghan King Amanullah Khan to Turkey*, 1928) 211
agriculture 99–101, 104
   economic reforms 185–6, 187
   educational function 101
   large-scale 186
   machine workshop 108–9
   small-scale 186
   tractors 107–8
AKP. *See* Justice and Development Party (Adalet ve Kalkınma Partisi)
Akyüz, Ali 210
alafranga (Western) lifestyle 36
Albanians 107
Alexander, King of Yugoslavia 141
Alexander the Great 206
Ali Efendi Sineması 24, 29, 31, 51
Alkan, Mehmet Ö. 174
Allied powers 3, 28–37, 54–5, 65, 66–7, 71, 74, 87, 100, 139, 165, 188
All Quiet on the Western Front (1930) 118
alphabet reform 172–3
American Friends of Turkey 113
American Patenior Cinematograph Company 64
Anadolu Ajansı 180
Anafartalar Group 204
Anatolian Railway 19
Anderson, Benedict 173
Angora (Ankara) 55
Ankara Independence Tribunal 171
Ankara Postası (*Ankara Post*, 1928) 207
Ankara- Serdtse Turtsii (*Türkiye'nin Kalbi Ankara* or *Ankara: Heart of Turkey*, 1934) 211
Ankara Sineması 76–7
Ar, Cezmi 51, 54, 55, 57, 66, 212, 217 n.24–5

Aras, Tevfik Rüştü 190
Araz, Nezihe 209
The Archeology of Knowledge (Foucault) 63
archives 7–11
Arıkan, Safvet 175
armed resistance 66–7
Armenian Revolutionary Federation 19
Armenians 66, 69, 77, 148–9
Armistice of Mudanya 54–5
Armistice of Mudros 33, 35
Arnshtam, Lev Oskarovich 211
Asaduryan 25
Asena, Orhan 209
Atatürk (film) 208
Atatürk, Mustafa Kemal 1–2
   Bryan meeting and filming 138–44
   on cinema 1, 76–7
   country trips 202–3
   as cult figure 213
   dress reforms 167–72
   early life 3
   economic reforms 185–8
   European fashion and 205
   family name/surname 174–5
   foreign policy 188–92
   Forest Farm 87–120
   interest in film 2
   language (theory and reform) 177–83
   letter to Roosevelt 134
   military career 3
   official media portrayal 206–10
   political agenda 3
   public image 3
   Roosevelt's letter to 133
   six-day speech (*Nutuk*) 69
   sixty-ninth death anniversary 150
   world peace and security 139–40
'Ata Turk' 175
Ataturk Entertains Grew on His Private Estate 8–9, 119
'Atatürk Film' 208–9
Atatürk's 4th Quarter Speech (1934) 212

Atatürk'ün Amerikan Büyükelçisi Joseph C. Grew'u Orman Çiftliğinde Kabulü (1930)   8, 9, 87–120
   cows (scene IV)   104–5
   fountain (scene II)   98–103
   garden (scene II)   103
   machine shop (scene VIII)   108–9
   making   89–90
   overview   87–8
   poultry (scene V)   106–7
   preliminary speeches (scene I)   90–8
   sheep (scene VI)   106–7
   tractors (scene VII)   107–8
   woman (scene IX)   109–11
Atatürk'ün Fedaisi Topal Osman (*Lame Osman the Bodyguard of Atatürk,* 2013)   69
Atatürk ve Sanat (*Atatürk and Art*)   208
Ateşten Gömlek (*The Turkish Ordeal,* 1923)   207
Austria-Hungarian Empire   29–30
Austria-Hungarian War Ministry Social Welfare Bureau   204
Axis powers   139–40, 164
Ayastefanos'taki Rus Abidesinin Yıkılışı (*The Demolition of the Russian Monument at San Stefano*)   29

Balkan Pact (Entente)   190
Balkan Wars (1912–3)   66
Banoğlu, Niyazi Ahmet   117
Baransel, Nurettin   61
Bardakçı, Murat   20
Barneys, Edward   115
Barnouw, Erik   39 n.9
bazaar   113–14
Belen, Fahri   61
Bellini, Gentile   201
Benjamin, Walter   116–17
Berger, Ludwig   118
Bey, Adnan (Adıvar)   64, 66
Bey, Ahmet Necati   32
Bey, Fazlı Necip   59
Bey, Fuad   112, 113
Bey, Mehmet Bolak   60
Bey, Tahsin   99, 101, 103, 104–6, 107, 127 n.57
Bey, Usakizâde Muammer   73
Bey, Vehbi   60
Bilginer, Haluk   150

Bilginer, Recep   209
bioscope   16
Bir Millet Uyanıyor (The Awakening of a Nation)   207, 212
Black Sea   101
Bloom, Sol   149
Bonaparte, Napoléon   163, 206
Boyar, Ebru   119
British Museum, London   17
British Pathé   65
broadcasting system   209
Bryan, Julien   8, 10, 12, 134–50
   afterlives of footage   144–50
   arrival in Istanbul   136–8
   meeting and filming Atatürk   138–44
   travel lectures   135–6
Bryan, Sam   8, 10, 136
Buğra, Tarık   209
Burke, Peter   14 n.14, 142, 162–3, 181

Caesar, J.   206
Calışlar, İpek   67–8, 84 n.110
cargo ships   188
Casetti, Francesco   27
censorship commission   208
Central Command   32–3
Central Intelligence Agency (CIA)   119
Central Office of Cinema   33–4, 35, 37
Chanel, Coco   205
Chaplin, Charlie   37, 85–6 n.124
Chapman, James   7
Charney, Leo   21
Cinecittà   213
cinema
   advantage over other media   58
   educational   135
   entertainment potential   22
   as a *gâvur* (non-Muslim or infidel)   22
   invention   57
   modern culture   21
   orphan   65–75
   Ottoman Muslims   24
   pioneers of   16
   propaganda   30, 31, 32, 78, 213
   public   20–8
   silent   118
   technological inventions   15–16
   universal language   27
   visual language   58
   wartime   28–37

cinématographe   16
Cine Theatrale d'Orient   26
civil society   97
Civil War in Spain   188
clothing style. *See* dress reforms
Cohen, Emanuel 'Jack'   65
Committee of Disabled Veterans   35–6, 37, 38, 47 n.146–7, 50, 58–61, 81 n.44
Committee of Disabled Veterans Film Factory   36
Committee of Union and Progress (CUP)   30, 31, 32, 35, 38, 50, 51, 58, 77, 148 n.47, 202, 203, 207, 208
Continsouza, Pierre Victor   18
cotton   187
cows   104–5
cuffed trousers   205
Cumali, Necati   209
Cumhuriyet (*The Republic*, 1998) (TV series)   209

David, Jacques-Louise   163
Declaration of Independence (US)   97
The Declaration of Jihad Proclamation   29
Delavallée, Henri   21, 22
democracy   96–8
The Demolition of the Moscow Monument   29
Derin, Haldun   141, 142, 143
Deringil, Selim   201
Derrida, Jacques   11, 56, 62–3
Der Sieg des Glaubens   213
d'Espèrey, Franchet   36
Die vierzig Tage des Musa Dagh (*The Forty Days of Musa Dagh,* 1933)   148–9
Dilaçar, Agop   143, 172, 178, 182
Dil Kurumu. *See* Turkish Language Association
Dilmen, Güngör   209
Diradour, Onnik   16, 39 n.8
Doane, Mary Ann   15, 22
domestic film producers   50–64
Dorsay, Attila   212
dress reforms   167–72
Dumlupınar Vekayi'i (*The Incidents of Dumlupınar,* 1922)   60
Dündar, Can   210

Eastman Kodak Co.   135
economic reforms   185–8

Edip, Halide   37
Edison, Thomas   15–16
educational films   135
education system   174
Edward, the Prince of Wales   168, 205, 216 n.17
Edward VII, King   205
Edward VIII, King   137
Efendi, Ali   24
Egeli, Münir Hayri   212
electricity   17, 18, 20, 23, 87
Elektra Sineması   54
The Emperor Napoleon in His Study at the Tuileries (1812)   56, 163
Emperyal Sineması   24
Empire Music Hall, London   16
Enlightenment   97
Enver Bey cigarettes   204
Enver Paşa Yazısı (Enver Pasha Writing)   173
Ercole, J.   64–5
Erduran, Refik   209
Erginsoy, Kenan Reşit   32, 202
Erksan, Metin   208–9
Ertegün Mehmet Münir   146–9, 152
Ertuğrul, Muhsin   206–7
Ethiopia, Italian invasion of   188, 191
Europe
  Axis aggression   139–40, 164
  civil society   97
  film screenings   22
European Union accession negotiations   209–10

farming. *See* agriculture
fascism   213
fashion   167–72, 205
'Father of All Turks'   9–10, 12, 161–3
Fehim, Ahmet   36
feudalism   97
Fevziye Kıraathanesi   22
fez   168
Fielding, Raymond   64–5
Filmarchiv Austria   29
Filmer, Cemil   33, 34, 51, 59, 75–6, 85 n.117, 85 n.119, 85 n.122, 85 n.124
film producers
  domestic   50–64
  foreign   64–5

films. *See* cinema
fires   40 n.13
First World War   24, 28–37, 49, 51, 58, 61–2, 66, 138–9, 173, 186, 187
Fleet, Kate   119
foreign film producers   64–5
Forest Farm   87–120. *See also Atatürk'ün Amerikan Büyükelçisi Joseph C. Grew'u Orman Çiftliğinde Kabulü* (1930)
Foucault, Michel   11, 26, 63
fountain   98–103
Fox Films Inc.   8–9
Fox Movietone News Collections   9, 119
France   190
Franco, Francisco   139
French Revolution   162–3
Freud, Sigmund   115

Gadmer   65
garden   103, 150
Gaumont   65
Gazi and Latife   209
Gazi Elifbası (Gazi Alphabet)   173
Gazi Mustafa Kemal, Atatürk Orman Çiftliği'nde (Ghazi Mustafa Kemal is on the Forest Farm)   9
Gazi Mustafa Kemal'in Amerikalılara Hitabı (Ghazi Mustafa Kemal's Address to the Americans)   9
Gazi'nin İzmir'e Gelişi ve Karşılanışı (*The Arrival and Reception of the Ghazi in Izmir*, 1922)   60
gender roles   26
gender segregation   76
Gérard, Francois   163
Germany   213
  Bryan in   150
  film industry   213
  Ministry of Propaganda   213
  Ottoman public opinion in favour of   30
Girls' Institute in Ankara   184
Glenn, Jack   150
Goebbels, Joseph   213
Goldschmid, J.   30
Goltz, Von der   204
Grand Café, Paris   16
Grandmother Despina   23
Great Fire of Izmir   64

'Great Man' theory   4
Greco-Turkish War of 1922   64–5
Greece
  Balkan Pact (Entente)   190
  treaty of friendship with Turkey   190
Greek army   49
Greek refugees   166
Grew, Joseph C.   8–9, 12, 87, 89, 109, 116–17, 120
Güneş Dil Teorisi (Sun Language Theory)   177

Hamid, Sultan Abdul, II   17–20, 22, 70, 200–2
Hamit, Baba   202
Hanım, Âfet   90, 98, 103, 109–10, 111
Hanım, Fikriye   209
Harf Devrimi (letter reform). *See* alphabet reform
hats   168–70
HBO archives   10
health care system   184–5
Hilal-i Ahmer Cemiyeti (Red Crescent Society)   59
Hindenburg Zeppelin   160
Hitler, Adolf   115, 138–9, 150, 152, 160, 161, 188, 213
Hoxha, Enver   203
Hrisos, Panayiotis   26
Hür Adam (Free Man, 2011)   210
Hynes, Samuel   61

Ice Age   176
Ileri   59
Illustration   64
İlmen, Vehice   31, 68
Incredible Turk (1958)   119
industries/industrialization   186–7
'Inside Nazi Germany'   150, 161
International Film Foundation   10
interpretative journalism   161
inventor-entrepreneurs   15–16
İran Şahı Rıza Pehlevi'nin Türkiye Ziyareti (*The Visit of the Iranian Shah Rýza Pehlevi to Turkey*, 1934)   211
Islamic civilization   72
I Stand for Your Dreams   208

İstiklâl (Independence)   61
İstiklâl Harbinin Başlangıcı, Devamı, Netayici (The Beginning, Continuation and Consequences of the Independence War)   61
Italy
    fascism   213
    invasion of Ethiopia   188, 191
    propaganda films and newsreels   213
    treaty of neutrality with Turkey   190
İzmir'deki Yunan Fecayii (The Disasters Caused by Greeks in Izmir, 1922)   60
İzmir'in İşgali (The Occupation of Izmir, 1922)   60
İzmir Yanıyor (Izmir in Flames, 1922)   60
İzmir Zaferi (The Victory of Izmir, 1922)   60, 61, 81 n.45

Janin, Louis   39 n.10
Jennings, Asa K.   113
Justice and Development Party (Adalet ve Kalkınma Partisi)   210

Kahn, Albert   65
kalpak (a lamb's-fur cap)   55–6, 65–6, 80 n.18–19, 84 n.115
Karagöz (a shadow play)   21
Kaya, Şükrü   117
Kellogg-Briand Pact   139
Kemal, Namık   180
Kemal Bey Sineması   51
Kemal Film   47 n.147, 50–5, 57, 58, 60–1, 66, 81 n.44, 117
kinetoscope   16
Kocatürk, Utkan   117
Krausz, Wilhelm Viktor   204
Kurtuluş (Liberation, 1994) (TV series)   209
Kuvâ-yı Milliye (National Forces)   67
Kvergić, Herman Feodor   177

language (theory and reform)   177–83
large-scale agriculture   186
L'Arrivée d'un Train en Gare de La Ciotat (The Arrival of a Train at La Ciotat Station, 1895)   16
La Sortie de l'Usine Lumière à Lyon (Workers Leaving the Lumière Factory in Lyon, 1895)   16

Latife   67–8, 73–5, 84 n.110, 209, 210
Latife Hanim (Çalışlar)   67–8
Latife Hanim (film)   68, 69
Latin   173
Law 5816 (The Law Concerning Crimes Committed Against Atatürk)   207–8
League of Nations   188–9, 190
Le Bon, Gustave   115
Lenin, Vladimir   142, 163, 213
Les Archives de la Planète   65
letter reform. See alphabet reform
Library of Congress, Washington, DC   17
LIFE   135
literacy rate   173
Locarno Treaties   139
Louis XVIII in His Cabinet (1824)   163
Lozan Sulh Heyetinin Karşılanması (The Reception of the Lausanne Peace Committee, 1923)   8, 11, 69–75, 83 n.90
Lumière brothers   16–17, 39 n.8

machine workshop   108–9
Magee, Patrick   208
Mahmud II (1785–1839)   201
Malûl Gaziler Cemiyeti. See Committee of Disabled Veterans
Malûl Gaziler Sineması   58
Manaki, Yanaki   42 n.54
Manaki brothers   23, 42 n.54, 70, 202
Mango, Andrew   69
The March of Time (newsreel series)   9–10, 12, 141, 159–93
    Atatürk's foreign policy (intertitle 4)   188–92
    Bryan's film footage   150
    'Father of All Turks'   9–10, 12, 161–3
    national movement (intertitle 2)   165–6
    Ottoman Empire (intertitle 1)   163–5
    Turkey as modern state and reforms (intertitle 3)   166–88
Marey, Étienne   15
Martanyan, Hagop   182
Martineau, Harriet   97
Meddah (storytelling)   22
medical reforms   184–5
Mehmed VI   71, 165, 203

Merkez Sinema Dairesi. *See* Central
    Office of Cinema
Messter, Oskar   29–30
Messter Film   29
Messter-Woche (newsreel
    series)   30, 31, 204
Metamorfoz (TV series)   209
MGM (Metro-Goldwyn-Mayer)   148–9
Michalakopoulos, Andreas   118
Milestone, Lewis   118
Mimar Sinan University   7
Ministry of Propaganda, Germany   213
mixed-gender education system   174
Montreux Convention   189
Mopty, Marc   208
motion pictures   15
Moving Image Research Collections
    (MIRC)   8–9
Müdafaa-i Milliye Cemiyeti. *See* Society of
    National Defense
Mudafaa-i Milliye Sineması. *See* Theatre
    of National Defense
multi-vocal cultural environment   209
Mürebbiye (Governess, film directed by
    Ahmet Fehim, 1919)   36
Mürebbiye (novel by Rahmi)   36
Mussolini, Benito   115, 139, 160, 161,
    188–9, 190, 213
Mustafa (2008)   210
Mustapha Kemal (1923)   8, 11
Mustapha Kemel (1920–9)   8, 11, 65–6, 69
Muybridge, Eadweard   15

namaz   166
National Archives, Washington, DC.   9
national cinema industry   24,
    34–5, 50, 77
National Forces   49
National Geographic Society   118
nationalism   4
National Movement   49–50, 56,
    64, 66–7, 165
national schools   173
Nazi party   138–9, 188
neutrality, treaty of   190
newspapers   57
newsreel/newsreel series   160–1. *See also*
    specific entries
    in cinemas   58
    Sorlin on   58

The New York Times   74
nitrate film base   7
Nursî, Said   210

The Oakparker   146
Odeon Theater   28
Oflazoğlu, Turan   209
Öke, Mehmet Sadık   31
Ordu Elifbası (Army Alphabet)   173
Ordu Film Çekme Merkezi *(The Army
    Film Shooting Center)*   60, 61
Oriental despotism   95
Orientalist image/discourse   94–6
orphan films   65–75
Ortaoyunu (Turkish comedia
    dell'arte)   21, 42 n.45
Osman, Topal (Lame)   66–9, 210
Osmanoğlu, Ayse   18
Ottoman Atrocities   19
Ottoman Empire   3, 11, 15–39, 163–5
    Armistice of Mudros   33, 35
    bourgeoisie   23
    electricity   17, 18, 20, 23
    modernization efforts   23
    Orientalist discourse   94–6
    public cinema   20–8
    Russians and   28–9
    wartime cinema   28–37
    women   183
    World War I   204
Özal, Turgut   208
Özen, Mustafa   19–20
Özön, Nijat   17, 29, 33, 47 n.146–7, 60,
    61, 81 n.44–5
Öztan, Ziya   209
Öztürk, Serdar   118–19
Özuyar, Ali   39 n.8, 51, 64, 131 n.141

Pahlavi, Reza Shah   61
*Paintings and Drawings from Turkey
    during World War*   204
Paramount Pictures   160
Pasha, Enver   30–1, 32, 34, 35, 58,
    173, 203–5
Pasha, Esat   204
Pasha, Fevzi Çakmak   56, 60, 66
Pasha, Ismet   67, 70, 71–2, 73, 74, 84–5
    n.115, 118, 166, 184
Pasha, İzzet   20
Pasha, Kâzım   56, 66

Pasha, Nureddin Ibrahim 56, 66
Pasha, Nurettin Baransel 2
Pasha, Said Halim 204
Pasha, Talat 28
Pathé Film 55, 66, 160
Pathé Frères 19
Pathé News 65
Peasant Petitioners Visiting Lenin (painting by Serov) 142
Pera Palace Hotel, Istanbul 57
performing arts 21–2
Philippe, Louis, I 163
photography 15, 21
photojournalism 135
Photo Reporter 10
The Pilgrim (1923) 85–6 n.124
Police (1916) 85–6 n.124
polygamy 110
poultry 105–6
Presidential Orchestra (Riyaseti Cumhur Orkestrası) 101
Promio, Alexandre 27, 39 n.9
Proodos 30
propaganda films 30, 31, 32, 78, 213

Rahmi, Hüseyin 36
Ramadan 22
Ramirez, Don 18
The Reception of the American Ambassador Joseph C. Grew by Atatürk on the Forest Farm. See Atatürk'ün Amerikan Büyükelçisi Joseph C. Grew'u Orman Çiftliğinde Kabulü (1930)
Refiğ, Halit 208, 209
Refik, Ahmet 206
refugees 185
religious dress 169–70
Repas de Bébé (Baby's Meal, 1895) 16
Republican People's Party (Cumhuriyet Halk Partisi, CHP) 118
Reşad, Sultan Mehmed V. 201–2, 204
Reshetnikov, F. 163
Rochemont, Louis de 64, 161, 166, 193 n.9
Roosevelt, Franklin D. 10, 133–5, 147, 163
Russians 28–9
Rüstü, Tevfik 118

Sadat, Anwar 203
Sanayi-i Nefise (Fine Arts) medal 18
Şarlo İdama Mahkum (Charlie is Sentenced to Death) 76
Sascha Film 29–30
Sauvegeot, Camille 65
Schub, Esfer 211
Schwartz, Vanessa R. 21
Scognamillo, Giovanni 40 n.24
Sea of Marmara 101
Second World War 139, 160
Section Photographiques et Cinématographiques des Armées (SPCA) 36
Seden, Kemal 51
Seden, Skir 51
Sekeroglu, Sami 212
Şemsi Efendi 23
Sener, Erman 49, 57, 60
Serov, Vladimir 142
Sharia law 110
silent film 118
single-sex education system 174
Skladanowsky, Emil 16
Skladanowsky, Max 16
small-scale agriculture 186
Society of National Defense 32, 34–5, 38
Sorlin, Pierre 58
sound newsreels 160
source materials 7–11
Soviet-Turkish friendship 211
Soviet Union 187, 213
Spain, Civil War in 188
Spanish Civil War 139, 188
Spiridis, Tilemahos 26
Stalin in His Office (1948) 163
struggle for independence 1, 49–77
  orphan films 65–75
sugar factories 187
Şükrü, Ali 67, 68, 69
Sultan-Galiev, Mirsaid 210
Sümerbank textile factory 186–7
Syria 190

Tahir, Kemal 208
Talu, Ercüment Ekrem 21
Tanin 29
Tanrısever, Mehmet 210
Tarama Dergisi (The Search Journal) 179
Tasvir-i Efkar 25, 51, 54

Teaching Film Division   135
technologies   15
Tepedelenlioğlu, Nizameddin Nazif   212
terrorist attacks   18
textile factory   186–7
Theatre of National Defense   31
Time-Life Incorporated   10, 12, 160–1
Time Warner Inc.   10
tobacco company   204
Tocqueville, Alexis de   97
Trabzon Society for the Defense of National Rights   66
tractors   107–8
Treaty of Lausanne   84–5 n.115, 139
treaty of neutrality   190
Treaty of Versailles   139
Triumph des Willens   213
Türkei (Konstantinopel): Kriegskundgebung der Bevölkerung bei der Fatih Moschee   29
Turkey
  agriculture (*See* agriculture)
  Allied occupation of (*See* Allied powers)
  alphabet reform   172–3
  American public opinion   148–9
  censorship commission   208
  civil code   110–11
  dress reforms   167–72
  economic reforms   185–8
  European Union accession negotiations   209–10
  foreign policy   188–92
  language (theory and reform)   177–83
  machine workshop   108–9
  medical reforms   184–5
  as modern nation   167
  national cinema industry   24, 34–5, 50, 77
  treaty of friendship with Greece   190
  treaty of neutrality with Italy   190
  Turk Tarih Tezi   175–7
  women   109–11
Turkey Reborn   10, 144–9
Türk İnkılabı'nda Terakki Hamleleri (Strides of Progress in Turkish Revolution, 1937)   211–12
Turkish Armed Forces Photo Film Center, Ankara   7, 8
Turkish Film & TV Institute at Mimar Sinan Fine Arts   1

Turkish Language Association (TLA)   141, 143, 145, 172
Turkish Language Congress   178
Turkish Market Day   114–15
Turkish Radio and Television Corporation (TRT)   209
Turkish Society for the Study of Language   179
Turkish War of Independence   208
Türkiye'de Meşrutiyet (The Constitutional Monarchy in Turkey)   28
Türkiye İş Bankası   150
Türk Sineması   24
Turks Still Smoke the Old Way (1930)   113, 114
Türk Tarih Tezi (Turkish History Thesis)   175–7

Ülkü   140–1, 145, 150
United States   15
  anti-Turkish groups   148
  Declaration of Independence (1776)   97
  democracy   97
  film screenings   22
  inventor-entrepreneurs   15–16
  public opinion about Turks   148–9
universal civilization   96
universal language   27
Ürdün Kralı Abdullah'ın Türkiye Ziyareti (The Visit of the Jordanian King Abdullah to Turkey, 1937)   211
Uzberk, Isfendiyar   61
Uzkınay, Fuat   24, 29, 30, 32–3, 34, 36, 51, 54, 59, 60, 61

Vafiadis, Théodore   16
The Vagabond King (1930)   118
Van Voorhis, Cornelius Westbrook   161
Venizelos, Eleftherios K.   118, 190
Victorian Internet   57
visual language   58
Vitagraphe Company   26
von Sanders, Liman   204
Vree, Frank van   26

Washington, George   206
Weinberg, Sigmund   19, 22–3, 24, 26, 28, 32–3
Werfel, Franz   148–9

Western civilization   72
White, Hayden   62
Wilhelm, Kaiser, II   18, 205
Winter, Jay   61
women   109–11
   cinema and   26
   emancipation   110–11
   enfranchisement   111
   image in liberated state   183–4
   Ottoman Empire and   183
   political rights   111
World War I. *See* First World War

World War II. *See* Second World War

Yorgun Savaşçı (Tired Soldier, 1978–83) (TV series)   208
You Can't Win 'Em All   208
Young Men's Christian Association (YMCA)   37, 113
Young Turk Revolution of 1908   19, 21, 22, 23, 25, 28, 70, 203
Yutkevich, Sergei Iosifovich   211

Zafer Yolları (Roads to Victory)   60

www.ingramcontent.com/pod-product-compliance
Lightning Source LLC
Chambersburg PA
CBHW072142290426
44111CB00012B/1955